What Dog?

What Dog?

A GUIDE TO HELP NEW OWNERS SELECT THE RIGHT BREED FOR THEIR LIFESTYLE

Amanda O'Neill

First edition for the United States and Canada
published in 2006 by Barron's Educational Series, Inc.

First published in 2006 by Interpet Publishing Ltd.
© Copyright 2006 by Interpet Publishing Ltd.

All inquiries should be addressed to:
Barron's Educational Series, Inc.
250 Wireless Boulevard
Hauppauge, NY 11788
www.barronseduc.com

ISBN-10: 0-7641-3272-5
ISBN-13: 978-0-7641-3272-8

Library of Congress Control No.: 2005921561

Printed in China.
9 8 7 6 5

About the Author

Amanda O'Neill was born in Sussex in 1951 and
educated at the University of Exeter, where she
studied medieval literature. She has written more
than 20 books including *The Best-Ever Book of Dogs*
and *Cats and Dogs* and was editor of *The Complete
Book of the Dog.* She is a regular contributor to a
number of dog magazines in the UK. Her current
menagerie consists of a teenage son, a hamster, an
assortment of fish, three Chihuahuas, a Pekingese,
and the world's worst-behaved Yorkie cross.

Dedication

For Edith Esland and Marilyn Fieldhouse, two
stalwarts of the rescue world, with much gratitude
for some wonderful dogs.

The information and recommendations in this book
are given without any guarantees on behalf of the
author and publisher, who disclaim any liability with
the use of this material.

Throughout the book silhouettes of the 100
selected breeds are shown in relation to the
profile of a Wire Fox Terrier (*above*) which
stands around 15 in. (38 cm) tall at its
withers. This is to allow the reader to get an
impression of the relative sizes of the dogs
being described. It should be understood
that the sizes given in the data tables are
averages and that inevitably some individuals
will grow to be smaller or larger than this at
maturity. The sizes are for general guidance
only. Where breed standards stipulate a
height, allowance has been made beyond
this to include the sizes of typical pets.

Contents

Introduction

No animal comes in such varied shapes and sizes as the dog, nor indeed with such a wide range of temperaments. Big or small, shaggy or bald, placid or dynamic, there are hundreds of breeds from which to choose the one that will best suit your own personality, circumstances, and lifestyle.

Before you choose a breed, ask yourself the following questions:

How much exercise (truthfully) will you give your dog? Are you content with a stroll around the park, do you enjoy long walks every day, wet or dry, or do you prefer short walks during the week and long country walks on weekends or in fine weather? Different breeds have different needs. Owners who love walking can pick from a wide range—even some of the Toy breeds thoroughly enjoy regular ten-mile hikes or more. Couch potatoes should look specifically at less-active breeds—a dog that needs lots of exercise and is denied this will be unfit and unhappy and will usually find something awful to do with its spare energy.

Do you really, really enjoy grooming? If not, pick a short-coated breed. If you don't mind some grooming, consider a medium coat. Adopt a long-coated dog only if you want to spend time daily with brush and comb. The demands of the show ring mean that some long-coated breeds nowadays have enormous coats that need hours of care and, if neglected, mat and tangle beyond redemption. Heavy-coated dogs like Poodles and Old English Sheepdogs are often passed on to rescue societies in pitiful states simply because their owners failed to consider their grooming needs.

Do you have young children living in, or regularly visiting, your home? If so, choose a calm, sensible,

reliable breed. If your children are badly behaved or will be left alone and unsupervised with the dog, buy them a computer game instead—no dog, however good-natured, should be expected to put up with ill-treatment.

Do you have the experience and strong personality to enjoy a challenging, dominant dog, or would you be happier with a gentler dog that is eager to please? It is important to make the right choice here. Most breeds fall into the middle range between dominant and submissive, the ideal temperament for a pet. Strong-minded dogs (often working breeds) are best suited to equally strong-minded owners who know how to be pack leader without bullying and who have plenty of time for training. Dominant breeds like Rottweilers and Pit Bulls can be wonderful dogs in the right hands. However, the increasing number of news reports of dog attacks on humans reflects what happens when they have owners unwilling or unable to commit to their training. At the opposite extreme, "soft" breeds like the Maltese lack nothing in personality, are great fun, and are certainly a better choice for the novice.

Must your home be immaculate? If heavy shedding or a dog that carries in a lot of mud and water would be a problem, you will need to think carefully about the type of coat you are looking at. Be aware that some short-coated breeds shed hairs even more profusely than some long coats.

Do you want a guard dog? You don't need to narrow your choice down to guard breeds such as Doberman Pinschers and Bullmastiffs—these certainly make great protection dogs but are best with experienced handlers who can keep their guarding instincts under control. Most people don't actually need a guard breed for this purpose—even small dogs are very effective burglar deterrents. Most dogs, however gentle, will defend their owners if a threat arises.

National crime statistics show that small dogs like this Shih Tzu deter burglars just as well as bigger breeds.

Breed standards are guidelines, not absolutes.
Broadly speaking, the standard of each breed tells
you what to expect in terms of appearance and
temperament. However, bear in mind that most
standards (and indeed breed books) are written
by people who love that particular breed and may
emphasize its virtues without, perhaps, preparing you
for its particular demands and difficulties. If you like
what you have read or heard about a breed, go and
meet as many examples as possible and talk to their
owners before making a decision.

Dogs are individuals. A breed standard sets out

Size at withers: Dog 9–10 in. (24–26 cm) Bitch 8–9 in. (22–24 cm)

● *As a show dog, this Brussels Griffon must conform to a
stipulated size; pet dogs may be bigger or smaller.*

TERRIER **e.g. Parson Russell Terrier,** **Cairn Terrier**	Lively, bossy, busy, willful; fun dogs with lots of character; strong hunting drive; can be fiery with other dogs; often great diggers and escapologists.
SIGHTHOUND **e.g. Greyhound, Whippet**	Gentle, affectionate; strong hunting and chasing drive, need opportunities to run; not particularly obedient and may not be trustworthy off leash; often escape artists.
SCENTHOUND **e.g. Basset Hound, Beagle**	Friendly, stubborn; strong hunting drive; need lots of exercise; not usually very obedient and usually hard to recall from a scent; often strong "houndy" smell.
GUNDOG **e.g. Labrador Retriever,** **Cocker Spaniel**	Good-natured, intelligent, highly trainable; need lots of exercise; generally good with children; European all-around breeds generally stronger willed.
HERDER **e.g. Border Collie, Belgian** **Sheepdog**	Highly intelligent and need lots of mental as well as physical exercise; very trainable; strong chasing drive; often very sensitive and need early socialization.

what dogs of that breed should be like, but that still leaves room for a lot of variation. Even within the same litter, puppies will show differences in character (the bold one, the timid one, the inquisitive one, and so forth) and even in looks (the big one, the one with funny ears or an unusual tail carriage). In terms of both physical appearance and temperament, much depends on the breeder's goals. Breeders who are aiming for the show ring will produce dogs that look as much like the show standard as possible, whereas breeders who want working dogs generally value performance over appearance. Indeed, in some breeds (e.g., Cocker Spaniels), working strains and show strains are quite different.

Nonetheless, breed standards are very useful guidelines, making it clear that most Border Collies are intelligent workaholics, most Basset Hounds will follow a scent instead of coming back when called, and so on.

A useful starting point when considering breeds is to look at their origins and function. Hounds have been bred for centuries to hunt, terriers to go down holes and kill, and sheepdogs to herd. A pet hound, terrier, or sheepdog that is not required to carry out his ancestral tasks will still have these instincts. So if you want a calm, gentle, laid-back dog, you don't want a terrier; if you want a dog that will leave an interesting scent the moment you call him, you don't want a hound.

GUARD e.g. **Rottweiler, Doberman Pinscher**	Strong willed and need confident, experienced owner; highly trainable in the right hands; protective drive needs to be controlled; socialization essential.
TOY e.g. **Pomeranian, Yorkshire Terrier**	Need lots of love and cuddles; despite small size, generally much more of a "real dog" than reputation suggests and most Toys enjoy long walks, opportunity for training, and so on.
SPITZ *(Northern dogs)* e.g. **Norwegian Elkhound, Keeshond**	Active, energetic, often noisy; tend to be independent and stubborn—not for obedience enthusiasts; need close relationship with owner, and dislike being left alone.
SLED BREEDS e.g. **Alaskan Malamute, Siberian Husky**	Active, not geared to obedience; need lots of exercise; strong prey drive and rarely to be trusted off leash; destructive if bored; great escapologists.
BULL BREEDS e.g. **Bulldog, Staffordshire Bull Terrier**	Strong-minded dogs of fighting ancestry but not nowadays generally aggressive—although most will not back down if challenged; smarter than reputation suggests.

Buy a puppy from a reputable breeder.
Backyard and commercial breeders (puppy mills) whose only interest is making money will be looking at quantity rather than quality. They may buy litters too young to leave their mothers or breed from unhealthy and ill-kept bitches to churn out puppies that may never recover from their bad start in life. Also, a breeder who doesn't care where the puppies end up is not likely to have gone to much trouble raising them. The most ideal situation would be for the puppy to go directly from his birth home to his permanent home without going through the trauma of a middleman.

Questions to ask the breeder:
- Have the puppies been raised in the house or in a kennel?
- What socialization have they had? (Have they been exposed to everyday household noises and activities? If not, they are poorly prepared for their new home.)
- What are the parents' temperaments and characters like?
- Have appropriate health checks for the breed been carried out, such as hip or eye testing? (If the breeder says these don't matter, go elsewhere.)

● *Puppies need a good start in life to grow into healthy dogs.*

- At what age can the puppies leave their mother? (Caring breeders won't let them leave too early.)

● *Puppies grow up fast. The progression from helpless infant to confident adult takes about two years.*

Puppy socialization: this pup is starting to learn that cats are part of the family too.

that you can offer a good, and permanent, home. Indeed, most responsible breeders will insist that the pup be returned to them if at any stage you are unable to keep him.

Don't buy a puppy if:

• You can't see its mother and assure yourself that she is fit, healthy, and of good temperament.

• You can see the mother and/or father and they are badly cared for or have poor temperaments.

• The breeder has multiple breeds and multiple litters—this suggests a money-making venture rather than a caring breeder.

• The puppy's environment is dirty and squalid, suggesting a poor level of care.

• The breeder is ignorant or dismissive of health issues in the breed.

• What paperwork is provided? This should include American Kennel Club (AKC) registration, pedigree, vaccination, and worming records, and in some breeds, certification for puppy or parents for hip scores or eye tests. Caring breeders will usually provide a diet sheet and offer after-sale advice.

Good breeders know their pups as individuals and will try to match each pup to the right owner. They will also care where their pups are going and be unwilling to sell you a puppy until they are satisfied

Time spent choosing the right breed and the right breeder is never wasted. You are picking a companion who may be with you for the next ten or twenty years—for his sake as well as your own, choose wisely.

Dogs from rescue organizations

You may prefer to adopt a "secondhand dog" from a rescue organization. As well as general rescue organizations, there are breed-specific rescues for almost every breed, from Great Dane Rescue to Chihuahua Rescue (details available from the AKC). Dogs come into rescue for all sorts of reasons. Some are cruelty cases, some have been abandoned, some are homeless through the death or changed circumstances of the owner, and many are passed on to rescue because their owners did not realize when they bought a cute puppy what it would turn into. Rescue workers are used to explanations ranging from, "I didn't expect my Wolfhound puppy to grow so big," to "The kids are too rough for my Chihuahua."

Some rescue dogs have been much-loved pets and need only to adapt to a change of home; others carry a lot of emotional baggage or even physical problems,

● *Rescue workers will try to ensure that families with active lifestyles are matched up with suitably energetic, fun-loving dogs.*

but with loving care they can become wonderful companions. Good rescue organizations aim to know each case as an individual before rehousing it and to match dogs to the right new owners.

Most rescue groups are run by dedicated volunteers. Single-breed rescues tend to be run by people who know the breed well, can advise you as to any problems, and will provide backup after you take your dog home. Sadly, a few groups are less than ideal, so be prepared to ask questions and assess the environment and people concerned. A good rescue group will grill you as to your suitability

● *Former racing greyhounds are always available for new homes. They make excellent pets, being friendly, gentle and undemanding—and are most appreciative of home comforts.*

for one of its dogs and will usually pay a home visit to satisfy themselves that you have a suitable environment. Don't be offended by tough questioning: it is the rescue worker's responsibility to ensure that a dog who has already lost one home is going to find a permanent, loving residence.

● *Before bringing your new dog home, make sure everything is ready for him, and try to make the journey as unstressful as possible.*

Most rescue homes do not charge for their dogs but require a donation to help keep the group running— the amounts vary from rescue to rescue. You are unlikely to find a puppy of your chosen breed via rescue—most of the dogs will be adults. Good rescue groups will be open about any behavioral problems of individual dogs—and eager to tell you about their virtues, which may be many. In some cases, old dogs may be guaranteed free medical treatment in exchange for a home for their twilight years, and such senior citizens can be very rewarding companions.

● *Dogs adapt amazingly well to owners' different lifestyles, but it pays to spend time on one's choice of breed.*

Rehoming a rescue dog may mean that you miss out on the fun of a puppy. However, many wonderful dogs are found through rescue, and you have the added satisfaction of having saved a life.

Before you bring your dog home, get everything ready for him.

Yards need to be dog proofed—check fencing, and look out for danger spots like ponds or sheds where garden chemicals are stored. Indoors, look out for hazards like trailing electrical wires or accessible upstairs windows that a dog might jump through. You may want to put up nursery gates across doorways or stairs so that you can control access until your new dog knows the ropes.

● A comfortable bed gives your dog a corner that he knows is his own as well as a place to sleep.

You will need to buy basics such as a bed, food and water bowls, grooming kit, collar and lead, and toys. A bewildering range of products is available in pet shops, but a new dog's needs are quite simple.

Decide where your new dog is going to sleep. He needs a comfy, easily cleaned bed in a secure draft-proof corner. You may want to train your dog to sleep in a crate, where he can be safely shut in when necessary, or you may prefer an open bed. Puppies are often best suited by a cardboard box of appropriate size, which can be replaced when chewed or soiled and succeeded by a permanent bed when they have finished teething. Different breeds have different needs: some like to disappear under a pile of warm blankets, while others don't feel the cold.

Food and water bowls should be of an appropriate size and easily cleanable—hygiene matters for dogs just as much as for people. Responsible breeders will provide an age-appropriate diet chart, and you should always stick to the breeder's diet for the first few weeks to avoid stomach upsets. Later on you can gradually switch

to whichever type of diet you favor: fresh, canned, or dry foods are all suitable for most dogs.

Your dog's grooming needs will depend on his breed, but if in doubt start out with a soft-bristle brush. Puppies don't need much grooming. If you accustom them to being brushed from day one, they will be much easier to tackle as adults. Grooming is important to keep the coat healthy but also a way of showing affection, an opportunity to carry out health checks, and a means of showing a bossy dog who is in charge.

The type of collar and lead also depends on breed. In general, puppies are best started out with soft puppy collars. Adults are usually most

● Providing toys for your dog makes it easier to teach him not to borrow your belongings for play sessions!

comfortable with a buckled leather collar; some breeds do better with a harness or a half-check collar. Don't forget to add a rabies tag—this is a legal requirement as well as a safety measure. The once-popular choke chain is not recommended as damaging a dog's neck with this type of collar is all too easy unless you really know what you are doing. Adults that pull on the lead may do better with a head collar, which gives you more control.

● *A dog is for life, not just for Christmas—a long-term, demanding, but rewarding commitment.*

Plan your new dog's social life and check out local training classes before you bring him home. For the first week or so (in the case of a puppy, until his vaccinations are complete), his new family and new environment will be enough for him to cope with. Once he is settled in, socialization is important. Puppies will benefit from meeting sensible visitors as well as from puppy socialization classes to accustom them to other dogs. For adult dogs, a weekly obedience class or similar activity will help you to build up a good relationship. Before you acquire your dog is also the best time to locate a good neighborhood veterinarian—don't leave it until you need one in a hurry.

How to use this book

This book aims to provide useful information for anyone who wants to choose the best companion breed for him/herself. It is not a guide to show standards. If you specifically want a show dog, you will need to look much more closely into details of colors, exact heights, grooming requirements, and so forth.

Breed attributes given are those of an average dog of that breed, and individual dogs will vary according to their upbringing. For example, "attitude to other dogs" will be affected by socialization (or lack of it). So where a breed is listed as being good with other dogs, a dog of that breed who has never mixed with other dogs will lack confidence with them and may be aggressive through fear. Similarly, "ease of training" will depend to some extent on the trainer (some breeds listed as "poor" in this area have produced obedience champions in the right hands). "Quietness" or "destructiveness" will depend on environment (most dogs can be noisy or destructive if neglected). "Protective behavior" (the likelihood of the dog sounding the alarm when it hears something unusual and barking at intruders) can be developed or partly repressed by an owner. Essentially this guide aims to show you the raw material with which you will be working: it is up to you to develop your dog's potential.

Small Dogs

Don't underrate small breeds.
Little dogs are as loving, intelligent,
and energetic as their bigger cousins. They enjoy
exercise, make great watchdogs, and have lots of
personality. Small size has practical advantages too:
little dogs need less space and cost less to maintain
than big ones, and they also have longer life spans.

Chihuahua

The world's smallest breed, the Chihuahua is nonetheless all dog and not a mere fashion accessory. Certainly it is the ideal lapdog, content to soak up affection and return it in kind. However, it is also a lively and playful little animal that enjoys country walks and outings. Alert, loving, and intelligent, it likes to be the center of attention and receive plenty of fuss and cuddles. Its small size and low exercise requirements suit this breed well for apartment life, but it still needs company and mental stimulation.

The Chihuahua is an all-American breed, originating in medieval South and Meso-America, where it is said to have been sacred to the Aztecs. In the 19th century, it was introduced to the US and subsequently worldwide. The popularity of the breed today means quality is variable—choose a breeder carefully to find a pet that is physically and temperamentally sound.

WHAT colors?

All colors acceptable, including red, cream, gold, fawn, sable, chocolate, blue, bicolor, tricolor, and black and tan. Merles (a sort of marbled effect distinguished by the presence of irregular dark blotches against a lighter background of the same basic pigment) are a recent introduction to the breed not universally approved.

WHAT grooming does the coat need?

Both types of coat are easy care. Smooth coats require minimal grooming—just an occasional combing to remove dead hair. Long coats need a little more time, but a weekly check for tangles and a gentle brushing will keep them looking and feeling good.

HOW suitable are they as family dogs?

Highly suitable—for the suitable family. They do tend to pick a favorite person, which is why many families end up with more than one Chihuahua. However, they are not recommended for households with very young children as their small size makes them vulnerable. In any case, they prefer to be the baby of the family themselves.

WHAT type of home?

These are essentially companion dogs that need company in order to thrive. So long as they can be with their owner, they can be just as happy in town or country. Apartment dogs will benefit from daily access to a park to provide both physical and mental stimulation, but they can exercise themselves quite well indoors playing with their owners.

WHAT type of owner?

Chihuahuas need affection and attention, so they need owners who are prepared to give, and receive, plenty of fuss. They make ideal companions for the house-bound elderly but can also enjoy a moderately robust family life with older, sensible children. This is not a suitable breed for part-time owners, as they crave company.

HOW compatible with other pets?

Chihuahuas enjoy the company of other pets (especially other Chihuahuas) if properly socialized in puppyhood. However, early socialization is essential to accustom them to bigger dogs—and also to control their hunting instincts as regards smaller pets.

Character Trait	Poor	Average	Good	Excellent
Attitude to other dogs		●		
Quietness	●			
Not destructive			●	
Protective behavior			●	
Not likely to stray		●		
Good with children		●		
Ease of training		●		

Original purpose: Companion; possibly edible; possibly sacred
Male height: 6–9 in. (15–23 cm)
Female height: 6–9 in. (15–23 cm)
Weight: not to exceed 6 lb. (1–2.8 kg)
Life span: 14–18 years

HOW much exercise?

Chihuahuas can thrive on little exercise but will also enjoy as much as you can offer. A healthy adult can walk for miles, and the breed also enjoys miniagility events.

HOW easy to train?

Chihuahuas don't rank high on the trainability scale—perhaps partly because owners of these minidogs are rarely obedience enthusiasts. In fact this breed responds surprisingly well to gentle, consistent training, but don't expect too much of them.

WHAT good points?

Devoted, responsive, nonaggressive, playful, alert, low maintenance in terms of exercise and food requirements, easily transported.

WHAT to be aware of?

Not the easiest breed to house-break. Can be yappy if untrained, and also can be fussy eaters if encouraged. Dislikes the cold.

● *A long coat will require a little more time for grooming.*

Small dogs

WHAT medical problems?

Chihuahuas are generally hardy little dogs. Possible problems include open molera (an opening at the top of the skull, like that of a newborn baby), leaving the head vulnerable, slipping kneecaps, and heart problems.

Pekingese

Imperious and self-assured, the Pekingese has been termed an "honorary cat," and indeed he has both a cat's dignity and a cat's playfulness. He is a dog of great personality, devoted to his owner, and naturally well-mannered but among the most stubborn and self-opinionated of all breeds. Despite his lapdog appearance, he is a sporty little dog who hates being left out of any activities. Sadly, modern show trends have exaggerated his foreshortened face and heavy coat so that he can no longer be as active a companion as he would wish, and his health and grooming needs are too much for many pet owners.

Recent genetic research shows that the Peke is among the oldest dog breeds. He originated in China, where he was the favorite of the imperial court and was unknown in the West until the mid-19th century. Today a glamorous show dog, he remains an enchanting companion.

WHAT colors?

Any color except liver or albino. Popular colors include red, fawn, brindle, black, white, parti-color. Self-colors usually have a black muzzle or mask.

WHAT grooming does the coat need?

The dense coat needs grooming daily, working right down to the skin with a bristle brush and comb, with special attention to the thick fur behind the ears and in the armpits. Grooming sessions must include checking and cleaning the facial wrinkle and checking the breeches for soiling. Many modern Pekes have so much coat that pet owners may prefer to clip it short, both for their own convenience and for their dog's comfort.

HOW suitable are they as family dogs?

Pekes tend to attach themselves most strongly to one person, but if brought up in a family, they will have plenty of affection to spare for

the whole household. They are not recommended for homes with young children as they are vulnerable to rough handling, but they thoroughly appreciate having considerate, older children to play and socialize with.

WHAT type of home?

Single family, condo, or apartment, a Peke will fit in anywhere so long as he has his owner with him. He does enjoy a yard where he can fill his coat with mud and burrs before settling down to enjoy the process of being brushed clean again.

WHAT type of owner?

Pekes need loving owners with plenty of time for them, and they are wasted on anyone who does not share their sense of fun. They are perhaps not for the house proud, as they cover carpets and furniture with shed fur and can carry in astonishing amounts of mud and water on their coats.

HOW compatible with other pets?

Pekes are great with other animals, though like all dogs they need to be introduced carefully to small pets. They should not be encouraged to play with boisterous breeds, as their eyes are vulnerable to injury if knocked. On country walks, watch out for livestock, as most Pekes consider themselves hunting breeds and will chase sheep if they have not been taught not to do so.

HOW much exercise?

The Peke enjoys walks and outings but his heavy coat and breathing difficulties make it hard for him to

Character Trait	Poor	Average	Good	Excellent
Attitude to other dogs				
Quietness				
Not destructive				
Protective behavior				
Not likely to stray				
Good with children				
Ease of training				

Origin
and st
Male !
Fema
Weig
Life :

go far. Daily walks at his own pace and for his own choice of distance will help to keep him healthy; but he should never be exercised in hot weather as he overheats easily.

HOW easy to train?

Pekes are intelligent and quick learners but prefer to train their owners rather than be trained; as the saying goes, "Nine out of ten Pekingese are disobedient; the tenth is really deaf." However, they are usually prepared to be cooperative if they believe their owner has a reason for asking them to do something. They do like showing off, and some individuals have even taken successfully to competitive obedience work for that reason.

● The massive coat is a crowning glory only if you are prepared to spend time on daily grooming.

WHAT good points?

Devoted, entertaining, intelligent, stable, dignified, alert, mischievous, playful, loving, sensitive, gentle.

WHAT to be aware of?

Heavy grooming requirements. Shortened nose leads to breathing difficulties. Pekes snore, wheeze, and tend to sneeze in your face.

Brus

vivacity wit
sensitivity t
he is a dem
Early sociali

WHAT col
Rich clear r
tan, the latte
A color vari
red and blac
as the Griffo
Continent an
accepted in t

the
Smooth coats n
attention, weekly
hound glove to

sels Griffon *Other names: Petit Brabançon, Griffon Belge, Griffon Bruxellois.*

A sturdy little dog with a monkey face and a monkey's curious, playful nature, the Brussels Griffon is an entertaining companion with a lot of personality. Intelligent and playful, he combines a terrier's ...n a toy's endearing self-importance and ...o his owner's needs—and his own, for ...anding companion who loves attention. ...zation and sensible training are important to prevent him from becoming either shy or spoiled. This lively little dog comes in two coat varieties, rough and smooth (Petit Brabançon), to suit all tastes.

The Brussels Griffon started out as Belgium's native ratter. By the 19th century he was the favorite of Brussels coachmen. With the addition of a dash of Pug blood and perhaps that of other toy breeds, he soon made the transition to fashionable pet. The first breed standard was drawn up in 1880s, and he became established as a delightful pet.

...ors?

...d, black, or black and ...r being least common. ...ety with a mixture of ...k hairs is recognized ...n Belge on the ...d in the US but not ...he UK.

hairs. Rough coats need vigorous brushing every other day with a bristle brush, scrupulous cleaning of facial hair, and hand-stripping twice a year to remove dead hair and keep the coat in good condition. In both cases, grooming sessions should include checking the wrinkle above the nose, which must be kept clean and dry to prevent soreness.

HOW suitable are they as family dogs?

The Griffon is a loving and entertaining family dog so long as children are old enough to treat him sensibly—young children are likely to be too rough for his comfort or safety. Early socialization is needed to ensure that he does not become timid or even snappy. He does need a lot of attention and can be jealous; owners with very young children may find him overdemanding.

WHAT type of home?

His owner matters to a Brussels Griffon more than his environment. He can thrive in a city apartment or enjoy an active country life.

WHAT type of owner?

This is a dog for a gentle, affectionate owner who enjoys playtime. Brussels Griffon owners should be committed to a close relationship with their dog, for this breed is affectionate to the point of clinginess.

HOW compatible with other pets?

With proper puppyhood socialization, these are friendly little dogs that can get along well with other dogs and cats. They were originally ratters, so it is not sensible to expect them to regard small pets such as rabbits and hamsters as anything other than prey.

HOW much exercise?

These adaptable little dogs can cope with little exercise or enjoy surprisingly lengthy country walks, although their short muzzles make them vulnerable to overheating in hot weather. What they do need is mental exercise and stimulation,

WHAT ...rooming does ...oat need?

...ed minimal ...brushing with a ...emove loose

Character Trait	Poor	Average	Good	Excellent
Attitude to other dogs			X	
Quietness		X		
Not destructive			X	
Protective behavior			X	
Not likely to stray			X	
Good with children			X	
Ease of training		X		

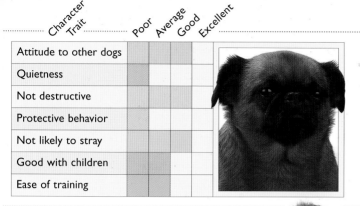

Original purpose: Small vermin hunting
Male height: 9–11 in. (23–28 cm)
Female height: 9–11 in. (23–28 cm)
Weight: 8–10 lb. (2.3–4.5 kg)
Life span: 12–15 years

● The Brussels Griffon, originally a ratter, has become a fashionable pet.

Small dogs

pupils' feelings and with a positive, reward-based, and above all fun approach to keep their interest.

WHAT good points?

Outgoing, lively, entertaining, sensitive, affectionate, responsive, playful, lots of personality, sturdy, and long-lived.

WHAT to be aware of?

Not the easiest breed to house-train. Tends to snore and can become a confirmed barker, especially if left alone. Perhaps not for keen gardeners—Brussels Griffons love digging.

WHAT medical problems?

This is a healthy and long-lived breed, although like all short-faced breeds vulnerable to the heat. Problems that have been reported include cataracts, dislocation of the kneecap (patellar luxation), heart murmurs, and hip malformation (dysplasia).

● Like other short-faced breeds, he may become overheated.

with plenty of playtime and training sessions.

HOW easy to train?

A challenging breed, Brussels Griffons are clever, quick to learn, and capable of a good performance in obedience or agility—also stubborn, willful, easily upset, and easily bored. Successful trainers need to think like good nursery school teachers, sensitive to their

Yorkshire Terrier

The Yorkie is a terrier in lapdog's clothing—a glamorous, miniature version of his ratting ancestors. Despite his small size and decorative coat, he retains the true terrier spirit—busy, bustling, and full of bounce. Devoted to his owner, he is an enthusiastic (sometimes overenthusiastic) watchdog, a keen hunter given the chance, and a lovable, if demanding, companion.

Don't make the mistake of seeing him as a lapdog: he needs mental and physical activity if he is not to become bored and frustrated. He refuses to acknowledge his small size and can be aggressive toward bigger dogs if not socialized from puppyhood. This is a small dog with a big personality.

There is considerable variation between show and pet Yorkies, both in size and in coat. Those bred as pets are often larger. The extravagant coat of the show ring, with its silky tresses decked with bows, is unlikely to be achieved by a family pet.

WHAT colors?
Dark, steel-blue body with golden-tan head, chest, and legs. Puppies start out black with tan points, gradually fading to the clear blue color and extending the tan areas—a process that may take up to three years.

WHAT grooming does the coat need?
The fine, silky coat needs daily brushing and combing to prevent tangles, and the hair over the eyes should be trimmed or tied back. Many pet owners prefer to keep the coat clipped short. In any case, the full-flowing show coat is achieved only by hours of labor, and is preserved between shows by being tied up in tissue paper.

HOW suitable are they as family dogs?
The Yorkie really comes into his own as a companion for adults, but he can be a great family pet with sensible, older children. He is not recommended for younger children, as his small size makes him vulnerable and he can become snappy in self-defense if teased.

WHAT type of home?
Small enough for apartment life and tough enough for the country, a Yorkie can fit in anywhere. As a country dog, he will need supervision to keep him out of mischief and rabbit holes. As a city dog, he will need access to a park or yard for exercise and an owner sensible enough to recognize that little dogs are easily trodden on in the street.

WHAT type of owner?
A devoted and demanding companion, the Yorkie needs an owner with plenty of time for him. He is an ideal pet for an active, older owner, providing encouragement to remain fit and active, but he can also be a fun dog for a sensible family. A nonshedding coat means this is a breed that can be suitable for asthmatics and others who are sensitive to dog hair.

HOW compatible with other pets?
Like most terriers, Yorkies will live happily with other animal members of their own household once properly introduced but should probably never be trusted with small prey animals such as mice and hamsters. They also need to be accustomed to strange dogs in puppyhood to prevent interdog aggression.

HOW much exercise?
Two short walks a day will keep your Yorkie healthy, but he will enjoy as much exercise as you are able to offer. This breed has a low boredom threshold, so the more activity available for them, the better.

Character Trait	Poor	Average	Good	Excellent
Attitude to other dogs		▓		
Quietness	▓			
Not destructive			▓	
Protective behavior			▓	
Not likely to stray		▓		
Good with children			▓	
Ease of training			▓	

Original purpose: Small vermin hunting
Male height: 8–9 in. (20–23 cm)
Female height: 8–9 in. (20–23 cm)
Weight: not to exceed 7 lb. (3.2 kg)
Life span: 14–16 years

HOW easy to train?

The Yorkie is intelligent and a quick learner as far as basic companion dog training goes. However, he can be stubborn and is usually too independent and easily distracted to be an ideal candidate for competitive obedience. However, his energy and enthusiasm can make him a star at miniagility.

WHAT good points?

Intelligent, lively, playful, alert, affectionate, adaptable in terms of exercise, long-lived, nonallergenic coat, easily transported.

WHAT to be aware of?

High grooming needs. Can be yappy if untrained, and can become snappy if teased or undersocialized. Males can be oversexed (usually resolved by castration). As with all highly popular breeds, beware commercial breeders who may produce physically and temperamentally unsound pups.

WHAT medical problems?

Generally a healthy breed. Reported problems include dislocation of elbow and kneecap, malformation of spinal vertebrae, Legg-Calvé-Perthes disease (affecting the hip joint), cataracts, epilepsy, heart murmurs.

● *A lively dog—and tougher than he looks.*

Small dogs

Dachshund *Other names: Teckel*

Originally bred as a hunter to pursue badgers (his name means "badger dog"), foxes, and rabbits underground, the Dachshund has made a successful career change to become a popular companion. A willful, self-opinionated charmer, he is a pet with personality plus. Despite his short legs, he is a sporting little character, active, playful, and always ready for a walk or a game, or indeed to set off hunting—but also perfectly capable of being quiet and sensible when necessary. He is an affectionate and devoted companion who wants to be close to his owner. One word of caution: his long back makes him vulnerable to spinal injuries.

Dachshunds come in two sizes, the ever-popular Miniature and the more substantial Standard, each of which has three coat varieties, Smooth, Longhaired, and Wirehaired. All have the same happy temperament, although Longhairs may be slightly more easygoing and Wirehairs a little more extroverted.

WHAT colors?

Red or black and tan are the most common colors, but Dachshund also come in chocolate and tan, cream, dapple (known as merle in other breeds), and brindle.

WHAT grooming does the coat need?

Smoothhairs need little maintenance: a weekly brushing to remove dead hairs will suffice. Longhairs and Wirehairs need brushing and combing two or three times a week to prevent matts and tangles. Wirehairs need their coats hand stripped two or three times a year to keep them under control.

HOW suitable are they as family dogs?

Dachshunds make delightful family dogs, who will fit in with a wide range of lifestyles. As long as they are not ignored, they are equally happy to join in activities or just enjoy being cuddled. Children must be taught how to pick up a Dachshund carefully to avoid the

● Time for a walk. To neglect exercise is to risk back trouble.

risk of back injury—and this breed is better in households with older, sensible children, as they can be jealous and may nip if teased or mishandled.

WHAT type of home?

Although they were bred for a sporting life in the country, Dachshunds can be just as happy in the city. Miniatures in particular make ideal apartment dogs, provided they have enough exercise.

WHAT type of owner?

Dachshunds are great companions for the elderly and equally well suited to a lively, young family. However, they are not for those who want a placid, malleable pet. Potential owners should be prepared for a feisty, stubborn, comical, loving little dog—and should be fairly strong-willed themselves, or they will find themselves at the bottom of the pack hierarchy!

HOW compatible with other pets?

Generally sociable and outgoing, Dachshunds usually get a long well with other dogs and indeed enjoy having a canine playmate in the same household. They do have a strong hunting drive. If they are to share a home with cats or small pets such as rabbits, they need to learn early on that these are also family members and not to be chased.

HOW much exercise?

Dachshunds need regular exercise: allowing them to become unfit is asking for back trouble. Two half-hour walks a day is all that is

Character Trait	Poor	Average	Good	Excellent
Attitude to other dogs				
Quietness				
Not destructive				
Protective behavior				
Not likely to stray				
Good with children				
Ease of training				

Original purpose: Hunting
Height (Standard): 8–10 in. (20–25 cm)
Height (Miniature): 5–6 in. (13–15 cm)
Weight (Standard): 16–32 lb. (7.2–14.5 kg)
Weight (Miniature): 9–11 lb. (4–5 kg)
Life span: 12–14 years

needed, but they will enjoy surprisingly long country hikes if that is their owner's choice. However, they should be discouraged from jumping, again because of their vulnerability to back injury.

HOW easy to train?

Smart and strong willed, the Dachshund will ride roughshod over an owner who lets him. Given an owner who can establish firm but kind leadership, he is perfectly trainable, though not a natural for formal obedience. Training should be positive, consistent, and reward based to encourage him to learn.

WHAT good points?

Intelligent, lively, courageous, faithful, versatile, good-tempered, playful, entertaining, adaptable, determined, brave; an alert watchdog.

WHAT to be aware of?

Tendency to bark—and they have a big bark for their size. Can be difficult to housebreak.

WHAT medical problems?

Dachshunds are prone to back problems. Other conditions to watch out for include elbow malformation (dysplasia), dislocation of the kneecap (patellar luxation), epilepsy, eye problems (cataracts and progressive retinal atrophy), diabetes, and epilepsy.

Small dogs

● Short legged but sporting: a loving but feisty pet.

Maltese

Ornamental and gentle, the Maltese has for centuries been considered the ultimate lapdog. His tiny size and luxurious snow-white tresses clearly identify him as a breed designed to be a lady's "comforter," and he has the sweet nature and happy temperament that go with this. Loving, playful, and responsive to his owner's moods, he makes an enchanting companion. He is also an intelligent little dog who benefits from training and enjoys walks just as much as cuddles. His coat takes a lot of care, so this is a breed only for those who enjoy grooming.

The Maltese is a toy breed of some antiquity with no traces of descent from any working breed—indeed, breed historians trace his origins back to Roman times. First exhibited in the UK in 1864 and in the United States in 1877, he is today equally successful as a glamorous show dog and as a delightful companion.

WHAT colors?

Pure white is the only color in this breed, although pale lemon markings are acceptable. Other colors were accepted at one time, but the colored strains died out altogether in the early years of the 20th century.

WHAT grooming does the coat need?

Daily grooming with a bristle brush is essential to keep the luxurious white tresses in good condition, and the facial hair needs tying back from the eyes. Pet Maltese are probably happier with the coat clipped down to a puppy trim, but it will still need daily brushing to avoid mats and tangles.

HOW suitable are they as family dogs?

Well tempered and reliable, they can be excellent family pets, although their small size makes them unsuitable for households with young or rough children. Older, sensible children will appreciate their sweet nature,

playfulness, and love of attention. They do need training as well as pampering, or they can become overdependent and clinging.

WHAT type of home?

These are essentially companion dogs that need company in order to thrive. As long as they can be with their owner, they can be just as happy in city or country and are small enough to fit in an apartment. They love country walks and hunting in hedgerows but can be perfectly content trotting around the block—though their flowing coats will pick up dirt anywhere, making daily grooming even more important.

WHAT type of owner?

The Maltese needs an affectionate and sensitive but sensible owner who will appreciate his desire for around-the-clock company and attention but also recognize that he is a dog, not an ornament, and requires proper training, exercise, and socialization. This is a high-maintenance breed not suitable for busy owners.

HOW compatible with other pets?

Maltese are friendly and gentle and will get along well with other household pets if brought up with them. Their small size means that they do need supervision with bigger dogs to prevent accidental injury. Small pets such as hamsters need careful introduction. Despite his cuddly appearance the Maltese does retain all of a dog's natural hunting instincts.

HOW much exercise?

This is a breed that will adapt to the owner's requirements. A daily stroll

Character Trait	Poor	Average	Good	Excellent
Attitude to other dogs				
Quietness				
Not destructive				
Protective behavior				
Not likely to stray				
Good with children				
Ease of training				

Original purpose: Lapdog and status symbol
Male height: 9–10 in. (23–25 cm)
Female height: 9–10 in. (23–25 cm)
Weight: 4–6 lb. (2–3 kg)
Life span: 12–14 years

around the park will suffice, but a fit adult Maltese will also enjoy surprisingly long country walks. Don't forget, however, to allow time after the walk to clean up your pet's coat, which will pick up an amazing amount of dirt on each outing.

HOW easy to train?

This is a bright, little dog who is eager to please and responds well to gentle training. Treat him like a toy, and he is likely to become demanding, clingy and over-dependent. Treat him like the intelligent creature he is, providing him with plenty of mental stimulus,

● *His flowing tresses need considerable care.*

and he will be a delight to live with. Many dogs have achieved excellent results in competitive obedience and agility.

Small dogs

WHAT good points?

Sweet tempered, lively, intelligent, affectionate, gentle, friendly, sensitive, alert, playful; nonshedding coat suitable for allergy sufferers.

WHAT to be aware of?

Time-consuming grooming needs. Prone to separation anxiety when left alone too much. Often hard to housebreak, and prone to barking.

WHAT medical problems?

Maltese are generally a healthy breed. Known problems include dislocation of kneecaps (patellar luxation), eye infections, lack of glucose in the blood (hypoglycemia), teeth and gum weaknesses, and liver shunt (an inherited defect whereby the liver does not get a proper blood supply and does not function properly).

Havanese *Other names: Bichon Habanero, Bichon Havanais, Havanese Silk Dog*

Barely known outside his native Cuba until the 1990s, the Havanese has come from nowhere to win hearts with his silky coat and sweet nature. A natural companion breed, he is bright, affectionate, playful, and devoted to his family. Although a toy breed, he is far from fragile but sturdy enough, both physically and mentally, to make a great children's playmate. Havanese are sociable and outgoing. They like people and get along well with other pets. Gentle, responsive, and willing to please, they are thoroughly endearing little characters. The downside is the heavy grooming requirements: the soft, flowing coat that gave them their earlier name of "Havanese Silk Dog" needs loving daily attention.

A member of the Bichon family, the Havanese was taken to Cuba by Spanish settlers and developed there as a distinct breed. By the 1950s they had become rare but are now enjoying a well-earned revival.

WHAT colors?

Any color or combination of colors, including black, white, chocolate, gray, silver, apricot, gold, champagne, sable, parti-color and tricolor.

WHAT grooming does the coat need?

The silky coat needs daily grooming with a soft bristle brush and wide-toothed comb to remove dead hair and prevent tangles. The long hair above the eyes needs to be clipped, braided or tied back to keep it out of the eyes. A neglected coat will mat into a disastrous mess and lead to skin problems and extreme discomfort. Show dogs are shown in full coat; pets can be clipped short for convenience but still need to be brushed every day.

HOW suitable are they as family dogs?

Havanese were made to be family dogs. They are happiest in a family atmosphere and have a natural affinity with children—especially children old enough to treat them sensitively, who will find them tireless playmates. As with any dog, young children must be supervised to prevent unintentional mistreatment of the pet.

WHAT type of home?

Robust enough for the country and compact enough for a city apartment, these undemanding dogs are at home wherever their family is.

WHAT type of owner?

Only those who enjoy grooming should consider a Havanese. Other than that, he makes a great companion for any loving owner, whether a single senior in need of friendship or a lively family with a vacancy for another playmate. He is not suitable for people who work full-time and would have to leave him alone a great deal nor for insensitive owners who are not interested in giving and receiving affection.

HOW compatible with other pets?

Havanese are as friendly toward other pets as they are toward people. They mix well with other dogs and live happily with cats or even smaller pets. If they are not accustomed to cats in puppyhood however, they cannot be expected to understand that cat chasing is not an acceptable game.

HOW much exercise?

Most of a Havanese's exercise

Character Trait	Poor	Average	Good	Excellent
Attitude to other dogs				
Quietness				
Not destructive				
Protective behavior				
Not likely to stray				
Good with children				
Ease of training				

Original purpose: Lapdog
Male height: 8.5–11.5 in. (22–28 cm)
Female height: 8.5–11.5 in. (22–28 cm)
Weight: 7–13 lb. (3–6 kg)
Life span: 12–14 years

needs will be met by play in the house and yard: an hour's walking a day, broken up into two or three brisk outings, will suffice. On the other hand, they have plenty of energy and stamina and will thoroughly enjoy long walks if that is what their owner's lifestyle requires of them.

HOW easy to train?

In the past, Havanese were popular circus dogs because they enjoy learning and showing off what they have learned. Bright and eager to please, they are among the easiest of toy breeds to teach. Training should be positive, gentle, and sensitive, as they are discouraged by harsh treatment and can be quite distressed if scolded.

WHAT good points?

Friendly, lively, outgoing, playful, gentle, affectionate, responsive, sensitive, intelligent, long-lived.

WHAT to be aware of?

Above-average coat care. Quite a dependent breed that may suffer from separation anxiety if left alone.

WHAT medical problems?

Havanese are hardy little dogs with few inherited disorders reported. Possible conditions include eye problems (cataracts, progressive retinal atrophy, and tear duct defects), lack of thyroid hormone (hypothyroidism), kneecap dislocation (patellar luxation), and liver shunt (an inherited defect whereby the liver does not get a proper blood supply and does not function properly).

Small dogs

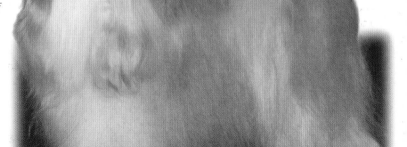

Papillon
Other names: Continental Toy Spaniel, "Butterfly Dog"

As early as the 14th century, the Papillon's ancestors were the favorite lapdogs of European courts. Bred for generations to be a decorative and charming companion, he makes a delightful pet, sweet tempered, playful, and devoted. For all his dainty appearance, he is one of the most trainable of the toy breeds, competing successfully against bigger breeds in obedience, agility, and tracking. Indeed, he is a very adaptable little dog who can be calm and restful or playful and energetic as required, as long as he can enjoy the company of his owner. He does, however, deserve an owner who will make use of his intelligence and keep him busy.

The Papillon takes his name from the French word for "butterfly," his wide-set erect ears resembling a butterfly's wings. There is also a drop-eared version known as the Phalène (French for "moth"), which is considered to be the original type but is less common today.

WHAT colors?
White with patches of any color other than liver, red, black, or sable being most common. Tricolors are white with black patches, tan spots over the eyes, and tan inside the ears, on the cheeks, and under the root of tail. Show dogs are required to have symmetrical facial markings.

WHAT grooming does the coat need?
The fine, silky coat is easy to keep in good condition, provided one is prepared to spend a few minutes each day with brush and comb to prevent tangles from forming—paying particular attention to ear fringes. Footpads may need trimming to keep the feet sound.

HOW suitable are they as family dogs?
Best for families with older children. Papillons are generally good with children, but younger children are often not so good with Papillons.

These are quite fragile little dogs, especially in puppyhood, and unsuited to the rough and tumble of hectic family life. Their tendency to be possessive with their toys may also lead to problems with young children.

WHAT type of home?
These are essentially companion dogs that need company in order to thrive. As long as they can be with their owner, they can be just as happy in city or country. They do need a securely fenced yard, as they can squeeze through tiny gaps and are also great jumpers.

WHAT type of owner?
Papillons are ideal companions for the elderly and indeed ideal dogs for families with older children. Their main function in life is to give and receive affection, so they need owners who are fully committed to spending time with them.

A gentle, sensitive owner who enjoys making use of a dog's intelligence will bring out the best in this breed.

HOW compatible with other pets?
These friendly, gentle little dogs get along well with other pets, especially cats and small dogs. They do need supervision with bigger dogs, as they are quite unaware of their size and can irritate larger animals by being bossy. Most are keen hunters of small prey and need careful introduction to small pets such as hamsters.

HOW much exercise?
Papillons don't need a great deal of exercise, and short walks will suffice

Character Trait	Poor	Average	Good	Excellent
Attitude to other dogs			■	
Quietness		■		
Not destructive			■	
Protective behavior		■		
Not likely to stray			■	
Good with children			■	
Ease of training				■

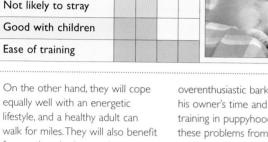

Original purpose: Lapdog and status symbol
Male height: 8–11 in. (20–28 cm)
Female height: 8–11 in. (20–28 cm)
Weight: 4–9 lb. (1.8–4.1 kg)
Life span: 12–15 years

On the other hand, they will cope equally well with an energetic lifestyle, and a healthy adult can walk for miles. They will also benefit from active playtime, and many breeders recommend having two Papillons who can play together.

overenthusiastic barker, so needs his owner's time and sensible training in puppyhood to prevent these problems from arising.

HOW easy to train?

Generally considered the most trainable of all toy breeds, the Papillon often excels at obedience work. In fact this breed responds surprisingly well to gentle, consistent training, but don't expect too much of them.

WHAT good points?

Lively, friendly, alert, playful, adaptable, highly intelligent and trainable, eager to please, neither shy nor aggressive, long-lived.

WHAT to be aware of?

This little dog's loving nature can lead to overprotectiveness or separation anxiety if he is over-coddled in puppyhood. He can also be possessive with toys and an

WHAT medical problems?

Generally a healthy and long-lived breed. Known problems include kneecap dislocation (patellar luxation) and eye problems (progressive retinal atrophy).

Small dogs

● *Alertness and intelligence on display.*

Pomeranian *Other names: Dwarf Spitz, Loulou*

This little ball of fluff looks like a child's toy, but he has a larger-than-life personality and is active, inquisitive, extroverted, and self-important. Tiny and decorative, he is also full of himself, interested in everything that is going on, and determined to be involved. He is one of the most independent of the toy breeds, intensely loyal and protective toward his owner but tending toward the bossy. For those who want a big character in a little package and who enjoy grooming, he makes an enchanting companion.

It is understandable that the Pom should consider himself a big dog, as the breed was not miniaturized until Victorian times. The original Pomeranian was a larger dog, about 30 lb. (13.6 kg) in weight, until a fashion for tiny specimens led to the creation of the modern Pom. His larger cousins are now known as German Spitz and come in a range of sizes.

WHAT colors?

All colors acceptable, including orange, orange sable, cream, wolf sable, black, chocolate, beaver, blue, and parti-colors. Merles (a sort of marbled effect distinguished by the presence of irregular dark blotches against a lighter background of the same basic pigment) are a recent introduction to the breed not universally approved.

WHAT grooming does the coat need?

Don't consider this breed if you don't enjoy grooming. The thick coat requires daily attention, using a stiff bristle brush to work through the fluffy undercoat and long, straight topcoat. Show dogs are delicately trimmed to emphasize the rounded shape.

HOW suitable are they as family dogs?

Highly suitable—for the suitable family. Their tiny size and high energy

● *Toylike in appearance—but the Pom displays remarkable energy.*

level makes them unsuitable for households with very young children, but they make great companions for older children and adults. He does need plenty of attention to keep him out of mischief, so he may not be ideal for a busy family.

WHAT type of home?

A Pom will fit in anywhere, from apartment to mansion. As long as he can be with his owner, he can be just as happy in the city or country. Apartment dogs will benefit from daily access to a park to provide both physical and mental stimulation, but they can exercise themselves quite well indoors playing with their owners.

WHAT type of owner?

Poms need affection and attention, but they also need training. An over-indulgent owner can turn this bossy little dog into a household tyrant. Given an owner who is prepared to spend time on gentle but firm and consistent training, he makes an ideal companion for the housebound elderly but can also enjoy a moderately robust family life with older, sensible children.

HOW compatible with other pets?

Poms are sociable little dogs that generally get along well with other household pets, although if kept with bigger dogs, they run the risk of accidental injury. They do need sensible socialization in puppyhood to curb their natural desire to

Character Trait	Poor	Average	Good	Excellent
Attitude to other dogs		■		
Quietness	■			
Not destructive			■	
Protective behavior			■	
Not likely to stray			■	
Good with children		■		
Ease of training		■		

*Place of origin: **Middle Europe***

Original purpose: Lapdog (but his ancestors were herders)
Male height: 8.5–11 in. (22–28 cm)
Female height: 8.5–11 in. (22–28 cm)
Weight: 3–7 lb. (1.4–3 kg)
Life span: 12–15 years

chase strange cats and bully strange dogs.

HOW much exercise?

The Pom's exercise requirements are minimal, and he can obtain all the exercise he needs running around a small yard or simply playing indoors. Having said that, he enjoys walks just as much as bigger breeds, and a healthy adult should be able to walk for miles.

HOW easy to train?

This breed responds surprisingly well to gentle, consistent training, but don't expect too much of them. They are intelligent and quick to learn; but they are also quite independent minded and mischievous, and not the breed for obedience enthusiasts.

WHAT good points?

Extrovert, vivacious, intelligent, active, loving, gregarious; good watchdogs; low maintenance in terms of exercise and food requirements; easily transported.

WHAT to be aware of?

Poms like the sound of their own voices and need sensible training to prevent them from being noisy. They shed profusely, so you will need a good vacuum cleaner. Watch out for unscrupulous breeders who may produce stock with untypical, poor temperaments..

WHAT medical problems?

Like other toy breeds, Pomeranians may suffer dislocation of the kneecaps (patellar luxation). Other disorders occurring in the breed include tracheal (windpipe) collapse, inward-turning eyelids (entropion), cataracts, and skin disease causing loss of hair.

Small dogs

Norfolk Terrier/Norwich Terrier

Two closely related breeds differing principally in ear carriage, these jaunty little terriers originated in East Anglia as working ratters and companions. In 1932 they were granted KC recognition as a single breed, the Norwich, with either erect or drop ears, but in 1964 they were divided into two breeds, the drop-eared Norfolk and prick-eared Norwich. The Norfolk's folded ears give him a softer expression, and some say he has a slightly softer temperament. However, both are friendly, outgoing characters whose breed standard stipulates a "lovable disposition," ideal companions for anyone who enjoys the busy, bustling terrier temperament but wants to avoid the more fiery breeds. Small enough to fit in anywhere and adaptable in terms of exercise, they make wonderful family pets, being very affectionate, responsive, and entertaining. They do need a moderate amount of exercise and coat care, but their primary need is for company—and entertainment.

WHAT colors?

All shades of red, wheat, black and tan, or grizzle (red mixed with black hairs).

WHAT grooming does the coat need?

The coat is quite dense and needs brushing with bristle brush and/or hound glove twice a week; dogs with heavier coats will also need facial and leg hair combing through. Twice a year the coat needs to be hand stripped to remove dead hairs and encourage the new coat to grow.

HOW suitable are they as family dogs?

These are great little family dogs for a household with children old enough to treat pets sensibly. Sociable, busy little dogs, they don't thrive without company and attention and want to be part of all family activities. No terrier is an ideal choice with very young children as terriers are rarely tolerant of rough handling.

● *A Norfolk puppy at rest—but he can quickly become a real ball of fire.*

WHAT type of home?

They would prefer a country home where there are hedges and ditches to investigate and local wildlife to bully but are small enough and adaptable enough to cope with city life provided they have enough to do. They do need access to a yard with terrier-proof fencing and a laid-back gardener who can put up with enthusiastic digging.

WHAT type of owner?

Both Norwich and Norfolk make great companions for active, easygoing owners who have plenty of time for play and exploration, are not looking for strict, formal obedience, and appreciate the busy, bossy terrier nature. They need company and activity and should not be considered by anyone who has to leave a dog alone for long periods.

HOW compatible with other pets?

With appropriate socialization, is important to ensure that terrier assertiveness does not go too far, they are generally friendly with other dogs and with cats in their own household. They are natural hunters, so they are likely to chase the cat next door and should not be trusted with small pets such as rabbits and hamsters.

HOW much exercise?

Active but adaptable, these small terriers will manage with a couple of brisk walks a day or will happily

Character Trait	Poor	Average	Good	Excellent
Attitude to other dogs		■		
Quietness	■			
Not destructive			■	
Protective behavior			■	
Not likely to stray		■		
Good with children			■	
Ease of training			■	

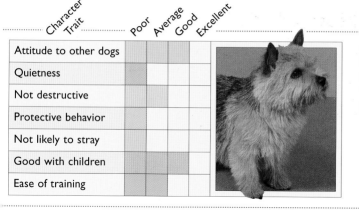

Original purpose: Ratting
Male height: 9–10 in. (23–25 cm)
Female height: 9–10 in. (23–25 cm)
Weight: 11–12 lb. (5–5.5 kg)
Life span: 13–15 years

walk their owners off their feet. Without a reasonable amount of exercise, they will easily become unfit and obese. Mental stimulation is equally important: a walk around the block is much less interesting than a chance to explore the farthest corners of the park.

HOW easy to train?

With firm, kind, sensible training starting from day one, the Norfolk or Norwich will become a well-behaved member of the household, but don't start thinking about obedience championships. They are terriers after all, bossy, self-willed, and prone to selective deafness when there is something interesting to investigate.

WHAT good points?

● *Folded ears characterize the Norfolk Terrier; the closely related Norwich Terrier is prick eared.*

Cheerful, sociable, friendly, lively, playful, fearless, inquisitive, entertaining, small yet tough, alert watchdog.

WHAT to be aware of?

Assertive little dogs who need firm but fair handling. Can be noisy; strong chasing instincts; great diggers and escape artists.

WHAT medical problems?

Generally healthy, with few reported health problems. Conditions reported occasionally include lack of thyroid hormone (hypothyroidism), epilepsy, and breathing problems.

Small dogs

Bichon Frise

Few breeds look as much like a fluffy toy as the Bichon, a cuddly, white snowball with jet-black eyes and nose. This is one of the liveliest of toy breeds, a playful extrovert with a great enthusiasm for life and affection for people. A delightful companion, he demands attention and is happy to reciprocate. He is tougher than he looks and with an active owner can enjoy long country walks or agility. He does take a lot of grooming and is a strong-willed little dog who can be manipulative and stubborn (and, if spoiled, a positive household tyrant), so sensible training in puppyhood is absolutely essential.

The Bichon's history displays his adaptability. He was an aristocratic lapdog in 17th-century France and Spain, later earning his living as the performing dog of street performers and circuses. In the mid-20th century he emerged from obscurity as a highly popular show dog and companion, a status this happy, affectionate, and intelligent dog well deserves.

WHAT colors?

Always white. Puppies under 18 months may show faint cream or apricot markings.

WHAT grooming does the coat need?

A lot—daily brushing and combing, regular baths, and clipping every four to six weeks. The face needs special attention to avoid brown tear stains and stains around the mouth. The natural coat (preferred in Europe) is a mass of soft loose curls, but in the UK and US the coat is trimmed to a sculptured shape. Pet owners often find a puppy clip more manageable.

HOW suitable are they as family dogs?

The Bichon's happy, people-loving nature makes him a great family dog in a household where there is plenty of time for him. He is not ideal for families with very young children, as he likes to be the center of attention himself. He is likely to compete for toys and affection and is also vulnerable to toddlers who cannot distinguish between stuffed toys and living creatures.

WHAT type of home?

Equally suited to city or country living, mansion or apartment, the Bichon can fit into most lifestyles as long as he has exercise and attention. Given the choice, he would prefer to have a yard so he can play outdoors.

WHAT type of owner?

A Bichon needs attention, attention, and attention—he is not a part-time dog but needs an owner who can be with him most of the time. He is best suited to a lively owner who will enjoy playing with him, who is loving but firm and patient enough not to allow this little charmer to turn into a spoiled brat, and who is happy to spend a fair amount of time on grooming.

HOW compatible with other pets?

This good-natured breed generally gets along well with other dogs and with cats in the same household. Puppyhood socialization is important to ensure that he knows how to behave with larger breeds. He may need watching with strange cats and also with other small pets, which he may see as toys.

HOW much exercise?

Bichons are very adaptable. They don't need a lot of exercise but will enjoy plenty if it is offered. They have lots of energy, which they can burn off in play and racing around the house. A couple of short walks a day will keep them fit, or they will enjoy longer walks if on a regular basis—but they may need a bath after a muddy country expedition.

Character Trait	Poor	Average	Good	Excellent
Attitude to other dogs			■	
Quietness		■		
Not destructive			■	
Protective behavior	■			
Not likely to stray		■		
Good with children			■	
Ease of training			■	

Original purpose: Companion
Male height: 9.5–11.5 in. (24–29 cm)
Female height: 9.5–11.5 in. (24–29 cm)
Weight: 7–12 lb. (3–5.5 kg)
Life span: 12–15 years

HOW easy to train?

The Bichon's natural liveliness can be a challenge. Like many toy breeds, they can be strong willed and stubborn but will respond to training as long as their interest is caught and maintained. Training needs to be gentle but firm, patient and persistent. This breed can be slow to mature, so don't expect rapid results.

WHAT good points?

Happy, lively, very friendly, affectionate, playful, outgoing, vivacious, intelligent, non-aggressive, ultra-companionable.

WHAT to be aware of?

A demanding little dog who may be too exuberant for owners who want a gentle lapdog temperament. Heavy grooming commitment. Can be noisy.

WHAT medical problems?

This is generally a healthy breed, but slipping kneecaps and hip malformation (dysplasia) can occur, as do hemophilia and heart defects. Progressive retinal atrophy (degeneration of the light receptor cells in the eyes) has been recorded in the US and Australia.

● *They look like fluffy toys and are almost as good-natured.*

Small dogs

Lhasa Apso

His name means "hairy barking dog," and the Lhasa Apso is indeed a keen watchdog covered with flowing hair. Beneath the abundant coat is a hardy little dog full of personality, who loves human company, is very attached to his owner, and will adapt to a range of lifestyles. Despite his glamorous appearance, he is no lapdog but an assertive character with the independence typical of Oriental breeds and a definite mind of his own. He will give you his heart, but don't expect him to obey your every command. As a companion, he is playful, affectionate, and attuned to his owner's mood—and requires a serious commitment to grooming.

Lhasa Apsos were developed in Tibetan monasteries as companions, sentinels, and "good luck dogs." Introduced to England in the late 19th century as "Lhassa terriers," they achieved KC recognition in 1902 and subsequently were recognized by the AKC in 1935.

WHAT colors?

Golden, sandy, honey, dark grizzle, slate, smoke, parti-color, black, white, or brown.

WHAT grooming does the coat need?

This is a high-maintenance coat needing thorough daily grooming with a firm brush and combing right down to the skin, paying special attention to the face and underparts. Although the hair is usually allowed to fall over the eyes, it can be tied back for comfort The coat can be cut down to a puppy clip every four to six weeks, although some daily grooming is still needed. A neglected coat mats and tangles, causing skin problems and real discomfort.

HOW suitable are they as family dogs?

Playful and affectionate, the Lhasa makes a great family dog so long as his needs are understood. He is very good with sensible children but dislikes rough handling and may snap if teased or accidentally stepped on. Not recommended for households with children too young to be gentle. He does like to be the baby of the household himself, and busy families may find that they do not have enough time for him.

WHAT type of home?

This adaptable little dog can be happy in the city or in the country. He would prefer a yard to play in, but if none is available can make do quite happily with three or four brief but interesting walks every day.

WHAT type of owner?

Lhasa owners should appreciate an independent, manipulative little dog and have plenty of time for grooming, play, and cuddles. He can be equally happy as sole companion to a senior or with a lively family—his main need is to be loved. Owners who don't actively enjoy grooming should probably look elsewhere as this is a major commitment with this breed.

HOW compatible with other pets?

Early socialization is essential to ensure good relationships with other dogs: Lhasas are naturally suspicious of strangers, and that includes strange canines. Males in particular can be aggressive toward other male dogs. They are usually good with cats and other small pets in their own household but often consider chasing strange cats to be great fun.

HOW much exercise?

Lhasas are very adaptable. They don't need a great

Character Trait	Poor	Average	Good	Excellent
Attitude to other dogs		■		
Quietness	■			
Not destructive		■		
Protective behavior			■	
Not likely to stray		■		
Good with children			■	
Ease of training		■		

Original purpose: Companion, watchdog
Male height: 10–11 in. (25–28 cm)
Female height: 8–10 in. (20–25 cm)
Weight: 13–15 lb. (6–7 kg)
Life span: 12–14 years

Small dogs

● Very obviously this is a high-maintenance coat.

deal of exercise and can stay fit with daily short walks; but they can thoroughly enjoy longer walks if that is your lifestyle.

HOW easy to train?
Moderate. Lhasas are smart little dogs who can learn anything they want; the trick is making them want to learn. Formal obedience is not their style, but good behavior needs to be taught. Training should start early and be firm, fair, consistent, and above all fun. Food rewards appeal to most Lhasas; a forceful approach will get you nowhere.

WHAT good points?
Merry, assertive, alert, steady, hardy, energetic, loyal, affectionate, intelligent

WHAT to be aware of?
Heavy grooming commitment. Can be difficult to housebreak.

WHAT medical problems?
Generally a healthy and long-lived breed, with some occurrence of progressive retinal atrophy; also rare juvenile kidney disease.

Australian Terrier

Affectionately nicknamed the "Little Terror," the Aussie is a classic short-legged, shaggy terrier born to hunt vermin and to be a lively companion. He is a busy little dog, full of spirit and fun, needing an active family who will enjoy his energy. Highly affectionate, he wants to be involved in family life and is unsuited to being left alone for long periods. For those who appreciate terrier high spirits, he is a wonderful pet, sometimes mischievous but also very responsive to his owner's moods. The breed is generally healthy and long-lived, with an easy-care coat and happy temperament. Although not a yappy dog, he is a keen guard who will announce visitors.

Developed in the Australian outback from ancestral British terrier breeds, the Aussie was imported to the UK in 1906 and recognized in the US in 1960. Slow to achieve popularity, his virtues have now won wider recognition, both as a lively and affectionate family pet and as a show dog.

WHAT colors?

Blue and tan (blue, steel blue, or dark gray blue with rich tan on face, ears, underbody, lower legs and feet, and around the vent), solid sandy, solid red.

WHAT grooming does the coat need?

This is an easy-care coat. Unlike many terriers, the pet Aussie does not require stripping, although show dogs are tidied with a stripping knife. A weekly brushing with a bristle brush to remove dead hairs will suffice, plus trimming the hair between the eyes for comfort. Particular attention needs to be paid to flea control, as allergies are common in this breed.

HOW suitable are they as family dogs?

The Aussie makes an excellent family pet. He is generally very good with children, although (as with any small dog) supervision with toddlers is essential. For sensible children he is the ideal fun-loving and tireless companion as well as a protective guard.

WHAT type of home?

Equally suited to city or country living as long as they have plenty to do these little terriers can fit into most lifestyles. They are not meant for kennel life for they need involvement with their human family and plenty to do—otherwise the devil will find work for idle paws. They will appreciate a yard, but secure fencing is a must to prevent solo hunting excursions.

WHAT type of owner?

If you like the sparky terrier temperament, you'll love the Aussie. If you prefer a more placid pet, look elsewhere. Like all terriers, he needs an owner with a firm, consistent approach to training, plenty of time for him, and a reasonably active lifestyle.

HOW compatible with other pets?

Terriers are naturally bossy little dogs and can be aggressive toward strange dogs—particularly big ones. They will accept dogs (and cats) that are members of the same household, although rivalry between adult males may be a problem. Small pets like rabbits and hamsters are best kept well out of the way of these enthusiastic hunters.

HOW much exercise?

This little terrier needs a great deal of exercise to keep him fit and to ward off boredom. Despite his

Character Trait	Poor	Average	Good	Excellent
Attitude to other dogs		■		
Quietness	■			
Not destructive		■		
Protective behavior			■	
Not likely to stray		■		
Good with children			■	
Ease of training		■		

Original purpose: Vermin control
Male height: 10–11 in. (25–28 cm)
Female height: 10–11 in. (25–28 cm)
Weight: 12–14 lb. (5.4–6.5 kg)
Life span: 12–14 years

short legs, he can run for miles. Particular attention needs to be paid to teaching him the recall, as his hunting instincts remain keen and he is not easily deflected from chasing anything that moves.

HOW easy to train?

Like most terriers, the Aussie can be willful and has a low boredom threshold, so training needs to be firm, consistent, and above all fun. Keep training sessions short, with plenty of rewards (treats, toys or verbal praise) to maintain his interest, and he is a quick learner. This breed has been trained to high levels of competitive obedience.

WHAT good points?

Friendly, extroverted, high spirited, alert, adaptable, fun-loving, affectionate, loyal, full of character, hardy; a good watchdog.

WHAT to be aware of?

Males can be aggressive toward other dogs and have the terrier tendency to take on much larger opponents. If left alone for long periods, they may become destructive or noisy. They are born diggers—not an ideal choice for dedicated gardeners.

WHAT medical problems?

The Aussie is generally a healthy breed. Disorders that have been noted include diabetes and thyroid disorder, some predisposition to skin allergies, dislocation of the kneecap (patellar luxation), Legg-Calvé-Perthes disease (a degenerative hip condition).

Small dogs

● *Although shaggy, the "Little Terror's" coat does not require great attention. Weekly grooming should suffice.*

Skye Terrier

The only terrier that can be described as glamorous, the Skye is a big dog in a small frame—long and low in body, with a flowing coat and a dignified air. As his looks suggest, he is a companion breed rather than a working terrier. This is a dog of great character who has a mind of his own and whose respect has to be earned. Intelligent, sensitive, and stubborn, he is calmer than most terrier breeds and very adaptable in terms of exercise. He is devoted to his owner, often tending to be a "one-man dog," but distrustful of strangers: early socialization is important to ensure that this trait does not become a problem. He is not to be trusted with small pets.

Skyes are descended from the tough working terriers of the Scottish Highlands. They became fashionable show dogs in the 19th century when Queen Victoria took up the breed but are sadly less popular today.

WHAT colors?
Black, dark or light gray, fawn, cream, all with black ears. A small white spot on the chest is permissible. Puppies (except creams) are born black, changing color at around three to four months old.

WHAT grooming does the coat need?
The flowing coat needs combing through twice a week to prevent mats, and the hair around eyes and mouth may need cleaning daily. Spayed bitches tend to grow softer, woollier coats that need extra combing. Pet owners may choose to have the coat clipped for ease of care.

HOW suitable are they as family dogs?
Some Skyes make great family pets, extending their love to the whole family, but on the whole this is not the obvious choice for a family. Although generally gentle and good-natured with their owners, Skyes dislike being teased, and some may snap if startled. So they are not recommended for households with young children.

WHAT type of home?
In general, the Skye will be happy where his owner is. Ideally he should have access to a secure yard where he can play. He will adapt to apartment life provided he has several walks a day to provide physical exercise and mental stimulation.

WHAT type of owner?
This is not a dog that will suit everyone. The Skye offers intense loyalty without servility and needs an owner who will appreciate the fun in this stubborn, self-opinionated character. He is best with an owner as strong willed as himself who has plenty of time for him. Skyes need company and become bored and destructive if left for long periods.

HOW compatible with other pets?
Terriers are naturally bossy and tend to be dominant, so early socialization with other dogs is essential if the Skye is to get on well with them in adult life. He will accept cats that are members of the same household if brought up with them. However, no terrier should be trusted with small pets like rabbits and hamsters.

HOW much exercise?
Moderate. Skyes are quite adaptable in terms of exercise, but an adult

Character Trait	Poor	Average	Good	Excellent
Attitude to other dogs	■			
Quietness	■			
Not destructive			■	
Protective behavior			■	
Not likely to stray	■			
Good with children	■			
Ease of training	■			

Original purpose: Fox and otter hunting
Male height: 9.5–10.5 in. (24–27 cm)
Female height: 9–10 in. (23–25 cm)
Weight: 25–40 lb. (11.3–18.2 kg)
Life span: 12–14 years

will enjoy an hour's walk every day. Puppies should not be over-exercised, as this can damage growing bones: build up the length of walks gradually from six months onward.

HOW easy to train?

Not easy. The Skye has a very strong character and no innate leaning toward obedience. He is intelligent and a quick learner, but he is not keen to do anything unless he can see good reason for it. Training needs to be firm, consistent, and rewarding for him. With the right handling, he will work with you but never for you.

WHAT good points?

Loving, faithful, plenty of personality, good watchdog, fearless, dignified, merry, and fun loving with his owners.

WHAT to be aware of?

Early socialization essential to prevent dislike of strangers and potential aggression toward other animals. Extremely stubborn and self-willed.

WHAT medical problems?

This is a robust breed with few inherited problems. Occasional early closure of growth plates in the forelegs (chondrodysplasia), causing lameness, may be caused by over-exercising immature youngsters.

Small dogs

● *The flowing locks that descend over the Skye's eyes and mouth demand daily attention.*

Border Terrier

One of the most sensible and good-natured of the terriers, the Border is a smart, functional little dog. He was bred to keep up with hounds and horses over a long day's hunting. He retains all the stamina, speed, and agility this required. However, nowadays it is his friendly nature that is most valued, and he has come into his own as a companion and family pet. This is a dog with all the terrier virtues, games, and love of family and fun, but without the aggressive edge of some terriers. He does need time, attention, and exercise for both mind and body to keep him out of mischief.

Borders love a close involvement with family life and hate being left alone all day—and a lonely, bored Border is likely to be noisy and destructive. In a loving home, however, this breed can be one of the best family dogs available since he has the reputation of being very good with children.

WHAT colors?

There are four approved colors: red, wheat, grizzle, and tan (the grizzle hairs being of agouti coloring with each hair banded in three colors), and blue and tan. White markings on the chest are acceptable.

WHAT grooming does the coat need?

The harsh, weatherproof coat is relatively low maintenance, needing a good brush through twice a week. To keep the coat good looking, it needs to be hand stripped two or three times a year, plucking dead hairs from the coat with finger and thumb—your pup's breeder can teach you the technique.

HOW suitable are they as family dogs?

The Border is an ideal family pet. He is generally very good with children, although (as with any small dog) supervision with youngsters is essential. He won't tolerate being teased or ill treated. For sensible

● Smart and alert, the Border is gentler than most terriers.

children, he is the ideal fun-loving and tireless companion.

WHAT type of home?

As long as a Border has reasonable exercise and plenty to interest him, he will be just as happy in the city as in the country. He will appreciate a yard, which needs to be securely fenced—most of this breed are champion escapologists who won't hesitate to scramble over or under obstacles in quest of adventure.

WHAT type of owner?

This is a great dog for active owners and families who want a lively, good-natured dog and have time for play and exercise—and who have no small pets that might be at risk. If you enjoy a busy, stimulating pet who wants to participate fully in family life and are prepared to put time into puppy socialization and training, the Border could well be the dog for you.

HOW compatible with other pets?

Borders are sociable creatures that usually get along well with other dogs and with cats within their own household—but probably not with other people's cats. They have strong hunting instincts and should not be trusted with smaller animals such as hamsters or guinea pigs.

HOW much exercise?

This active breed will take all the exercise you can offer. A daily stroll once around the block is not enough to keep a Border fit and happy—a fit adult can run for miles. He needs regular, brisk walks,

Place of origin: **Scotland and northern England**

Character Trait	Poor	Average	Good	Excellent
Attitude to other dogs	■			
Quietness		■		
Not destructive		■		
Protective behavior	■			
Not likely to stray		■		
Good with children				■
Ease of training			■	

Original purpose: Vermin control
Male height: 10–11 in. (25–28 cm)
Female height: 10–11 in. (25–28 cm)
Weight: 11.5–15.5 lb. (5–7 kg)
Life span: 12–15 years

including off-lead exercise, which should be supplemented with games in the yard and training exercises to occupy his mind.

HOW easy to train?

No terrier would be the first choice for an obedience enthusiast. The Border is easier to train than most provided his interest is engaged—though his strong streak of independence means that he is likely to obey in his own time rather than instantly. Keep training sessions short, challenging, reward based, and above all fun for best results.

Small dogs

WHAT good points?

Sensible, affectionate, active, devoted, sweet natured, alert, playful, good-natured with strangers, gentle for a terrier.

WHAT to be aware of?

Like most terriers, has a tendency to bark excessively and, if left to his own devices, will dig up the yard. Strong instinct to chase anything that moves.

WHAT medical problems?

Generally a healthy breed without significant health problems. Occasionally reported are dislocation of the kneecap (patellar luxation), eye problems including glaucoma and cataracts, and skin problems.

Miniature Pinscher

The "King of the Toys" is a smart, elegant little dog with clean lines, a classy high-stepping gait, and dainty, even fragile appearance. In temperament, however, he is far from fragile. More terrier than lapdog in character, this is an alert, bossy, and dynamic character. He is highly active, energetic, fearless, and inquisitive; an enthusiastic watchdog, and a loving companion. This busy little dog is perhaps not suitable for the novice as he is strong willed and, given the chance, can become a household tyrant. He needs socialization to prevent his innate suspicion of strangers from escalating into overt aggression, exercise and mental stimulation to keep him happy, and constant supervision to keep him out of mischief.

The Min Pin dates back to at least the 16th century. Despite the name, he has no connection with the Doberman Pinscher, although they share the same stylish build—on a different scale.

WHAT colors?

Black and tan, chocolate and tan, blue and tan, or solid red. Slight white marking on chest permissible but not desirable.

WHAT grooming does the coat need?

The easy-care coat needs only weekly brushing to remove dead hairs and the occasional polish with a soft cloth.

HOW suitable are they as family dogs?

The Min Pin makes a great addition to a family who want a little dog with a big character. He is very loving, good with sensible children who treat him with respect, and enjoys participating in family activities. He is not recommended for households with young children as he is too fragile to withstand rough handling and may nip if teased.

WHAT type of home?

This compact little dog makes an ideal apartment pet, but he can be just as happy burning off energy in the country. Min Pins are great escapologists who need absolutely secure fencing and screens on windows and doors: they will take advantage of any opportunity to run out and investigate the world outside. With their fine coats, they feel the cold and need a warm home.

WHAT type of owner?

Min Pins do best with experienced, confident owners who appreciate a high-energy breed and can cope with a dog with the attitude of an adventurous toddler who is into everything. They need firm but gentle handling by owners who are neither harsh nor overindulgent, and they should not be left alone for long periods, as they need company and supervision.

HOW compatible with other pets?

Like terriers, Min Pins are bossy little dogs descended from

"Let's play," suggests an energetic Miniature Pinscher.

Character Trait	Poor	Average	Good	Excellent
Attitude to other dogs		▓		
Quietness	▓			
Not destructive			▓	
Protective behavior				▓
Not likely to stray		▓		
Good with children			▓	
Ease of training		▓		

Original purpose: Small vermin hunting
Male height: 10–12 in. (25–30 cm)
Female height: 10–12 in. (25–30 cm)
Weight: 8–10 lb. (3.5–4.5 kg)
Life span: 12–14 years

generations of ratters. They are usually fine with cats and dogs within their own household but can be dominant and aggressive with strange dogs and will chase strange cats. They are unlikely to be safe with small pets like rabbits and hamsters.

HOW much exercise?

Min Pins are adaptable. They don't need a lot of exercise but will enjoy as much as is offered. Ideally they should have a good walk every day and burn off the rest of their energy in play. This breed really feels the cold and will need a warm coat for winter walks.

HOW easy to train?

Training the Min Pin is not easy but can be achieved with time, patience and persistence. He has a short attention span and a low boredom threshold, so training needs to be firm, consistent, and above all fun. Keep training sessions short, with plenty of rewards to maintain his interest. A sense of humor is vital as this breed loves to play the clown.

WHAT good points?

Loyal, loving, alert, excellent watchdog, fearless, animated, curious, active, entertaining, sound, intelligent, convenient size.

WHAT to be aware of?

Can be difficult to housebreak, and likes the sound of his own voice. His curiosity can lead him into trouble, so care needs to be taken to pinscher-proof the home—he can jump onto furniture and steal hazardous items such as medication as well as being able to run through the smallest of gaps. The yard, too, should be escape proof.

WHAT medical problems?

This is generally a healthy breed, with occasional kneecap dislocation (patellar luxation) the only real concern.

Small dogs

Pug

Supremely dignified on the outside and a natural clown on the inside, the Pug is a custom-built companion for less-active owners. He is far from sedentary himself but a busy, curious little dog full of personality who loves to play and requires plenty of interaction with his owner. However, he is a low-maintenance dog needing relatively little exercise or grooming. Sociable, equable, and affectionate, he will adapt to most lifestyles as long as he has his owner's company. The breed does have quite a few health problems and needs special consideration in hot weather.

Pugs originated in China in ancient times and reached the West by trade in the 16th or 17th century to become great favorites in Holland and later England, reaching the height of their popularity in the 18th century. Although Pugs have been out of fashion for some time, they are now enjoying a well-merited comeback.

WHAT colors?

Silver, apricot, fawn, or black. The lighter colors have a dark mask, ears, thumb mark, or diamond on forehead, and trace (a line down the back from head to tail).

WHAT grooming does the coat need?

The short, smooth coat requires regular brushing to remove dead hairs—Pugs shed a surprising amount. In addition, the facial wrinkles need checking and cleaning daily. If this task is neglected, they become damp, smelly, and even infected.

HOW suitable are they as family dogs?

The Pug is an ideal dog for a family whose lifestyle does not revolve around long walks. He tends to regard himself as one of the children. His even temperament and playful nature make him a wonderful choice for children old enough to understand how to handle a living creature. However, preschool children are likely to be too rough for a small dog.

WHAT type of home?

Any home that has a Pug-lover will suit a Pug. He is compact enough for a small apartment and sturdy enough to prosper in the country. He would not be happy kennelled outside, however, as he needs to be with people.

WHAT type of owner?

This is a wonderful breed for any-one who wants a close, affectionate relationship with a dog and will appreciate a lively, demanding little character. Pugs won't suit owners who want a dog to go for long, energetic walks or to work at competitive obedience, but they are adaptable and can adopt a wide variety of lifestyles.

HOW compatible with other pets?

Pugs will happily extend their friendship to other animals of all kinds—but be careful with kittens or aggressive cats as the Pug's bulging eyes are vulnerable to scratches.

HOW much exercise?

Pugs have boundless energy but will use most of it up in play and don't need a great deal of exercise. However, two brisk walks a day are recommended to keep them fit. If your lifestyle includes regular exercise, a fit adult Pug will enjoy accompanying you for several miles.

Character Trait	Poor	Average	Good	Excellent
Attitude to other dogs			●	
Quietness		●		
Not destructive			●	
Protective behavior	●			
Not likely to stray			●	
Good with children				●
Ease of training		●		

Original purpose: Lapdog
Male height: 10–11 in. (25–28 cm)
Female height: 10–11 in. (25–28 cm)
Weight: 14–18 lb. (6.5–8 kg)
Life span: 12–15 years

This breed should never be walked in hot weather as they overheat easily.

HOW easy to train?
If you want an obedience champion, look elsewhere. Pugs are strong-minded little dogs who can be taught good behavior reasonably easily but have little interest in responding snappily to commands. However, they are intelligent and can learn if they wish—individuals have performed well at obedience, flyball, agility, and even as support dog for a disabled owner, carrying out tasks like fetching the telephone and unloading the washing machine.

WHAT good points?
Friendly, affectionate, tolerant, well-tempered, lively, playful, entertaining, sociable, intelligent, lots of personality, adaptable.

WHAT to be aware of?
Snorting, snuffling, wheezing, snoring, and flatulence. Susceptibility to overheating.

Constant heavy shedding. May be hard to housebreak.

WHAT medical problems?
Breathing problems associated with the short face, including elongated soft palate; hip malformation (dysplasia); kneecap dislocation (patellar luxation); Legg-Calvé-Perthes disease (lack of blood supply to the top of the femur resulting in bone death); hemivertebrae (congenital spinal deformity); eye problems (cataracts,

● His flat face and bulgy eyes have great charm.

ulcers, vulnerability to injury), and inward-turning eyelids (entropion); tendency to mast-cell skin tumors.

Small dogs

● The Pug's facial wrinkles should be checked every day.

Scottish Terrier

At first glance, the Scottie gives the impression of being more serious minded than most terriers—indeed, he is often described as "dour." Those who know him would disagree. Reserved and even suspicious with strangers, in the heart of his family he is a devoted companion, lively, playful, and surprisingly sensitive. He is not, however, a dog for the faint-hearted. Strong willed and downright stubborn, he needs an equally strong-minded owner or he will take over as leader of the household. He has strong hunting instincts, a tendency to be territorial, and a low tolerance of anything he considers mistreatment.

The terriers of the Scottish Highlands have a long history but were not separated into distinct breeds until well into the 19th century. The Scottie breed standard was written in 1880, and it was not long before he had become as much of a Scottish icon as the kilt and the bagpipes.

WHAT colors?

The most common color is black, but Scotties can also be wheat (pale gold to red gold) or brindle.

WHAT grooming does the coat need?

Quite a lot: thorough brushing twice weekly with a hard bristle brush plus hand stripping or clipping every few months. If left untrimmed, the coat grows too long for comfort. Show dogs are trimmed short on the back with flowing skirts and shaggy beard and eyebrows; pets can be clipped short for convenience, although clipping rather than stripping affects coat texture.

HOW suitable are they as family dogs?

Scotties can be good family dogs if sensibly raised within the family, but in general they are a better choice for adults. They often tend to be one-person dogs. They can also be quite jealous little dogs who may object to children competing for attention. They are not recommended with young children as they do not tolerate rough treatment or mishandling.

WHAT type of home?

The Scottie is a dog for city or country, even apartment life as long as he has company and exercise. He needs a yard, though keen gardeners may not need a Scottie as he is an enthusiastic digger. Secure fences are a must: he can jump four times his own height or burrow under barriers if he feels the need to investigate the outside world.

WHAT type of owner?

Not recommended for the novice, the Scottie suits an experienced, strong-willed owner who appreciates a dog with an independent nature and can be boss in the household without being a bully. Prospective owners should not be obedience enthusiasts but should enjoy walking and playing with a dog. This breed needs company and is not for people who are out at work all day.

HOW compatible with other pets?

Early socialization is important to ensure that Scotties are not aggressive with other dogs. Good with cats in their household if brought up with them, they tend to regard strange cats as fair game. They are enthusiastic hunters, so small pets should be kept well out of their way.

Character Trait	Poor	Average	Good	Excellent
Attitude to other dogs				
Quietness				
Not destructive				
Protective behavior				
Not likely to stray				
Good with children				
Ease of training				

Original purpose: Vermin control
Male height: 10–11 in. (25–28 cm)
Female height: 10–11 in. (25–28 cm)
Weight: 18–22 lb. (8.1–10 kg)
Life span: 11–13 years

HOW much exercise?

Medium. Scotties are energetic dogs who need at least half an hour's brisk walk a day and active playtime. Beyond that, they are adaptable. They can amuse themselves at home, or they can enjoy long country hikes, although their short legs mean they are not suitable jogging or running companions.

HOW easy to train?

Difficult. Scotties don't do obedience. For a handler who can establish firm but kind leadership, they are perfectly prepared to be cooperative—in their own time. They need to respect their owners and also to be treated with respect: they are sensitive dogs who resent affronts to their dignity and react badly to rough handling.

WHAT good points?

Loyal, faithful, intelligent, protective, dignified, bold, sensible, vigilant, playful, independent.

WHAT to be aware of

Can be territorial and/or aggressive to strangers or other dogs if not properly socialized. Above-average coat care.

Small dogs

WHAT medical problems?

Basically a healthy breed, the Scottie may suffer from problems of the skin and flea allergies, cranio-mandibular osteopathy (a painful disease of the lower jaw), von Willebrand's disease (a bleeding disorder), lack of thyroid hormone (hypothyroidism), and "Scottie cramp."

● *Full of Scottish dignity, the Scottie needs a strong-willed owner.*

Shih Tzu

China's "Chrysanthemum Dog," with his flowerlike face and cascade of fur, looks like a glamorous toy, but he is a sturdy little dog bursting with personality. The Shih Tzu is a merry extrovert, playful, highly sociable, and affectionate without being clingy. The independent character typical of Oriental breeds makes him a great companion but a poor choice for obedience fanatics. He is highly adaptable, happy to recline on a cushion or enjoy country walks. His only real disadvantage is his flowing coat, which requires a lot of time and an owner who sincerely enjoys grooming.

One of the Oriental "lion dogs" representing the lion of Buddha in canine form, the Shih Tzu developed in China from Tibetan lion dogs presented to the emperor. Reaching the West in the early 20th century, he was initially identified with Tibet's Lhasa Apso; recognized as a distinct breed in the 1930s, he rapidly achieved popularity.

WHAT colors?

All colors are allowed, including gold, black, gray, silver, brindle, and particolor.

WHAT grooming does the coat need?

A major commitment, half an hour every day brushing down to the skin, combing face furnishings, and tying up the topknot to keep hair out of the eyes. Regular baths are also needed, monthly or even every two weeks depending on the environment. The coat can be cut down to a puppy clip every four to six weeks, although some daily grooming is still needed. A neglected coat tangles and mats, causing skin problems and real discomfort.

HOW suitable are they as family dogs?

Sturdy, well-tempered and playful, the Shih Tzu is an ideal choice for a family who appreciate his willful charm, are prepared to involve him in all family activities, don't expect obedience, and enjoy grooming. He is good with children and a fun playmate as long as they are good with dogs. Not recommended for households with children too young to be gentle; parents of little ones may not have enough time for grooming and attention.

WHAT type of home?

This adaptable little dog is ideal for city life but can live anywhere. He would prefer a yard for outdoor games, but if none is available can make do quite happily with three or four daily walks around the block.

WHAT type of owner?

The Shih Tzu is an ideal breed for anyone who wants a playful, entertaining companion and who enjoys grooming. He needs an affectionate but sensible owner, strong minded enough not to allow a small dog to become a household tyrant, and with time for socialization and play.

HOW compatible with other pets?

If well socialized in puppyhood, the Shih Tzu is normally friendly with other animals of all species.

HOW much exercise?

This very adaptable breed will fit in with his owner's requirements. He can enjoy lengthy hikes but is equally happy with short outings and plenty of time for active play in the yard. If confined to an apartment, think in terms of four walks a day to keep him healthy.

● *Delightful to look at and an ideal companion dog in city or country.*

Character Trait	Poor	Average	Good	Excellent
Attitude to other dogs				
Quietness				
Not destructive				
Protective behavior				
Not likely to stray				
Good with children				
Ease of training				

Original purpose: Lapdog
Male height: 8–11 in. (25–28 cm)
Female height: 8–11 in. (25–28 cm)
Weight: 9–16 lb. (4.1–7.3 kg)
Life span: 11–14 years

HOW easy to train?

Moderate. With a firm, kind, consistent approach, the Shih Tzu is perfectly ready to cooperate and learn good behavior. However, he is a strong-minded, willful little dog, and formal obedience is not his natural style. Training for fun rather than for competition is well worthwhile to keep him entertained, otherwise he may find less-acceptable ways of amusing himself.

● *These lovely locks require a lot of maintenance, 30 minutes of grooming each day plus regular baths.*

WHAT good points?

Playful, happy, friendly, loving, loyal, attentive, active, full of character, small but not fragile, adaptable, good with children, decorative.

Small dogs

WHAT to be aware of?

Heavy grooming commitment. Can be difficult to housebreak. Prone to eye injuries.

WHAT medical problems?

Generally a healthy, long-lived breed, the Shih Tzu may suffer from heart conditions, kidney problems, intervertebral disk disease, certain blood disorders, and a number of eye problems including ulcers and conjunctivitis.

Pembroke Welsh Corgi

Among the smallest working breeds, the Pembroke originated as a cattle dog, driving livestock by "heeling" (nipping cows' heels to keep them moving)—a task that required an active, strong-minded dog. Although a convenient size for modern homes, he is a "big dog in a small body," a cheerful companion and an enthusiastic watchdog who likes to keep busy. Bossy, and often excitable, he needs sensible handling and an outlet for his intelligence and energy. Corgis often perform well at obedience, agility, and indeed herding trials, but above all they need an active sense of involvement in family life.

The Corgi's origins are obscure, possibly dating back to the Dark Ages. KC recognition came in 1925. Nine years later the different types from north and south Wales were separated into two breeds, Pembroke and Cardigan. The Pembroke, the smaller and more extroverted, is the more popular, probably because of its adoption by the British Royal Family.

WHAT colors?
Red, sable (red with black-tipped hairs), or fawn, with or without white markings on legs, brisket, neck, head, or foreface, or tricolor (mostly black, with tan and white markings).

WHAT grooming does the coat need?
This is an easy-care coat, needing brushing only weekly (daily during the twice-yearly molt) to remove dead hairs.

HOW suitable are they as family dogs?
Pembrokes enjoy family life and are fun companions for older, sensible youngsters though often too excitable to be recommended with young or very boisterous children. Nipping the heels of livestock was once their profession. As youngsters they often need to be taught not to nip ankles or this can become a habit.

● *An appealing trio of Cardigans.*

WHAT type of home?
A country home is ideal, but the Pembroke will adapt to city life provided he has enough activity. He should have access to a yard where he can burn off some energy and preferably a park.

WHAT type of owner?
The Pembroke is a good choice for anyone who likes big dogs but doesn't have room for one. He needs a fairly strong-minded owner, or he can take over the household. Corgis fare best with active owners who enjoy walking, training, and play and can keep them busy—it is a shame to let their intelligence go to waste.

HOW compatible with other pets?
Pembrokes generally get along well with other dogs, and with cats in the own household, subject of course to early socialization. Males from some bloodlines can be aggressive toward dogs of the same sex. Take care with small pets such as rabbits and hamsters: Corgis were originally farm dogs and natural ratters, and have not lost their innate prey drive.

HOW much exercise?
Moderate. These short-legged dogs do not need as much exercise as most working breeds and can keep fit with a daily walk in the park. They do have plenty of stamina and will enjoy long walks, free running, and active play.

HOW easy to train?
Given an owner who can establish

Character Trait	Poor	Average	Good	Excellent
Attitude to other dogs				
Quietness				
Not destructive				
Protective behavior				
Not likely to stray				
Good with children				
Ease of training				

Original purpose: Herding
Male height: 10–12 in. (25–30 cm)
Female height: 10–12 in. (25–30 cm)
Weight: 20–26 lb. (9–12 kg)
Life span: 11–13 years

kind but firm leadership, this intelligent dog is easily trained—but also easily bored. As a working dog, he was expected to use his initiative rather than follow commands blindly, and he sees little point in repetitive exercises. Reward-based techniques of training work best to motivate him. Get him interested, and his desire to show how clever he is will take him the rest of the way.

WHAT good points?

Outgoing, alert, friendly, active, people oriented, playful, energetic, long-lived, hardy, good watchdog.

WHAT to be aware of?

Can be noisy. Tendency to nip ankles if not discouraged in puppyhood. Watch out for a tendency to put on weight, which can put too much strain on his long back.

WHAT medical problems?

Corgis are generally a healthy and long-lived breed. Short legs and a long back make them vulnerable to back problems, and occasional inherited defects include hip malformation (dysplasia), von Willebrand's disease (a bleeding disorder), and progressive retinal atrophy (degeneration of the light receptor cells in the eyes).

Small dogs

● In the US, Welsh Corgis almost always have cropped tails.

West Highland White Terrier

One of the most popular breeds, the Westie has taken his transformation from working terrier to household pet in his stride. This is a busy, happy little dog and probably the only breed whose standard calls for him to be "possessed of no small amount of self-esteem." Less fiery and hyperactive than some terrier breeds, he makes a great companion who is prepared to enjoy almost any lifestyle, equally successful as smart city dog or sporty country companion. He has a great sense of fun and, like all terriers, likes to keep busy. This is an affectionate and adaptable breed, friendly and extroverted. He is hardy and relatively easy care, although his trademark white coat requires attention to keep it looking good.

The Westie originated from the same stock as the Cairn and other Highland terriers. He was recognized as a distinct breed in 1907, and he has never looked back.

WHAT colors?
White only.

WHAT grooming does the coat need?
Brush with stiff bristle brush at least twice a week to prevent tangles from forming. The coat needs stripping about every four months, a task probably best left to a professional. Show dogs have the coat sculpted into a stylized shape with a stripping knife; pets can be left shaggy but may need the hair around eyes and ears trimmed for health and comfort.

HOW suitable are they as family dogs?
These fun-loving little dogs enjoy family life and want to be involved in family activities. They are generally great companions for sensible children who treat them with respect, although they won't tolerate being teased or otherwise mistreated.

WHAT type of home?
The Westie is highly adaptable. He is perfectly happy as a city dog,

● The Westie: a true fun dog.

provided he has regular walks (not just quickly around the block). He will also thoroughly appreciate country life, where his sporting instincts and love of exploration will come to the fore.

WHAT type of owner?
A fun dog for a lively family, the Westie can also be an ideal companion for an active, older owner, providing encouragement to remain fit and active. Best for those who appreciate the busy, enthusiastic, loving, and sometimes maddening terrier character, he needs an owner who can apply a firm, consistent approach to training and has time for play, exercise, and cuddles.

HOW compatible with other pets?
Generally good with other animals, the Westie is nonetheless a terrier, with strong hunting and chasing instincts and a tendency to be bossy with other dogs. Sensible early socialization is important, and other pets should be introduced with care and plenty of supervision.

HOW much exercise?
These active little dogs love exercise and long country walks, but they are quite adaptable and can burn off a lot of energy playing in the yard. City dwellers should think in terms of two or three good walks a day, preferably including time off leash in the

Character Trait	Poor	Average	Good	Excellent
Attitude to other dogs		■		
Quietness	■			
Not destructive			■	
Protective behavior			■	
Not likely to stray	■			
Good with children			■	
Ease of training		■		

Original purpose: Vermin control
Male height: 10–11 in. (25–30 cm)
Female height: 9–10 in. (23–28 cm)
Weight: 15–21 lb. (6.8–9.5 kg)
Life span: 12–14 years

park. Work on the recall is important: this is a dog who will disappear over the horizon in pursuit of an interesting scent once his hunting instincts are aroused.

HOW easy to train?

No terrier would be the first choice for an obedience enthusiast, and Westies are as obstinate and willful as any. With firm, consistent, reward-based training, he will become a well-behaved household pet, but training needs to start early to establish who is in charge. Keep training sessions short, challenging, and above all fun to retain his interest.

WHAT good points?

Affectionate, loyal, active, hardy, versatile, fun loving, family loving, curious, friendly, plenty of personality, convenient size.

Small dogs

WHAT to be aware of?

Overpopularity has made this breed a target for puppy mills: buy only from reputable breeders or risk health and temperament problems. Coat care is an ongoing commitment.

WHAT medical problems?

Most Westies are healthy, but (as with other white breeds) chronic skin problems are not infrequent. Other disorders include Legg-Calvé-Perthes disease (hip problems), hernias, liver disease, and craniomandibular osteopathy (Westie jaw), a painful bone deformity in puppies.

● *Early socialization will be important when training these young Westie puppies.*

Cavalier King Charles Spaniel

An absolute winner in the toy dog category, the Cavalier has a gentle and courteous nature that seems utterly appropriate to its history as the favorite dog of King Charles II of England. His ancestors may have originated in the East, making their way by the Middle Ages to Europe, where they were crossed with spaniels. In the 16th century they reached England, to develop there into today's toy breed.

Part of the secret of this breed's success underlies the reason why it was so popular as a ladies' lapdog. It dotes on its owner and will repay the care you lavish on it with absolute devotion. This is no living room wimp—the sporting ancestry and typical spaniel energy ensure that Cavaliers are also lively and playful companions who are just as much fun to be with out of doors. Graceful and balanced in movement and possessing a charming, docile expression, this is an ideal family dog—good spirited, polite and friendly, and full of enthusiasm!

What colors?

Black and tan, ruby, Blenheim (rich chestnut markings, well broken up, on pearly white ground), tricolor.

What grooming does the coat need?

The coat is long, silky, and free from curl. A slight wave is permitted by the breed standard, and there is plenty of feathering. This breed is a delight to groom and does not require a lot of attention. Ten minutes or so a day working with a slicker brush and comb, paying particular attention to the areas that are heavily coated, should be quite sufficient.

How suitable are they as family dogs?

A great choice as a family pet, Cavaliers are some of the nicest and best-mannered toy dogs available. They get along well with children, are easy to handle, and make loving companions for the elderly, being good-natured, home loving, and affectionate.

What type of home?

These sturdy and appealing little dogs are very adaptable and suit a variety of lifestyles. While their size and nature mean that they can be treated as lapdogs by people who lead their lives predominantly indoors, they are also happy running vigorously after scents in the wide open and so are well adapted to country dwellers.

What type of owner?

This breed in many ways offers the best of both worlds—it is a toy-sized dog that enjoys the social life of a family but also embodies the virtues of a sporting breed with a good nose and hunting instinct. So the Cavalier King Charles can be equally at home with a large, energetic family as with a single owner, whatever their age. Sometimes called a "people's dog," Cavaliers enjoy human company of all kinds. Indeed the owner must be prepared to let the dog participate in family life and enjoy the companionship of people—it would be cruel to own a Cavalier King Charles and leave it locked up on its own for long periods.

How compatible with other pets?

Cavaliers generally mix well with other pets, rarely showing signs of possessiveness or jealousy. Take care when introducing them to large dogs as their tolerant, gentle nature means they can be overwhelmed by the rough and tumble of bigger breeds. Two or more Cavaliers will usually live happily together.

How much exercise?

While a Cavalier loves snoozing in comfort at home, its sporting

Character Trait	Poor	Average	Good	Excellent
Attitude to other dogs			■	
Quietness		■		
Not destructive			■	
Protective behavior	■			
Not likely to stray		■		
Good with children				■
Ease of training			■	

Original purpose: Lapdog
Male height: 10–12.5 in. (25–32 cm)
Female height: 9–12 in. (24–30 cm)
Weight: 12–18 lb. (5.5–8 kg)
Life span: 9–14 years

Small dogs

ancestry means that it does need to get outside and run off excess energy at least once day. A regular walk around the park or a play session in the yard will be enough to keep a Cavalier in good condition. If you have a chance to enjoy a longer walk in the country, the dog will remain eager to keep you company.

How easy to train?

This breed ranks somewhere around the middle of the rankings for trainability and working intelligence, so you will not find it the fastest to learn and respond. It is at its best as a family companion, so owners do not generally look to the breed to star in high-level agility and obedience tests.

What good points?

Friendly, nonaggressive, fun loving, sporting, active, fearless, charming, and gentle expression.

What to be aware of?

Has a tendency to become distracted by scents when out on a walk, so you need to keep an eye on a dog that may wander off; little road sense so keep on a lead in public places. While not "yappy," will tend to bark at strangers. However, its friendly nature means that it is not a good guard dog.

What medical problems?

While generally vigorous and fit dogs can sometimes live to 14 years of age, Cavaliers can be susceptible to a hereditary heart condition—mitral valve disease. Other typical health problems include malformation of the hip (dysplasia) and eye problems like cataracts and retinal atrophy.

Löwchen *Other names: Little Lion Dog*

With its traditional lion clip haircut, the Löwchen was the designer lapdog of 16th century Europe. The breed dwindled in popularity in modern times and almost died out after World War II. However, it was rescued at the last moment by dedicated breeders and now enjoys a revival as a companion breed. Merry, affectionate, intelligent, and lively, the "Little Lion Dog" deserves his return to popularity. He is emphatically a companion dog who loves affection, needs company, and hates being left alone. His sociable and playful nature makes him a fun dog for families with sensible children and a true comforter for those who live alone, although this is a time-consuming breed as regards both attention and coat care.

Show dogs are always presented in the classic lion clip, which requires careful, regular maintenance, but pet owners often prefer the "shaggy dog" effect of an unclipped coat or a more easy-care "teddy bear" puppy trim.

WHAT colors?

Any color or combination of colors is permitted. Puppy coats often bear no resemblance to the final adult color because of a "fading gene" in the breed.

WHAT grooming does the coat need?

The long, fine coat needs thorough daily combing with a wide-toothed comb to prevent tangles. The traditional clip needs regular maintenance, with a trim every four to six weeks, while an unclipped "natural" coat takes a lot of care.

Some owners clip the hair around the eyes for the dog's comfort, and many pet owners prefer an all over short puppy clip for easy care.

HOW suitable are they as family dogs?

Löwchens are delightful family dogs who enjoy the company of responsible children. They are equally happy being cuddly lapdogs and active playmates and are a convenient size for children to handle. They are nonaggressive and not snappy, although puppies can be quite rowdy and mischievous and need sensible supervision to become well-behaved members of the family.

WHAT type of home?

This is a breed that will adapt to almost any circumstances except neglect. As long as he is allowed to participate fully in his owner's life, the Löwchen will be happy in city or country, with a single owner or in the heart of a large family. He is perfectly suited to apartment life as long as he can enjoy plenty of exercise both indoors and outside.

WHAT type of owner?

Löwchen owners need a sense of humor to appreciate the fun-loving nature of the breed. This is a demanding little dog who can be self-willed, stubborn, and downright mischievous, so his owner should be prepared to be patient and firm in order to get the best out of him. He should not be left alone for long periods—not a breed for those who are out at work all day.

HOW compatible with other pets?

The typical Löwchen likes other animals just as much as he likes humans and will get along well with other family pets. He will enjoy playing with other dogs in the household and is not aggressive with strange dogs. Like every other breed, he does need proper socialization as a puppy.

Character Trait	Poor	Average	Good	Excellent
Attitude to other dogs				
Quietness				
Not destructive				
Protective behavior				
Not likely to stray				
Good with children				
Ease of training				

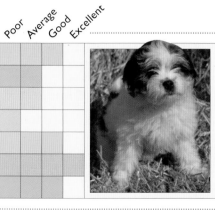

Original purpose: Companion
Male height: 12–14 in. (30–35.5 cm)
Female height: 10–13 in. (25–33 cm)
Weight: 8–18 lb. (3.6–8.2 kg)
Life span: 13–15 years

HOW much exercise?

These little dogs don't need a great deal of exercise but will enjoy as much as you can offer. A couple of short walks will keep them fit and make life more interesting for them. They have plenty of energy and enjoy hours of play.

HOW easy to train?

Like many toy breeds, Löwchens can be strong willed and stubborn but respond well to training as long as it is made fun and interesting for them. Reward-based training with plenty of praise will encourage them to use their natural intelligence and learning ability, and they can perform well at obedience work and agility.

WHAT good points?

Friendly, active, intelligent, sweet natured, non-aggressive, active, playful, affectionate, nonshedding coat unlikely to cause allergies.

WHAT to be aware of?

Early socialization is important for this breed. They like to be the center of attention and need sensible training to prevent them from taking over the household. A demanding breed that repays attention.

WHAT medical problems?

Löwchens are generally healthy. Minor concerns include dislocation of the kneecaps (patellar luxation) and eye problems, such as progressive retinal atrophy (degeneration of the light receptor cells in the eyes) and cataracts.

Small dogs

Schipperke

Intensely active and full of insatiable curiosity, the Schipperke is a merry little busybody, always on the alert. Though small, he is robust, sturdy, and energetic—a big dog in a little dog's body. He is very people oriented and makes a fun companion, devoted to his owner, friendly to children, and an alert (and vocal) watchdog. His compact size and easy-care coat suit him well for modern lifestyles, but he is not a dog for busy owners as he needs plenty of company, attention, and occupation. He is a master of mischief if left to make his own entertainment.

The Schipperke's's ancestry is a puzzle; his name means either "little captain" (a barge dog) or "little shepherd" (a herder). Certainly the breed dates back to at least the 1600s when they were exhibited in Brussels. He was introduced to the UK and US in the 19th century but has never achieved the popularity he merits.

WHAT colors?
Usually black (the only color acknowledged in many countries, including its native Belgium and the US), but cream, fawn, and other solid colors are also accepted in the UK.

WHAT grooming does the coat need?
A thorough weekly grooming with a hard bristle brush will keep the dense coat in good condition. Extra attention is required during the heavy molt (at least twice a year).

HOW suitable are they as family dogs?
The Schipperke is a great dog for an active family who want a dog to participate fully in their lives and can keep him amused. He enjoys the company of children and makes a great playmate and protector—but children must learn to treat this little dog with the respect he deserves.

WHAT type of home?
Robust enough for the country, compact enough for a city apartment, the Schipperke will fit in wherever his people choose to live. However, he is too active to be happy without a yard, which must be completely secure—otherwise this little escape artist will almost inevitably set off over or under the fence to investigate the world outside.

WHAT type of owner?
This active, affectionate little dog is suited to an active, affectionate owner with plenty of time for play and training. As long as he has plenty of attention, he can be a great companion for a lively senior or a large household with school-age children. He is not a dog for couch potatoes or anyone who favors a calm, sedate pet.

HOW compatible with other pets?
Early socialization is important to ensure that this bossy little dog learns appropriate canine manners and can enjoy the company of other dogs (and cats, if the household includes them). Small pets such as rabbits and guinea pigs should be protected from him, as he is descended from enthusiastic ratters and has a high prey drive.

HOW much exercise?
Always on the go, the Schipperke will burn off some of his abundant energy running around the house. He needs a moderate amount of outdoor exercise as well and greatly enjoys walks on a leash and

Character Trait	Poor	Average	Good	Excellent
Attitude to other dogs				
Quietness				
Not destructive				
Protective behavior				
Not likely to stray				
Good with children				
Ease of training				

Original purpose: Companion, watchdog, ratter, and farm dog
Male height: 11–13 in. (28–33 cm)
Female height: 10–12 in. (25–30 cm)
Weight: 12–16 lb. (5.5–7.25 kg)
Life span: 13–15 years

running free in the park. He is a suitable breed for agility, which will provide him with both physical and mental exercise.

HOW easy to train?
Schipperkes are quick learners but also independent, stubborn, and bossy, liking to do things their own way. They respond best to a reward-based approach with plenty of positive reinforcement. Lessons should be varied to maintain their interest—these bright little dogs are easily bored. Training should start early and be firm, patient, kind, and consistent.

Small dogs

WHAT good points?
Devoted, protective, courageous, lively, alert, responsive, playful, affectionate, good watchdog.

WHAT to be aware of?
Fond of their own voices and have a loud and penetrating bark. Destructive if bored. Can be hard to housebreak.

WHAT medical problems?
This is generally a healthy and long-lived breed, with occasional occurrence of hypothyroidism (lack of thyroid hormone), epilepsy, hip malformation (dysplasia), and Legg-Calvé-Perthes disease (lack of blood supply to the top of the femur resulting in bone death).

Cairn Terrier

The Cairn takes his name from the rocky outcrops (cairns) of the Scottish Highlands where his ancestors dug out foxes, badgers, and other predators. Although today his primary role is as a companion, this is one terrier breed that has not been prettied up for the show ring and retains the appealingly scruffy, workmanlike appearance of his forebears. As a companion, he is ideal for those who want a small, active dog who will walk for miles. A true terrier, bossy, busy, and merry, he will never be content to be a mere couch potato and needs exercise for both mind and body. Provided he is kept occupied, he makes a great household pet who is devoted to his family.

While retaining all the terrier courage and assertiveness, the Cairn is less dog aggressive and more amenable to training than many terrier breeds and indeed can perform well in obedience events.

WHAT colors?

Cairns come in a range of colors including cream, wheat, light or dark red, gray and nearly black. Brindling (black hairs mixed with the base color) is acceptable in any of these colors.

WHAT grooming does the coat need?

The harsh, weatherproof coat is relatively low maintenance, needing perhaps ten minutes a day with brush and comb or a more thorough session once a week. Cairns should never be clipped but hand stripped, plucking dead hairs from the coat with finger and thumb—your pup's breeder will be happy to teach you the technique.

HOW suitable are they as family dogs?

The Cairn makes an excellent family pet. He is generally very good with children, although (as with any small dog) supervision with toddlers is essential. He won't tolerate being teased or ill-treated.

For sensible children, he is the ideal fun-loving and tireless companion as well as doubling as a protective guard.

WHAT type of home?

The Cairn will adapt to most lifestyles. He is in his element in the country, with hedges and ditches to explore, but will be just as happy bustling about the city. He will appreciate a yard, which needs to be securely fenced—a bored terrier won't hesitate to scramble over or under obstacles in search of adventure.

WHAT type of owner?

This is a great dog for an active owner who enjoys country walks and who is prepared to maintain a firm, consistent approach to training. If you enjoy a busy, stimulating pet who wants to participate fully in family life and are prepared to be "pack leader," the Cairn is a great choice—but if you prefer a more placid companion, look outside the terrier group.

HOW compatible with other pets?

Cairns will get along with other pets in the household better than some terrier breeds but need careful introduction. They have strong chasing instincts and should not be trusted with smaller animals such as hamsters or rabbits.

HOW much exercise?

This active breed needs a fair amount of exercise for its size. A daily stroll once around the block is not enough to keep a Cairn fit and happy—a fit adult can run for miles

Character Trait	Poor	Average	Good	Excellent
Attitude to other dogs		X		
Quietness	X			
Not destructive			X	
Protective behavior			X	
Not likely to stray		X		
Good with children			X	
Ease of training			X	

Original purpose: Vermin control
Male height: 11–12 in. (28–30.5 cm)
Female height: 11–12 in. (28–30.5 cm)
Weight: 14–16 lb. (6.5–7.25 kg)
Life span: 13–14 years

He needs regular brisk walks, including off-lead exercise, which should be supplemented with games in the yard and training exercises to occupy his mind.

● *Cheerful and friendly, the Cairn, with its harsh, weatherproof coat, retains the attractively workmanlike appearance of its working forebears.*

Small dogs

HOW easy to train?

No terrier would be the first choice for an obedience enthusiast, but Cairns respond better than most to firm, sensible, reward-based training to become well-behaved household pets. Training sessions should be short, challenging, and above all fun to retain his interest. It is vital to start training at an early age to ensure that your Cairn knows who is in charge.

WHAT good points?

Cheerful, friendly, intelligent, lively, resourceful, confident, small yet tough, a keen watchdog, not a heavy shedder.

WHAT to be aware of?

Like most terriers, has a tendency to bark excessively and, if left to his own devices, will dig up the yard. Can be possessive of food and toys.

WHAT medical problems?

Generally a healthy breed. Some problems with dislocation of the kneecap (patellar luxation), eye problems including glaucoma and cataracts, and skin problems.

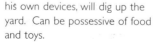

Chinese Crested

The Chinese Crested is a hairless dog with decorative trim—flowing crest, "socks," and plumed tail setting off a bare body. Although some find the idea of a bald dog off-putting initially, he is an attractive little dog, elegant, graceful, and reminiscent of a miniature pony with flowing mane and tail. His skin is soft and warm to the touch, lacking any "doggy" odor and ideal for many allergy sufferers. Gentle, playful, and absolutely devoted to his owner, this breed was designed to be a companion. He also comes in a "powder puff" variety that is very hairy indeed, veiled in a long, silky coat. Both types can appear in the same litter.

The breed was common in China in the 1880s, when it came to the attention of the western world. Its origins are obscure, although it may be connected with the hairless dogs of Africa and Central America.

WHAT colors?

Any color or combination of colors. The skin of hairless dogs may be lilac, blue, gold, or pink, often spotted or dappled, and tends to darken in summer and lighten again in winter. Spotted specimens are usually born plain pink, developing the spots after the first week.

WHAT grooming does the coat need?

Hairless dogs need the same skin care as a child, cleansing and moisturizing, and the protection of sunblock in summer. Like teenagers, they can suffer from acne and blackheads if the skin is neglected. Powderpuffs need daily grooming of the soft coat to prevent tangles and often have the face clipped to show the sweet expression.

HOW suitable are they as family dogs?

Ideally suited for life with a considerate family, this breed actively enjoys the company of children. He loves play and cuddles and is devoted to family members. However, he is physically dainty and not suited to rough games and temperamentally too gentle to be happy in a rowdy family.

WHAT type of home?

Home is where the heart is for this loving little dog, and he will adapt to any environment as long as he has his owner's company. His compact size makes him suitable for apartment life. He does need protection from extremes of temperature—a warm coat in winter and sunblock in summer are essential.

WHAT type of owner?

The Chinese Crested can be a wonderful companion for a single person or happy in the heart of the family. He needs a sociable, affectionate owner who is willing to provide plenty of companionship and to receive devotion in return. Owners of this vivacious breed should make time for play and affection as well as for daily skin care.

HOW compatible with other pets?

This breed is generally very good with other pets, although, like other breeds, he needs to be properly socialized with them while young.

HOW much exercise?

Like most toy breeds, the Crested can thrive on minimal exercise but will relish a surprising amount. Short, frequent walks will keep him happy and interested, but he will enjoy walking for several miles if that is his owner's preferred lifestyle.

	Poor	Average	Good	Excellent
Attitude to other dogs				
Quietness				
Not destructive				
Protective behavior				
Not likely to stray				
Good with children				
Ease of training				

(Character Trait)

Place of origin: **China**

Original purpose: Lapdog
Male height: 11–13 in. (28–33 cm)
Female height: 9–12 in. (23–30 cm)
Weight: Under 12 lb. (2.3–5.5 kg)
Life span: 13-15 years

● A contrast: hairless and "powder puff."

HOW easy to train?

Intelligent but not always easy to train—aim for cooperation rather than strict obedience. He has a mind of his own and tends to be stubborn. However, he does need directing toward good behavior from an early age to prevent him from becoming a household tyrant.

WHAT good points?

Affectionate, intelligent, loyal, happy, playful, gentle, entertaining, friendly, alert, good watchdog, no "doggy" odor.

WHAT to be aware of?

Regular skin care is a must, and protection from chills and sunburn is important. Can be yappy and has a tendency to high-pitched "singing" that some find endearing, others off-putting.

Small dogs

WHAT medical problems?

As a breed extremely healthy and hardier than they look. Recorded problems include dislocating kneecaps, Legg-Calvé-Perthes disease (crippling hip disorder), and skin allergies.

French Bulldog *Other names: Bouledogue Francais*

This bat-eared, frog-faced charmer is about as far removed from his big, fierce, bull-baiting ancestors as a Bulldog can be. A sweet-natured clown, he was made for the role of companion and entertainer. He fits well into modern lifestyles, being compact in size, lively without being boisterous, naturally quiet, and with an easy-care coat and low exercise requirements. He is a highly sociable, very loving dog who needs company and hates being left out of family activities. More energetic than he looks, he is nonetheless not built for a very active lifestyle. Overexertion or overheating cause breathing difficulties because of his foreshortened face.

Despite his name, the Frenchie originated in Britain as an unwanted by-product of mid-19th-century bulldog breeding programs. It was left to the French to recognize the potential of this comical little dog, which became a fashionable pet in Paris—and subsequently across Europe and the US.

WHAT colors?
Brindle, fawn, or pied (predominantly white with brindle markings).

WHAT grooming does the coat need?
This is an easy-care coat, needing only occasional (weekly) brushing to remove dead hairs. However, the face should be cleaned daily with a damp cloth, paying particular attention to the area around the eyes. The short coat has the advantage of minimal shedding.

HOW suitable are they as family dogs?
The Frenchie certainly has the temperament to be an ideal family pet, a role he enjoys as long as children are old enough to respect his needs. Indeed, he makes a truly fun companion for sensible children. Physically, however, he is unsuitable for a very active family, and his vulnerability to overheating can be a problem in summer.

WHAT type of home?
This adaptable breed can be happy

in city or country as long as he has his owner's attention. He appreciates a yard to play in but needs shade in summer. Wherever he lives, care must always be taken to protect him from extremes of temperature.

WHAT type of owner?
This is a breed that needs human companionship, so he must have an owner who can spend time with him—an ideal choice for retirees or people who can take their dog to work with them. He is unsuited to energetic types who love long walks or to obedience fanatics but is perfect for gentle, affectionate owners who value character and a sense of humor in a dog.,

HOW compatible with other pets?
Puppyhood socialization is important, as Frenchies can be very possessive of their owners and regard other dogs as competitors. Some dominant males can be very territorial. Having said that, they are good-natured and will generally get along well with other pets in their own household, although they may find it amusing to chase cats.

HOW much exercise?
Although the Frenchie's exercise needs are very moderate, he does need regular outings, about half an hour twice daily. Avoid exercise in hot weather, as this breed overheats very easily. The adult Frenchie can easily become a couch potato, which will not do his health any good. Puppies are generally very lively, and walks

Character Trait	Poor	Average	Good	Excellent
Attitude to other dogs				
Quietness				
Not destructive				
Protective behavior				
Not likely to stray				
Good with children				
Ease of training				

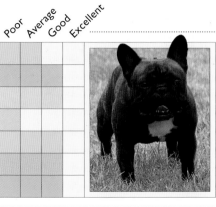

Original purpose: Lapdog
Male height: 11–13 in. (28–33 cm)
Female height: 11–13 in. (28–33 cm)
Weight: 24–28 lb. (11–12.5 kg)
Life span: 9–11 years

should be built up gradually from about six months.

HOW easy to train?

Quite easy, as long as you don't expect Collie-style formal obedience. Frenchies think life should be fun. If training sessions are treated as a game, they will learn quickly. Several of this breed have even succeeded in competitive obedience trials.

Small dogs

WHAT good points?

Vivacious, deeply affectionate, intelligent, sociable, great sense of fun, adaptable, well suited to city life.

WHAT to be aware of?

Like all short-faced dogs, Frenchies may have breathing difficulties when exposed to heat or over-exertion and are liable in any case to snort, snuffle, wheeze, and snore. They also have a tendency to flatulence.

WHAT medical problems?

Breathing problems are inevitable with short-faced breeds: avoid overheating and overexertion. Other problems include spinal disk trouble, hip malformation (dysplasia), and cataracts.

Miniature and Toy Poodles

The two smaller Poodle breeds look like fluffy toys, but they are no mere fashion accessories. The Miniature and Toy are smaller versions of the Standard Poodle, originally a working water retriever of great intelligence and versatility. They share his brains, energy, and sense of fun. Overpopularity has led to puppy mills churning out specimens (Toys in particular) that are physically and temperamentally unsound, but a well-bred Poodle is capable of a great deal. Lively, loving, and extroverted, they make endearing companions and are highly trainable. They do need a great deal of coat care and are not dogs who thrive without plenty of company.

Poodles date back to at least the 15th century, and the smaller versions were certainly known by the 18th century and possibly well before that time. Miniatures (then called Toys) were formally recognized in 1907, while Toys had to wait until 1957 for recognition.

WHAT colors?

Any solid color, including white, cream, brown, apricot, black, silver, and blue. Parti-colors occur but are not recognized by the AKC.

WHAT grooming does the coat need?

The thick, curly coat does not molt and keeps growing if not clipped. Daily grooming with slicker brush and wide-toothed comb is essential to prevent the coat from matting. It needs clipping every six to eight weeks. Show dogs are presented in an elaborate lion clip that requires a great deal of maintenance; pets are usually more comfortable with a practical short trim (lamb or puppy clip).

HOW suitable are they as family dogs?

Toys are vulnerable to rough handling by children and are happier as the companion of adults. Miniatures are sturdier and make great family dogs as long as they are treated as a member of the family and not denied attention. Most Minis love children and make great playmates. However, they are sensitive, excitable, and easily stressed and not well suited for a noisy, rowdy household.

WHAT type of home?

Miniatures are particularly adaptable and can be happy in city or country. Toys are ideal for city life and make great apartment dogs, although they will do just as well as their bigger cousins in a country home, enjoying walks and exploring hedges and ditches with enthusiasm.

WHAT type of owner?

These little Poodles need owners who recognize that they are more than fashion accessories and can provide affection, attention and mental stimulation. They are fun dogs with a lot to offer. Miniatures in particular thrive on more exercise than they are often offered. Owners do need to be committed to grooming or, at the very least, to regular trips to a groomer.

HOW compatible with other pets?

These friendly little dogs usually get along well with other animals, especially any that can be persuaded to join them in a game. They remain very puppyish throughout life and, like children, can

Fancy haircuts are not compulsory!

Character Trait	Poor	Average	Good	Excellent
Attitude to other dogs				
Quietness				
Not destructive				
Protective behavior				
Not likely to stray				
Good with children				
Ease of training				

Original purpose: Lapdog
Miniature height: 11–15 in. (28–38 cm)
Toy height: Under 10 in. (25 cm)
Miniature weight: 26–30 lb. (12–14 kg)
Toy weight: 4–8 lb. (1.8–3.6 kg)
Life span: 12–14 years

become overexcited and annoying to older, more sedate pets if not reminded of their manners.

HOW much exercise?

Moderate. Miniatures should have at least half an hour's walk every day and plenty of active play. Toys don't need a great deal of exercise, but they can walk a great deal farther than one might expect and will benefit both in mind and body.

HOW easy to train?

Miniature and Toy Poodles are bright dogs whose capacity to learn should not be wasted. They can be excitable, so training needs to be calm, gentle, and sensitive, but they are quick learners and keen to please. Handlers need a sense of humor. Poodles are easily bored by repetition and often have a creative approach to obedience.

WHAT good points?

Intelligent, well tempered, obedient, eager to learn, affectionate, reliable, lively, sensitive, adaptable, fun loving, nonaggressive, convenient size.

WHAT to be aware of?

Above-average coat care requirements. Tends to enjoy the sound of his own voice. Some bloodlines can be very high strung and oversensitive. Choose breeder with care.

WHAT medical problems?

Inherited disorders include kneecap dislocation (patellar luxation), Legg-Calvé-Perthes disease (degeneration of the head of the thighbone due to insufficient blood supply), epilepsy, and progressive retinal atrophy (degeneration of the light receptor cells in the eyes). There is also some occurrence of other eye problems. Toy bitches occasionally suffer from a malformed ureter, causing incontinence. If grooming is neglected, skin problems may possibly arise.

Small dogs

● The dense curly coat lends itself to sculpturing.

Italian Greyhound *Other names: Piccolo Levrieri Italiani*

Daintiest of all breeds, this miniature greyhound has all the grace of his full-size cousin plus the charm of a true toy dog. Mini-greyhounds have been treasured pets since at least Roman times, so they have been bred for generations to specialize in the role of loving companion. Gentle, affectionate, and entertaining, they need to be with their owner as much as possible and cannot have too much attention. They are highly dependent, even clinging, and need plenty of gentle socialization to give them confidence. When properly brought up, however, they are lively, playful, and often mischievous.

Despite their delicate appearance, they are quite hardy. Puppies under 18 months old have fragile bones and need special care to protect them from the risk of breaking a leg. They have very little awareness of how small they are and are quite capable of leaping from a dangerous height and doing themselves damage.

WHAT colors?
Black, blue, cream, fawn, red, white, or pied (white with colored patches).

WHAT grooming does the coat need?
The fine satiny coat sheds little and needs very little care, just an occasional brushing with a soft bristle brush or simply "polishing" with a piece of silk or velvet cloth.

HOW suitable are they as family dogs?
The Italian Greyhound can make a delightful pet for a quiet family with considerate, older children. A busy, noisy household is not the right environment for him. He is simply not safe with young or careless children as he can easily be injured in rough play.

WHAT type of home?
The Italian Greyhound will be happy anywhere that suits his owner. His small size and low exercise requirements make him an ideal pet for an apartment.

However, he is just as much at home in the country, where he will walk miles, chase rabbits, and generally hark back to his sighthound ancestry.

WHAT type of owner?
This is a dog for quiet, gentle owners who want a constant companion and are prepared to lavish affection on him. He needs a lot of attention and consideration. A lover of warmth and comfort, he would prefer an owner who is willing to share a bed with him. Not for owners who want formal, prompt obedience as this is not his style.

HOW compatible with other pets?
In general this charming little dog is prepared to be friendly with other animals of all kinds but common sense needs to be applied. His sighthound heritage means that he can be tempted to chase cats or other small animals, and his fragility means that he is at risk of injury from boisterous larger dogs. Early socialization is important, or he may become timid.

HOW much exercise?
How much would you like? This is a truly adaptable little dog who can exercise himself playing in the house and yard or who can enjoy long country walks, depending on your lifestyle. Remember that despite his size, he has all the instincts of a sighthound and will disappear into the distance if he spots a rabbit. Puppies under a year old should have restricted exercise to avoid the risk of injury to fragile bones.

Character Trait	Poor	Average	Good	Excellent
Attitude to other dogs				
Quietness				
Not destructive				
Protective behavior				
Not likely to stray				
Good with children				
Ease of training				

Original purpose: Lapdog
Male height: 12–15 in. (30–38 cm)
Female height: 12–15 in. (30–38 cm)
Weight: 7–14 lb. (3.2–6.4 kg)
Life span: 12–15 years

HOW easy to train?

Moderate. These are sighthounds, therefore they have a short attention span and no predisposition toward formal obedience. However, basic training and lots of socialization are important to increase their confidence as well as to encourage good behavior. Training should be broken up into frequent, short sessions and motivated by praise and tidbits.

Small dogs

WHAT good points?

Intelligent, affectionate, trusting, vivacious, sweet natured, playful, good-tempered, devoted, entertaining.

WHAT to be aware of?

Very sensitive to the cold. Provide a snug bed and a sweater for cold weather. Puppies are very fragile and can break a leg just wriggling out of your arms. No sense of heights, may recklessly jump out of a window or off a balcony.

WHAT medical problems?

Generally a healthy breed, Some epilepsy, hair loss (alopecia), and dislocation of kneecaps (patellar luxation) reported. Broken bones are the main hazard. These dogs should be supervised at all times to prevent injury.

● *Less fragile than its delicate appearance suggests, the Italian Greyhound makes one of the most loving canine companions imaginable.*

Miniature Schnauzer *Other names: Zwergschnauzer*

The smallest of the three Schnauzer breeds, the Miniature was a 19th-century creation intended to present the virtues of the versatile Standard Schnauzer in a conveniently sized package. Small but sturdy, he makes an excellent companion and family dog, adaptable to most lifestyles and very people oriented. He is an intelligent, active dog who needs company and attention and repays it with affection

and loyalty. Sometimes described as "a terrier without attitude," he has a terrier's liveliness and enjoyment of life but not the fire and aggression associated with many terriers. He can be quite bossy if allowed but is very responsive to training and indeed benefits from the mental stimulation of obedience or agility.

Originating in Germany, the breed reached the United States in the 1920s and soon became popular there. In Britain, interest did not really take off until the 1960s, since then the Miniature Schnauzer has become very well established.

WHAT colors?

Black, black and silver (black with silver points), or salt and pepper (dark to light gray, the hairs being banded). In Europe, the Féderation Cynologique International has recently accepted pure white, but this color is not recognized in Britain or America.

WHAT grooming does the coat need?

This is quite a high-maintenance coat, needing at least weekly grooming (ideally ten minutes a day) with a stiff brush for the body and a comb for the whiskers and leg hair. The beard usually needs cleaning after every meal! Twice a year the coat should be hand stripped. Clipping is unacceptable for show dogs as it affects coat texture, but pet owners may find it simpler.

HOW suitable are they as family dogs?

The Miniature Schnauzer makes

an excellent family dog who is devoted to his family and wants to be fully involved in all their activities. He enjoys the company of sensible children who have been taught to treat him with respect and makes a fun playmate.

WHAT type of home?

This conveniently sized little dog fits in anywhere and is equally at home in city or country. He can adapt perfectly well to apartment life as long as he has regular exercise.

WHAT type of owner?

The Miniature Schnauzer needs a loving, responsible owner who appreciates a lively dog with character and has plenty of time for him—this breed is miserable if left alone for long periods. A good choice for someone wanting to take up obedience or agility with a small breed—as long as they are prepared to spend time on coat care.

HOW compatible with other pets?

Generally friendly with other animals in the same household, this cocky little dog can sometimes be a bit too bossy with strange dogs for his own good, so early socialization is recommended.

HOW much exercise?

This very adaptable breed will adapt to his owner's lifestyle. He can stay fit with quite moderate exercise—say three brisk walks a day—or he can enjoy regular, long country rambles. He has plenty of energy for

Character Trait	Poor	Average	Good	Excellent
Attitude to other dogs		▓		
Quietness	▓			
Not destructive			▓	
Protective behavior				▓
Not likely to stray			▓	
Good with children			▓	
Ease of training				▓

Original purpose: Ratter and companion
  Male height: 13–14 in. (33–36 cm)
  Female height: 12–13 in. (30.5–33 cm)
  Weight: 13–15 lb. (6–7 kg)
  Life span: 13–14 years

play and is a suitable choice for obedience work or agility.

HOW easy to train?

Miniature Schnauzers are very trainable, given calm, firm, consistent handling. They do need to be persuaded that lessons are fun, and a reward-based approach will achieve best results. Quick to learn, they are equally quickly bored by repetition, so keep lessons short and stimulating.

WHAT good points?

Intelligent, active, versatile, adaptable, playful, alert, reliable, docile, inquisitive, affectionate, responsive.

WHAT to be aware of?

Above-average grooming requirements. Tend to like the sound of their own voices.

WHAT medical problems?

This breed suffers from two hereditary eye disorders, cataracts and progressive retinal atrophy (degeneration of the light receptors cells in the eyes). All breeding stock should be eye tested. Otherwise this is generally a healthy breed, with occasional incidence of bleeding disorders (hemophilia and von Willebrand's disease), heart murmurs, diabetes, Legg-Calvé-Perthes disease (degeneration of the head of the thighbone due to insufficient blood supply), and liver shunt (an inherited defect whereby the liver does not get a proper blood supply and does not function properly).

Small dogs

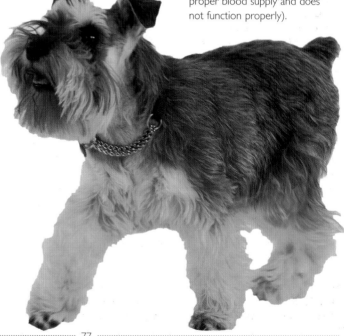

Parson Russell Terrier

The identity of the Parson Russell has been a source of confusion for some time. These merry little dogs originated as a strain of Fox Terrier, bred to keep up with hounds and horses and then to bolt the fox from its earth. Like Fox Terriers, their lively, fun-loving, and affectionate nature also made them popular pets. However, until recently they were not officially recognized by any kennel club, and the name "Jack Russell" was often applied to any mainly white mongrel terrier.

1990 saw the recognition of the original long-legged type (resembling the original Fox Terrier before it became a show dog) as the Parson Jack Russell (later Parson Russell). Short-legged specimens have since achieved recognition in some countries as a separate breed, the Jack Russell. Whatever the name, like most terriers, they are great, if energetic, companions who enjoy life and want to investigate every part of it.

WHAT colors?

All white or white with black, tan, or lemon markings, typically confined to the head and root of tail.

WHAT grooming does the coat need?

Parson Russells may have rough or smooth coats, but both are easy to groom, needing only a brisk weekly brushing with a stiff bristle brush. Show dogs are neatened up by hand stripping.

HOW suitable are they as family dogs?

These are great dogs for active families who will include them in all their activities. They can be a bit too fiery for the comfort of small children but are fun dogs for sensible older children, full of energy and never tired of playing. They do need a lot of supervision. If bored, they will certainly find some mischief to occupy themselves.

WHAT type of home?

These energetic dogs are ideal for country life, but will adapt to an urban lifestyle, even in an apartment, as long as they have a reasonable-sized yard and access to a local park for exercise. Yards must be securely fenced as, like most terriers, these are escape artists always on the look-out for adventure.

WHAT type of owner?

Terrier enthusiasts only should apply! Parson Russells are best suited to active, experienced, strong-willed owners who expect a dog to be involved in all family activities, and will not allow a clever, bossy little dog to rule the household. Not suitable for owners who are out all day, as they will get into mischief if bored. Not recommended for avid gardeners: they dig!

HOW compatible with other pets?

Early socialization with other dogs is essential to prevent the natural terrier fire escalating into aggression. Parson Russells have very strong chasing and hunting instincts. They will usually be friendly with cats in their own household, but strange cats and small pets are definitely at risk.

HOW much exercise?

These active little dogs are very adaptable and will obtain a lot of exercise through play, but they benefit from a brisk walk at least twice a day plus time for free galloping. Their intense hunting drive means that they should not

Character Trait	Poor	Average	Good	Excellent
Attitude to other dogs	■			
Quietness	■			
Not destructive		■		
Protective behavior			■	
Not likely to stray	■			
Good with children		■		
Ease of training		■		

Original purpose: Hunting vermin
Male height: 13–14 in. (33–35 cm)
Female height: 12–13 in. (30.5–33 cm)
Weight: 13–17 lb. (5.9–7.7 kg)
Life span: 13–15 years

be trusted off leash in any place where they might start chasing, especially near roads.

HOW easy to train?

Moderate. Owners of these stubborn, active, and mischievous dogs need to be firm, patient, and consistent, prepared to respect the independent terrier spirit while insisting on reasonable standards of behavior. A Parson will never be the first choice for formal obedience work, but sensible training will produce a dog who is a pleasure to live with rather than a hooligan.

WHAT good points?

Active, lively, alert, friendly, forthcoming, fearless, loving, playful, vigilant, convenient size, hardy.

● Socialization with other dogs in puppyhood is crucial for Parson Russells.

WHAT to be aware of?

Excitable, stubborn, territorial; strong hunting instinct. Can be noisy, and can be dog aggressive.

WHAT medical problems?

Generally hardy and healthy, though some eye problems (primary lens luxation), deafness, dislocation of the kneecaps (patellar luxation), and Legg-Calvé-Perthes (disease of the hip joints).

Small dogs

Beagle

The Beagle is the smallest of the pack hounds and was developed to hunt hares, with huntsmen following on foot. His convenient size and merry nature have also made him deservedly popular as a companion breed. Like all scenthounds, he has a strong hunting instinct and will follow a scent regardless of his owner's calls. He is more amenable than most of his kind and fits in well with family life. Lively and affectionate, he is friendly toward everyone and gets along well with children. As long as he has company and exercise, he is an easy dog to live with, sensible and well-behaved at home, low maintenance, and generally robust and healthy.

Dedicated hunter, loving companion, and smart show dog, the Beagle is a real all-around dog who is also employed worldwide as a sniffer dog, using his keen nose to detect anything from drugs or fire accelerants to termites.

WHAT colors?

Any accepted hound color, such as lemon and white, red and white, tricolor (black, tan, and white), and mottled—never black and tan.

WHAT grooming does the coat need?

The short coat is easy care but benefits from regular brushing (at least once a week) with a hound glove or bristle brush to remove dead hairs. Grooming sessions should include checking that the floppy ears are clean to prevent infections.

HOW suitable are they as family dogs?

This is an ideal family dog for an active household. He loves to be part of the family and is generally very good with older children. His bounciness and tendency to mouth hands and clothes in play mean he may be too robust for the comfort of toddlers. In any case, few households with pre-school children will have the time

● *Born to run, the Beagle is most likely to flourish in a country setting.*

and energy to cope with the mischievous whirlwind that is a Beagle puppy.

WHAT type of home?

The Beagle is best suited to a country home but can be just as happy living in a city provided his exercise needs are catered for. He is not a suitable apartment dog as he should have access to a yard—with a good, secure fence as he is quite an escapologist when bored.

WHAT type of owner?

This is a breed for an active, easy-going owner who wants an affectionate companion and enjoys long walks. Beagles are happy as part of a lively family or living alone with an active older person. Not a breed for those who are out at work all day, as they do not like being left alone for long periods, nor for those who want strict obedience.

HOW compatible with other pets?

These friendly dogs get along well with other dogs and with pets of different species within their own household. However, they were bred to chase, so expect them to do just that.

HOW much exercise?

Moderate. Beagles are built to run and can keep going for miles, but a couple of half-hour walks each day plus active playtime will keep them fit and happy. A stroll around the block is not enough! Without sufficient regular exercise, they easily become obese and unhealthy.

Character Trait	Poor	Average	Good	Excellent
Attitude to other dogs				■
Quietness	■			
Not destructive		■		
Protective behavior		■		
Not likely to stray	■			
Good with children				■
Ease of training		■		

Original purpose: Hunting hares in packs
Male height: 13–15 in. (33–38 cm)
Female height: Slightly smaller
Weight: 18–30 lb. (8–14 kg)
Life span: c.14 years

● This Beagle is a trim fellow, in fine condition, but a tendency toward greediness can sometimes result in obesity.

HOW easy to train?
Moderate. Training needs to start early, and trainers need to be patient and persistent as Beagles are naturally both stubborn and easily distracted if they pick up a scent. They respond well to reward-based training, but don't overdo the tidbits. Its strong chasing instinct means that extra attention must be paid to teaching the recall.

Small dogs

WHAT good points?
Intelligent, playful, loving, friendly, energetic, nonaggressive, happy, bold, even tempered, physically very sound.

WHAT to be aware of?
May be hard to control off lead. Tends to be greedy and prone to obesity. Some are very vocal. The short coat has a noticeable "doggy" smell and sheds surprisingly profusely over carpets, furniture, and clothes.

WHAT medical problems?
Generally free from major defects, but epilepsy and seizures, eye problems, and "Beagle pain syndrome" (neck pain and fever in youngsters) have been reported.

Shetland Sheepdog *Other names: Sheltie*

The enchantingly pretty Shetland Sheepdog resembles a miniature Rough Collie and shares many of the virtues of that breed. Loyal, affectionate, and responsive, he requires sensitive handling to bring out the best in him. The Sheltie is naturally standoffish with strangers, and lack of proper socialization in puppyhood may allow this to develop into timidity. Like most herding breeds, he has a high

intelligence and needs to be allowed to use this. If denied mental stimulation such as obedience training or agility, he can become neurotic, noisy, and destructive. In the right hands, however, he is an affectionate and rewarding pet, with a sweet temperament and a strong desire to please.

The Sheltie originated in the Shetland Isles, probably in the early 19th century, as a herder and general farm dog. Today the breed has become more elegant and more heavily coated in line with his cousin the Rough Collie.

WHAT colors?

Sable (from pale gold to mahogany), tricolor (black, tan, and white), and blue merle (a kind of two-toned marbled effect) are the most common colors, all with white markings that may include blaze, collar and chest, frill, legs, and tail tip. Less frequently seen are black and white or black and tan.

WHAT grooming does the coat need?

That glamorous coat needs regular, preferably daily, brushing and combing, paying special attention to the soft hair behind the ears, inside the thighs, and in the armpits, where it mats easily. Shelties molt heavily, once or twice a year, at which time the coat comes out in handfuls and is best tackled with a bath to remove as much dead hair as possible.

HOW suitable are they as family dogs?

Fantastic—with the right family,

generally a calm family with sensible, older children. Shelties dislike boisterous play and loud noises and if harassed by children may be driven to nip. These highly sensitive little dogs react badly to a tense or hectic environment and need a peaceful home.

WHAT type of home?

A country home is probably every Sheltie's ideal, but this breed will adapt perfectly well to life in a town house or apartment as long as they are given sufficient daily exercise to keep them active.

WHAT type of owner?

The Sheltie is a wonderful companion for calm, sensitive, affectionate owners who have time for the necessary exercise, training, and grooming. This is definitely not a "home alone" dog. Shelties need company and owners who will not leave them alone for long periods.

HOW compatible with other pets?

Shelties are gentle dogs who are generally good with other animals. They do have a strong instinct to chase (and sometimes nip) things that move, so they may not be good with neighbors' cats.

HOW much exercise?

These are active little dogs that need at least a couple of walks a day in the park and plenty of playtime. It is advisable to seek a secure place for off-lead exercise because of their extreme sensitivity to loud noises, which may cause them to bolt if startled.

Character Trait	Poor	Average	Good	Excellent
Attitude to other dogs			X	
Quietness		X		
Not destructive			X	
Protective behavior		X		
Not likely to stray			X	
Good with children		X		
Ease of training				X

Place of origin: **Shetland Islands**

Original purpose: Herder
Male height: 13–16 in. (33–40.5 cm)
Female height: 13–16 in. (33–40.5 cm)
Weight: 14–16 lb. (6–7 kg)
Life span: 12–14 years

HOW easy to train?

Shelties are very intelligent, willing to please, and easy to train in the hands of a sensitive owner. This breed needs encouragement and reward-based training. Harsh training techniques and scoldings will be counterproductive, but gentle, patient, and consistent training will achieve admirable results.

● Since its days as a working dog in the Shetlands, the Sheltie has become more heavily coated and elegant. Its coat now benefits from daily attention.

WHAT good points?

Gentle, very affectionate, responsive, alert, loyal, intelligent, non-aggressive, devoted to owner, good watchdog , eminently trainable, and willing to please.

Small dogs

WHAT to be aware of?

Demanding in terms of coat care— and company. Early socialization vital to prevent shyness. Extreme sensitivity to stress. Can be very clinging. Not recommended for hectic homes or for homes with young children. Strong chasing instinct.

WHAT medical problems?

Eye problems including progressive retinal eye disease (PRA) and collie eye anomaly, for which puppies should be eye tested. Von Willebrand's disease (a blood disorder), hip malformation (dysplasia), kneecap dislocation (patellar luxation), epilepsy, heart valve defects, and thyroid disease also occur in this breed.

Cocker Spaniel

From the 1920s, the Cocker Spaniel in America evolved along such different lines from the English type as to become a distinct breed in its own right, achieving separate status in 1946. The Cocker Spaniel is smaller than his English cousin, with a shorter back, more domed head shape with shorter muzzle, and much more profuse coat. He has the same sweet nature and abundant energy as the English Cocker and is, if anything, even more of a companion breed. Despite his glamorous looks, he retains his working intelligence, which should be sensibly channeled to avoid him from becoming bored and destructive.

His crowning glory in the show ring and major drawback as a pet is his voluminous coat, which needs a great deal of care. Prospective owners must recognize that this is a high-maintenance breed. Professional assistance with grooming may be needed, even when the coat is clipped short.

WHAT colors?

Black, chocolate, red, buff, cream, sable, black and tan, roan, and parti-color (white with distinct markings in any accepted color, with or without tan markings).

WHAT grooming does the coat need?

Maximum. Maintaining a full show coat in good condition is a skilled and time-consuming task, and most pet owners will need professional help. Reputable breeders will recommend a good grooming service or may provide this. Many pet owners opt to have the coat clipped short, but remember that this entails a substantial cost every six to eight weeks.

HOW suitable are they as family dogs?

This happy little dog makes a wonderful pet for an active family with plenty of time for exercise, play, and training and whose members are prepared to commit themselves wholeheartedly to his grooming needs. Gentle and playful, he is great fun for sensible children and greatly enjoys participating in family activities.

WHAT type of home?

A country home is ideal for this active breed. However, the Cocker Spaniel will adapt to city and even apartment life so long as he has access to a park where he can enjoy a good run every day.

WHAT type of owner?

This breed needs an active, affectionate owner who has plenty of time for energetic walks, enjoys the stimulus of training a responsive dog, and is committed to time-consuming coat care. Cocker Spaniels are happy as part of a family or as companions for the active elderly. They dislike being left alone, however, and are not recommended for owners who are out at work all day.

HOW compatible with other pets?

These friendly little dogs usually get along well with other dogs and with cats in their own household. They were bred to hunt and have a strong chasing instinct, so strange cats had better watch out. Smaller pets, such as rabbits and hamsters, should be introduced with great care, and contact should always be supervised.

Character Trait	Poor	Average	Good	Excellent
Attitude to other dogs				
Quietness				
Not destructive				
Protective behavior				
Not likely to stray				
Good with children				
Ease of training				

Original purpose: Finding and retrieving game
Male height: 14.5–15.5 in. (37–39.5 cm)
Female height: 13.5–14.5 in. (34–37 cm)
Weight: 24–28 lb. (11–13 kg)
Life span: 12–15 years

Small dogs

HOW much exercise?

Regular, energetic walks are essential for these very active little dogs—at least an hour's walk a day and more if possible, together with free exercise and active playtime. An underexercised spaniel is likely to be bored, badly behaved, and overweight.

HOW easy to train?

These working dogs are intelligent, enthusiastic, and eager to please. Given a consistently firm but gentle, positive approach, they are highly trainable. They are sensitive and easily put off by harsh treatment, but they can also be willful and easily distracted if their interest is not maintained, so handlers need to keep lessons fun and rewarding.

WHAT good points?

Happy, sweet natured, loyal, playful, gentle, affectionate, even tempered, intelligent, responsive, energetic.

WHAT to be aware of?

Demanding in terms of coat care and company. Does not like being left alone. Beware commercially bred pups that may have temperament problems.

WHAT medical problems?

This breed has a number of potential health problems, so choose pups only from healthy stock. Various eye problems including hereditary cataracts (breeding stock should have current eye certificates), hip malformation (dysplasia), tendency to ear infections, skin ailments, and allergies.

● *A shorter back, more domed head, shorter muzzle, and more profuse coat distinguish the Cocker Spaniel from his English cousin.*

Welsh Terrier

Smart, neat, and workmanlike in appearance, the Welsh Terrier has the true terrier nature, cheerful, energetic, and inquisitive, while being less fiery and quarrelsome than some terrier breeds. He is a great "people dog" and makes an affectionate, entertaining companion for those who appreciate a lively, fun-loving pet with a will of his own. This is a dog who likes to keep busy and needs to be involved with family activities. If left to his own devices, he will get into mischief. He is tireless on walks, always ready to play, and an alert house guard who will challenge any intruder.

Rough-haired black and tan working terriers were used throughout Britain since before the Middle Ages. The Welsh representative of this type was chosen for Kennel Club recognition in 1886. Today the breed has been smartened up for the show ring to resemble a miniature Airedale.

WHAT colors?

Black and tan, or black, grizzle, and tan. Puppies born predominantly black, developing the tan gradually.

WHAT grooming does the coat need?

It is essential to groom at least weekly with a hard bristle brush and steel comb. If neglected, it will mat and tangle. The coat should also be stripped every three months or it will end up looking like a scruffy old doormat. Pet owners may find it easier to have the coat clipped, but this does mar both texture and color.

HOW suitable are they as family dogs?

The Welsh Terrier is an excellent choice for an active family with older children. He loves family companionship and is a great children's playmate, although he is not recommended for households with very young children since he will not tolerate mishandling. Busy families may not have the time to keep this busy terrier out of mischief.

WHAT type of home?

This is an ideal country dog who will be just as happy in the city, given enough exercise. He will appreciate a yard, which needs to be securely fenced—most terriers are escape artists whose interest in the outside world will direct them through any gap. He does love to run free and explore, so in a city he will be happier living near a reasonably sized park.

WHAT type of owner?

This is a great dog for an active owner who enjoys country walks and who is prepared to maintain a firm, consistent approach to training. If you enjoy a busy, stimulating pet who wants to participate fully in family life and are prepared to be "pack leader," the Welsh Terrier is a great choice. If you prefer a more placid companion, look outside the terrier group.

HOW compatible with other pets?

The Welsh Terrier is less aggressive than many terriers but won't back down if challenged by another dog. He retains all his original hunting instincts and should not be trusted with small pets like rabbits and

Character Trait	Poor	Average	Good	Excellent
Attitude to other dogs	■			
Quietness		■		
Not destructive		■		
Protective behavior			■	
Not likely to stray	■			
Good with children			■	
Ease of training		■		

Original purpose: Vermin control
Male height: 14–15.5 in. (35.5–39 cm)
Female height: 14–15.5 in. (35.5–39 cm)
Weight: 20–21 lb. (9–9.5 kg)
Life span: c.14 years

hamsters. He usually gets along well with cats in his own household if brought up with them, but next-door's cat is likely to be considered fair game.

HOW much exercise?

This is an active breed that needs regular exercise and active play. A daily stroll around the block is not enough, and a fit adult doesn't know the meaning of too much.

HOW easy to train?

Moderate. This is a terrier, a strong-willed dog with no built-in predisposition toward obedience. With firmness, patience, consistency, and a reward-based approach, he certainly is trainable. However, he is easily distracted and has a mind of his own. There will always be times when he decides to ignore you.

WHAT good points?

Affectionate, lively, inquisitive, adaptable, playful, full of character, convenient size, hardy, a good watchdog.

WHAT to be aware of?

Excitable, stubborn, territorial, strong hunting instinct. Can be trouble with other dogs of the same sex. If left alone for long periods, they may become destructive or noisy.

WHAT medical problems?

This is a healthy breed with no major problems, although glaucoma (increased pressure in the fluid in the eyeball), skin allergies, epilepsy, and thyroid problems have been reported.

Small dogs

Tibetan Terrier _Other names: Dhoki Apso_

The Tibetan Terrier is the classic shaggy dog in miniature. Despite his name, he has no terrier characteristic, but rather resembles a small-scale Old English Sheepdog. His attractive shaggy appearance and happy temperament make the Tibetan Terrier an appealing companion. Under the glamorous coat, he is a sound, unexaggerated, medium-sized dog capable of fitting into any home environment, with an outgoing, affectionate nature that makes him an excellent family dog. Tibetans are "people dogs." What they do need is their owners' time, both in terms of the company they love and the grooming that the flowing coat requires.

The breed evolved as a companion, guard, and herder in the harsh conditions of the Tibetan mountains, where it was greatly prized. It was not introduced to the West until 1926 and was initially overshadowed by its close relative, the Lhasa Apso, but today has achieved a deserved popularity.

WHAT colors?

All colors, including black, gray, smoke, cream, gold, white, parti-colored, and tricolored. Liver and chocolate colors occur but are not accepted in the show ring.

WHAT grooming does the coat need?

The profuse double coat needs a great deal of attention. Daily brushing is essential to avoid knots and tangles, the facial hair needs cleaning after each meal, and on top of that a trip to the groomer every eight to ten weeks is advisable. Some owners prefer to keep the coat clipped short for the dog's comfort and for ease of care.

HOW suitable are they as family dogs?

This breed makes an ideal family dog. He is devoted to his family, likes to be involved in their activities, and has endless energy. Children need to learn to treat him with respect, but he will respond in kind. He is a sensible size to be managed easily by older children.

WHAT type of home?

Adaptable to most circumstances, the Tibetan Terrier can be just as happy in the city or country. What matters to him is the company of his human family.

WHAT type of owner?

Tibetan puppies can be very exuberant and need a fairly firm hand, so this may not be the ideal first dog. A sensible, experienced owner will bring out the best in them. Their prime need is to be part of the family, receiving plenty of time and attention.

HOW compatible with other pets?

Normally Tibetan Terriers get along well with other dogs. Although usually sensible as adults, they can be very bouncy as youngsters and need to be taught how to behave around cats and other pets.

HOW much exercise?

The Tibetan will adapt to its owner's lifestyle in terms of exercise needs, content to enjoy short walks or long ones. However, he is a lively dog with plenty of stamina who will enjoy as much exercise as his owners can offer.

HOW easy to train?

This is a strong-willed little dog, willing to please but needing sensible, consistent, and above-all early training. He has a great deal of energy that needs to be directed and is well suited to advanced

Character Trait	Poor	Average	Good	Excellent
Attitude to other dogs				
Quietness				
Not destructive				
Protective behavior				
Not likely to stray				
Good with children				
Ease of training				

Original purpose: Companion and guard
Male height: US not above 17 in. (43 cm),
UK about 14–16 in. (35.5–40.5 cm)
Female height: Slightly smaller than males
Weight: 18–30 lb. (8–13.6 kg)
Life span: 13–14 years upward

training disciplines like agility and competitive obedience.

WHAT good points?

Hardy, family oriented, loyal companion, intelligent, quick learner, alert, lively, not nervous or aggressive, excellent watchdog.

WHAT to be aware of?

These are active dogs who jump and climb. If neglected and left to their own devices, youngsters can easily become hyperactive and noisy. They demand attention.

WHAT medical problems?

Generally a very healthy breed. However, prospective puppy owners should check that breeding stock has been tested for hip dysplasia and for two eye conditions, progressive retinal atrophy (degeneration of light receptor cells) and dislocation of the lens (primary lens luxation). Dislocation of the kneecaps (patellar luxation) and hernias also occur.

Small dogs

Boston Terrier *Other names: Boston Bull*

The smart and stylish Boston is a delightful companion who suits most modern lifestyles. A compact little dog who fits well into apartment living, he has an easy-care coat and low exercise requirements, and his sunny disposition wins him friends everywhere. His only demand is for company. This is not a dog who will be happy on his own as he needs plenty of love and attention (and repays this generously). He is gentle enough to be chosen as a companion for an elderly person, lively enough to flourish as a child's playmate, and sociable enough to enjoy family life. Physically, however, he does not cope well with extremes of temperature and needs extra care in hot weather to prevent breathing difficulties.

The Boston is an all-American breed. Hard though it is to believe, this gentle and friendly pet descends from early 19th-century fighting dogs, deriving from the same bulldog-terrier crosses that produced the Bull Terrier.

WHAT colors?

Brindle or black with even white markings. Ideally these markings comprise white muzzle, blaze, collar, breast, part or whole of forelegs, and hindlegs below hocks. However, mismarked pups make just as good pets.

WHAT grooming does the coat need?

This is an easy-care coat, needing only occasional (weekly) brushing to remove dead hairs. However, the face should be cleaned daily with a damp cloth, paying particular attention to the area around the eyes. The short coat has the advantage of minimal shedding.

HOW suitable are they as family dogs?

With a considerate family that appreciates his needs, the Boston is a marvelous family dog. If raised with children, they will usually become a child's best friend. As with any breed, children need to be supervised and taught to

● *Alertness, intelligence, and self-confidence radiate from this all-American Boston Terrier.*

respect the dog's needs, but they will appreciate the Boston's playful and responsive nature and bold personality.

WHAT type of home?

Created in the city of Boston, this compact little dog was designed for city life and can be quite comfortable in an apartment. However, he is quite prepared to enjoy the delights of the country as well. Wherever he lives, care

must always be taken to protect him from extremes of temperature.

WHAT type of owner?

Any loving, responsible owner who wants a close companion and is not too keen on long walks will suit the Boston. He is an excellent companion for children and the elderly and a great family dog, provided always that care is taken to avoid circumstances where over-heating may cause distress.

HOW compatible with other pets?

Bostons are just as friendly with other animals as with people, although some dominant males may display intermale aggression with other dogs. As with all breeds, they benefit from early socialization with their own kind and with any other household pets with which they may be expected to share a home.

HOW much exercise?

Bostons are active dogs who need daily exercise, but they are not great walkers. A short, daily walk will

Character Trait	Poor	Average	Good	Excellent
Attitude to other dogs		▓	▓	
Quietness		▓		
Not destructive		▓	▓	
Protective behavior	▓			
Not likely to stray		▓		
Good with children			▓	▓
Ease of training			▓	

Original purpose: Stable dog
Male height: 15–17 in. (38–43 cm)
Female height: 15–17 in. (38–43 cm)
Weight: 10–25 lb. (4.5–11.5 kg)
Life span: 10–14 years

suffice, supplemented by playtime indoors or in the yard. Avoid exercise in hot weather, as this breed overheats very easily. Bostons like to go everywhere with you but would often prefer to be carried rather than walk.

HOW easy to train?
Bostons are strong-minded, stubborn little dogs who need to be persuaded that training sessions are fun, but they are also highly intelligent and quick to learn if it suits them. They enjoy learning tricks and, with patience, can achieve impressive levels of obedience.

WHAT good points?
Companionable, lively, intelligent, affectionate, sociable, gentle, playful, nonaggressive, entertaining, well-suited to city life.

WHAT to be aware of?
Like all short-faced dogs, Bostons may have breathing difficulties when exposed to heat or over-exertion, and are liable in any case to snort, snuffle, wheeze, and snore. They also have a tendency to flatulence.

WHAT medical problems?
Breathing problems are inevitable with short-faced breeds but should not be a problem if care is taken to avoid overheating or overexertion. Youngsters should be tested for inherited juvenile cataract; lack of thyroid hormone (hypothyroidism), and skin tumors also occur in this breed.

Small dogs

● *Like other short-faced breeds, the Boston can develop breathing problems and also overheats quite easily. Strenuous exercise in hot weather should be avoided.*

English Cocker Spaniel *Other names: Cocker Spaniel*

The nickname of the "Merry Cocker" is well-deserved, for he is a happy, friendly, enthusiastic character whose tail never stops wagging. A keen worker, he is just as ready to pour his energy into the role of family pet. This is a lively and loving breed that needs, and revels in, company. He is devoted to his owners, sociable with visitors, and good with children. Indeed, his kindness and working intelligence make him a great hearing ear dog, support dog for the disabled, and therapy dog. Outgoing yet gentle, he is however highly demanding in terms of attention, exercise, and grooming.

Spaniels developed to assist falconers and later shooters by finding, flushing, and retrieving game. The smallest of the land spaniels, the English Cocker was recognized as a separate breed in 1892. Today show and working strains have diverged, the latter being stockier, less heavily coated, and even more energetic.

WHAT colors?

English Cockers come in a wide range of colors including golden, red, liver, black, blue roan, black and white, orange and white, lemon and white, tricolor, and black and tan.

WHAT grooming does the coat need?

The thick, silky coat needs quite a lot of attention, ideally a daily brushing and combing plus a thorough grooming at least once a week. The long ears and ear fringes need particular care. In addition, the coat needs regular stripping or clipping. Professional grooming may be needed. Neutering can cause coat changes, leading to a thicker, softer coat needing extra work.

HOW suitable are they as family dogs?

This is a wonderful breed for an active family. English Cockers thrive on family life. They are generally good with children but won't tolerate teasing or rough

● Friendly and energetic, the English Cocker is happiest with an active family.

treatment. Younger members of the family should be supervised.

WHAT type of home?

A country home is idea. As long as they have the exercise and attention they need, English Cockers will adapt happily to life in a city and are compact enough to live in an apartment.

WHAT type of owner?

This breed is best suited to active, sociable owners who expect a close relationship with their dogs and have time and the inclination for exercise, grooming, and training. English Cockers are happy as part of a lively family but make equally good companions for the active elderly. Not a breed for those who are out at work all day as they may suffer separation anxiety.

HOW compatible with other pets?

English Cockers are usually as friendly with other animals as with people. This is a sporting breed, so don't expect them to resist chasing the neighbor's cat until fully trained.

HOW much exercise?

English Cockers have boundless energy and need regular walks, free exercise, and active playtime. When denied exercise, they are likely to become frustrated, destructive—and overweight.

HOW easy to train?

Intelligent and eager to please, this working breed is highly trainable and indeed needs the mental stimulation of training lessons. Start early to prevent

Character Trait	Poor	Average	Good	Excellent
Attitude to other dogs				
Quietness				
Not destructive				
Protective behavior				
Not likely to stray				
Good with children				
Ease of training				

Original purpose: Finding and retrieving game
Male height: 15–17 in. (38–43 cm)
Female height: 14–16 in. (35.5–41 cm)
Weight: 26–34 lb. (12–15.5 kg)
Life span: 12–15 years

puppy mischief from escalating into disregard of your wishes. Training must be gentle but firm. They are sensitive to harsh treatment but can also be quite independent, headstrong, and easily distracted by scents when outdoors.

WHAT good points?
Happy, sweet natured, loyal, playful, gentle, affectionate, even tempered, intelligent, responsive, energetic.

WHAT to be aware of?
Demanding coat care. Does not like being left alone. "Rage syndrome" (sudden outbreaks of unprovoked aggression, possibly an inherited condition) has been an occasional but alarming problem in the breed, mostly in reds and goldens, but is quite rare.

Small dogs

WHAT medical problems?
English Cockers are generally a healthy breed. Hereditary problems include progressive retinal atrophy (degeneration of the light receptor cells in the eyes)—breeding stock should be eye tested—kidney disease, heart problems, and dislocating kneecaps (patellar luxation).

Basenji

A dog who washes his face like a cat, climbs like a monkey, and crows like a cockerel, the Basenji is a breed with a difference. Classed as a "primitive" breed, he originated as the hunting dog of Central-African tribesmen. As a pet for the modern household, he is endearing but distinctly challenging. Catlike in character, he is fastidiously clean, fond of comfort, affectionate but independent, and not geared toward obedience. He is also an active hunting dog who needs plenty of physical and mental exercise. Company, stimulus, and supervision are essential. A bored Basenji gravitates toward mischief. Famously barkless, he is certainly not mute but yodels, chortles, crows, and, if distressed, shrieks like a siren.

First known to the West in the 19th century, the Basenji was not established in Britain until 1936, reaching the US five years later. Since then it has become well-known but not overpopular.

WHAT colors?
Red and white, tan and white, black and white, brindle, black. Feet, chest, and tail tip are white, and white legs, blaze, and collar are also acceptable.

WHAT grooming does the coat need?
The short, fine coat requires very little attention. A weekly rubbing with a hound glove is sufficient. Basenjis are very clean dogs who wash themselves like cats, shed very little, and have no "doggy" smell.

HOW suitable are they as family dogs?
Not recommended for inexperienced families as these dogs are demanding, challenging, and require a lot of input. They can be very good with older children if raised with them but are usually too active and impish for households with toddlers.

WHAT type of home?
The Basenji is best suited to a country home but can cope with

● *Although barkless, the Basenji has a wide range of vocal skills.*

city life, even in an apartment, if he has enough exercise and attention. Homes need to be Basenji proofed as this breed is highly inquisitive and often destructive. High, secure fencing is a must. Basenjis are escape artists who can burrow under obstacles and scramble up chain-link fences with ease.

WHAT type of owner?
This is one for dedicated owners only, who appreciate the challenge of an independent, willful catlike charmer with plenty of energy and a sense of mischief. Basenji owners need patience, stamina, and a sense of humor and should be prepared to spend time on socializing, training and daily exercise. Not a dog for obedience enthusiast, or for anyone who will be seriously upset by damage to household items.

HOW compatible with other pets?
Basenjis are generally fine, even playful with other dogs, provided they are well socialized in puppyhood, although some are aggressive toward dogs of the same sex. They have strong hunting and chasing instincts, and most should not be trusted with small pets.

HOW much exercise?
Basenjis are active dogs who need a fair amount of daily exercise. Their keen hunting drive and low obedience instinct mean that they should not be trusted off leash in the vicinity of livestock and are difficult to recall if they discover an interesting scent. If there is a local lure chasing or racing society, this is an ideal way of using up a Basenji's abundant energy.

Character Trait	Poor	Average	Good	Excellent
Attitude to other dogs		■		
Quietness			■	
Not destructive	■			
Protective behavior	■			
Not likely to stray	■			
Good with children			■	
Ease of training	■			

Original purpose: Hunting
Male height: 16–18 in. (41–46 cm)
Female height: 15–17 in. (38–43 cm)
Weight: 21–24 lb. (9.5–11 kg)
Life span: c.12 years

HOW easy to train?

Difficult. Basenjis are intelligent and quick to learn but have no innate predisposition toward obedience. They are independent thinkers who need positive, firm, consistent, and reward-based training and even then will generally obey only when it suits them. It is important to persist, even if only to keep them entertained and out of mischief.

Small dogs

WHAT good points?

Affectionate, gentle, quiet, clean, neat, independent, spirited, curious, self-confident, friendly, lacks "doggy" odor.

WHAT to be aware of?

High energy level, very demanding of time and attention, easily bored, can be very destructive, and can be noisy.

WHAT medical problems?

Generally healthy, but known disorders include hemolitic anemia, eye disorders (cataracts, progressive retinal atrophy), kidney disease, and lack of thyroid hormone (hypothyroidism).

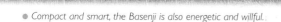

● Compact and smart, the Basenji is also energetic and willful.

Medium Dogs

This group contains some of the most popular family dogs, animals that are big enough to play with the children but not too big for the average home. They include a selection to suit all tastes, from the elegant Whippet to the lumbering Basset Hound and from the live-wire Border Collie to the laidback Bulldog.

Bulldog

A controversial breed, the Bulldog is physically exaggerated to an unusual degree, with his big head, foreshortened face, thickset body, massive chest, and bowed legs. These exaggerations are associated with health problems such as breathing difficulties, impaired activity, and whelping problems. A poor specimen of Bulldog (of which there are sadly many) often has a reduced quality of life. Having said that, a well-bred, well-raised Bulldog is nothing like as handicapped as some claim and should be happy, healthy, and quite active. They are great characters, amiable, affectionate, strong-minded, and humorous, though probably not the best choice for a novice owner.

The Bulldog's ancestors were fighting dogs, longer legged and more agile than today's breed, which developed in the 19th century. Modern variations such as Regency, Victorian, and Old English Bulldogs are reconstructions of the old type, not recognized by the Kennel Club but growing in popularity.

WHAT colors?

Practically any color except black or black and tan; commonly brindle, red and fawn, with or without black mask or muzzle, white, and pied (white and another color).

● *A great character—but he may have some health problems.*

WHAT grooming does the coat need?

Minimal; regular brushing with a hound glove to remove dead hairs is all that is needed. Facial wrinkles should be cleaned daily with cotton to prevent them from becoming damp and sore or developing eczema.

HOW suitable are they as family dogs?

With his kind temperament and affectionate nature, the Bulldog is a great pet for a considerate family who want a less-active dog but are prepared to give him the loving care and company he needs. He is excellent with sensible children, though puppies under two years old can be too exuberant and clumsy for the comfort of toddlers and indeed the frail elderly.

WHAT type of home?

As long as he has his family, the Bulldog can be happy in country or city. He enjoys access to a yard, which should provide plenty of shade in summer.

WHAT type of owner?

The Bulldog is ideal for owners who don't want to walk miles but have plenty of time to spend with him, who appreciate a dog who is an individual, and are not expecting rigid obedience. Owners also need to be confident and experienced and have plenty of patience with a dog who likes his own way, is physically strong, and as a puppy can be boisterous and mischievous.

HOW compatible with other pets?

This good-natured breed generally gets along very well with other pets. Some males can be rather challenging with other males.

HOW much exercise?

With their short legs, heavy muscles, and potential breathing problems, Bulldogs don't need a great deal of exercise, but they should not be allowed to become couch potatoes. Two half-hour walks a day at a steady pace, avoiding hot or humid weather, will keep them fit and sound.

HOW easy to train?

Difficult. Bulldogs are strong-minded, not to say obstinate, and have no innate tendency to obedience, although they are sensible dogs who are willing to

Character Trait	Poor	Average	Good	Excellent
Attitude to other dogs	■	■		
Quietness	■	■	■	■
Not destructive	■	■	■	
Protective behavior	■	■	■	
Not likely to stray	■	■	■	
Good with children	■	■	■	■
Ease of training	■	■		

Original purpose: Bull baiting and companion
Male height: 12–15 in. (30–38 cm)
Female height: 12–15 in. (30–38 cm)
Weight: 40–50 lb. (18.2–22.7 kg)
Life span: 8–12 years

cooperate if it makes sense to them. With firm, loving handling, some individuals have even been trained for competitive obedience and agility. Bullying a Bulldog will get you nowhere. Training needs to be positive and reward based (most Bulldogs are highly motivated by food rewards).

WHAT good points?

Loyal, affectionate, good humored, brave, protective, reliable, tenacious, fun-loving, excellent watchdog.

WHAT to be aware of?

Snorting, wheezing, snoring, and flatulence. Many health problems. Essential to choose breeder with care and locate a vet who knows the breed.

Medium dogs

WHAT medical problems?

Bulldogs have more health problems than most breeds, including eye disorders (inturned eyelids, out-turned eyelids, cataracts, and faulty tear ducts), breathing difficulties, dental and skin problems, heart defects, elbow and kneecap dislocation (luxation), hip malformation (dysplasia), and vertebral deformities. They are prone to overheating and to bloat. Some have malformed (screw) tails so tight that the dog has difficulty defecating. Buying a puppy from anyone but a reputable breeder is asking for trouble.

Basset Hound

The Basset Hound is a gentleman – peaceful, mild and naturally well-behaved–and also a dog of great character. Good-humored and affectionate, he fits well into family life. He is first and foremost a hound, so he needs more exercise than those short legs might suggest and is hard to recall once he starts following a scent. He also needs the company of his human "pack." A lonely Basset will make his feelings known loud and clear across the neighborhood. However, his equable temperament and engaging personality make him a delightful family member.

The Basset is an ancient breed developed in France as a pack hound to be followed on foot, and introduced into the UK and the US in the late 19th century. Show standards have led to exaggeration of type. Today working Bassets are longer-legged and less deep in the chest than the average pet or show dog.

WHAT colors?
Any recognized hound color; typically tricolor (black, white, and tan) or bicolor (lemon and white).

WHAT grooming does the coat need?
The short, easy-care coat needs brushing only about twice weekly with a stiff bristle brush. However, the pendulous ears need frequent checking and cleaning, and folds of loose skin and wrinkles also need regular checks to ensure they are dry and not developing sores.

HOW suitable are they as family dogs?
Bassets make great family dogs. They are peaceful, sensible and nonaggressive, gentle with children and devoted to their family and friends. However, they may be too powerful and too stubborn for children to take for walks without parental supervision, and time must be made for their exercise requirements.

WHAT type of home?
The Basset is a fairly big dog, and he needs space. He is happiest as a country dweller, but will adapt to apartment life and is quiet and sensible indoors, as long as he has several long walks a day. He does need company, or neighbors are likely to complain about his deep, musical voice.

WHAT type of owner?
Bassets are not for the house proud. They molt, drool, have quite a strong doggy smell, and, being low to the ground, pick up a lot of dirt. They need patient owners who appreciate a dog of independent character, enjoy long walks in all weather, and can provide plenty of company–Bassets hate being left alone.

HOW compatible with other pets?
The Basset's friendly nature means that he will usually get on well with other dogs. However, his innate hunting drive means that small household pets like cats and rabbits should be introduced with care.

HOW much exercise?
Bassets need a great deal of exercise–two good walks a day, including the opportunity to run free off lead. Allowing a Basset to become overweight and unfit is likely to lead to back problems. However, growing puppies should not be overexercised. Build up walks gradually from six months onward.

HOW easy to train?
The Basset's reputation for being stubborn and self-willed is well earned. This is not a suitable breed

Character Trait	Poor	Average	Good	Excellent
Attitude to other dogs				●
Quietness	●			
Not destructive			●	
Protective behavior	●			
Not likely to stray	●			
Good with children				●
Ease of training		●		

Original purpose: Hunting as pack hound
Male height: 13–15 in. (33–38 cm)
 Female height: 11–14 in. (28–36 cm)
Weight: 40–60 lb. (18–27 kg)
Life span: 10–12 years

for obedience enthusiasts. It is important to work on training the recall, or your Basset will follow his nose whenever he is off lead, happily deaf to your calls.

WHAT good points?
Good-natured, cheerful, companionable, gentle, peaceful, friendly, reliable, affectionate, sensible, great with children, oodles of personality.

WHAT to be aware of?
Physical exaggeration means potential health problems. Stubborn nature means that sensible discipline is essential—males can be quite dominant if not adequately trained from puppyhood.

WHAT medical problems?

Medium dogs

The long back means a risk of back problems, especially if a dog is allowed to become overweight. Elbow deformity (dysplasia) occurs in the breed, as do eye problems, and skin wrinkles may develop dermatitis. The breed is prone to gastric torsion (bloat), so avoid taking a Basset out for a strenuous walk immediately after mealtime.

● *A dog of great character, the Basset is good humored but more stubborn than his sweet expression may suggest.*

Petit Basset Griffon Vendéen

This mouthful of a name, often shortened for convenience to PBGV, means "small, short-legged, rough-coated hound of the Vendée" (western France). The PBGV is more lightly built and much livelier than the more familiar Basset Hound, who is no relation. He is a merry, friendly extrovert, as busy as a terrier and as fond of attention as any toy breed, and makes a delightful family pet. However, being a hound, he is also independent, stubborn, and ruled by his nose. Pursuing an exciting scent will always matter more to him than following orders.

France's short-legged wirehaired hounds may date back to the 16th century, but it was not until 1951 that Bassets Griffon Vendéen were divided into two breeds, Petit ("small") and Grand ("large"). The PBGV is relatively new to both Britain and the US, but his appealing looks and charming nature have led to a rapid rise in popularity.

WHAT colors?

White with any combination of lemon, orange, tricolor, or grizzle markings.

WHAT grooming does the coat need?

The PBGV needs grooming daily, or at least twice a week, with a wire pin brush and comb to prevent mats and tangles, paying special attention to the ears and the hair around eyes and mouth. The rough, harsh coat will need a quick check after country walks as it tends to pick up burrs and other debris.

HOW suitable are they as family dogs?

This is a great choice for an active family who want a loving, lively, sweet-natured pet. PBGVs are good with children and friendly with visitors. They do need a lot of attention: if bored or lonely, they are likely to be destructive and noisy. As youngsters (up to about two years old) they can be too boisterous for the comfort of pre-school children.

WHAT type of home?

This energetic dog is happiest in the country. He would not be happy in an apartment unless provided with a great deal of daily exercise. He needs a very secure garden—PBGVs are great escapologists who specialize in digging their way out if the world beyond if the fence looks (or smells) interesting.

WHAT type of owner?

This breed needs an active owner who enjoys long walks in all weather and can provide plenty of company and attention—PBGVs hate being left alone or ignored. They are not a good choice for anyone who wants a placid, patient pet, as they are real live wires. Potential owners should appreciate the basic hound nature, with its independence and strong innate hunting drive.

HOW compatible with other pets?

The PBGV's friendliness extends to other dogs and, with training, to other animals in the same household. However, it is important to remember that his strong hunting and chasing instincts embrace anything that runs away, which could well include cats, rabbits, and hamsters.

HOW much exercise?

These hounds were bred to enjoy a full day's hunting, so they have a

Character Trait	Poor	Average	Good	Excellent
Attitude to other dogs			●	
Quietness	●			
Not destructive		●		
Protective behavior	●			
Not likely to stray	●			
Good with children			●	
Ease of training		●		

Original purpose: Hunting
Male height: 13–15 in. (33–38 cm)
Female height: 13–15 in. (33–38 cm)
Weight: 25–35 lb. (11.5–16 kg)
Life span: 11–14 years

great deal of energy and stamina and need plenty of exercise—say an hour's walk twice a day for an adult, more if possible. Most PBGVs cannot be trusted for off-leash exercise. If they pick up a scent, they will be deaf to the recall and disappear over the horizon.

HOW easy to train?

Moderate. Hounds are not programmed by nature for obedience. They are independent and often stubborn and willful. If it comes to a choice between following a scent or hearing his master's voice,

the average PBGV will be stone deaf. However, this breed is intelligent and likes to please, so consistent firm but gentle training from an early age will have an impact.

WHAT good points?

Happy, extroverted, independent, willing to please, intelligent, playful, active, affectionate, sociable, friendly.

WHAT to be aware of?

High exercise requirements and very lively—more entertaining than restful. Likes the sound of his own voice.

WHAT medical problems?

Generally a healthy breed, but reported problems include hip malformation (dysplasia), kneecap dislocation (patellar luxation), eye disorders (corneal dystrophy, persistent pupillary membrane, retinal folds), lack of thyroid hormone (hypothyroidism), and epilepsy.

Medium dogs

Staffordshire Bull Terrier

The Staffordshire Bull Terrier is an impressive and imposing sight—it has well-defined musculature, strong jaws and large teeth, a broad chest, and loose shoulders allied to a low-slung body. It should come as no surprise to know that its ancestors were bred for fighting and bull baiting. They were prized for their courage and tenacity, of course, but also for their level headed and obedient nature. This dog was not a hot-headed brawler but a cool, calculating, and big-hearted opponent who would not flinch from taking on a larger animal and then hanging on for grim death.

The breed derives from the crossing of an Old English Bulldog with a type of terrier, possibly the extinct Black and Tan. The resulting dog combined the strength and tenacity of a Bulldog with the agility and quick-wittedness of a terrier. When bull baiting and dog fighting were banned, the Staffy was developed as a reliable companion breed. It was recognized by the Kennel Club in 1935 and by the AKC in 1974.

What colors?
Red, fawn, white, black, blue, or brindle or any one of these colors with white.

What grooming does the coat need?
The coat is smooth, short, and close. A daily five-minute grooming session with a bristle brush or a hound glove will remove dead hair and encourage the coat to shine. Most Staffies like water and enjoy the occasional bath.

How suitable are they as family dogs?
A marvelous family pet, Staffordshire Bull Terriers are devoted and loyal companions. They dote on their owners and are remarkably fond of children—not for nothing are they nicknamed "the nanny dog." They have a tremendous sense of fun and love playing games of chase and fetch. They are also very protective of their family circle and so are an excellent choice of companion for women who live alone.

What type of home?
These are highly adaptable dogs. Despite their pronounced musculature and very powerful, athletic outline, they do not have to be kept in acres of open country-side. Staffies are happy living in an urban environment, even in an apartment, provided that they get regular exercise every day and can have access to open spaces for uninhibited play and recreation.

What type of owner?
For the right owner, this breed is an absolute prince among dogs, offering unswerving loyalty and constant devotion. Prospective owners must be aware that they have to make an equal commitment to the dog; this is not the right breed for a "hands-off" owner. They are athletic and vigorous animals that seek companionship and entertain-ment. The ideal owner should also be an active individual who will enjoy energetic bouts of exercise with their four-legged friend—certainly not the right choice for the infirm or housebound.

How compatible with other pets?
Staffordshire Bull Terriers are not afraid to fight and so care should be exercised when introducing them to other pets or when out walking when you are likely to come across other dogs. Provided that puppies have been properly socialized during their formative weeks of growth, they should respond positively to other animals and members of the family circle. If you are unsure of your dog's likely reactions to other dogs, it makes sense to walk him on a lead while you assess his reactions to the outside world.

Character Trait	Poor	Average	Good	Excellent
Attitude to other dogs				
Quietness				
Not destructive				
Protective behavior				
Not likely to stray				
Good with children				
Ease of training				

Original purpose: Fighting dog and companion
Male height: 14–16 in. (35.5–41 cm)
Female height: 14–16 in. (35.5–41 cm)
Weight: 24–38 lb. (11–17 kg)
Life span: 12–14 years

How much exercise?

Staffies need more exercise than many other breeds. Regular walks and play sessions are a must, and they will thrive on an even more energetic regime. Staffies need to be well-exercised both to maintain their physical condition and to keep them mentally stimulated.

How easy to train?

This breed is highly intelligent and responds well to training. Owners, however, have to be firm (not harsh) and consistent in their training exercises as Staffies can display a stubborn streak. They respond best to praise and encouragement; reprimands and anger will dampen their spirits.

What good points?

Tenacious, strong, fun loving, devoted, fearless, reliable and even tempered, easy to groom.

What to be aware of?

While this is a friendly and companionable breed, its history means that it has a combative and fearless character that can lead to confrontations with other dogs if you are not in control of the situation. This dog demands a lot of attention; don't consider a Staffordshire if you are not 100 percent committed to the breed.

What medical problems?

These terriers are strong and robust dogs that happily do not suffer from many congenital illnesses. Tumors can be a problem, as can cataracts and kidney stones.

Medium dogs

Keeshond *Other names: Wolfspitz*

The Keeshond is among the prettiest of the Spitz breeds, with his smiling face and abundant, beautifully shaded coat, and he has a sweet nature to match. A happy, friendly dog who enjoys life and likes people, he makes a delightful family pet with an affinity for children. Like most Spitz, he has a mind of his own, but he responds well to positive training. He is a great watchdog but a poor guard—he will bark his head off at suspicious sounds but is more likely to welcome a burglar in and show him around the house than to bite him.

In their native Holland, Keeshonds (named for national hero Cornelius "Kees" de Gyzelaar) worked on farms and boats as watchdogs and ratters but had fallen from favor by the 1920s, when British admirers revived the breed. Popular in Britain and America, they are not recognized in Europe but come under the category of Wolfspitz.

WHAT colors?
A mixture of gray and black with a pale gray or cream undercoat. The muzzle should be dark, and there should be characteristic black "spectacles" around the eyes.

WHAT grooming does the coat need?
The dense coat is easier to groom than it looks but requires a regular commitment of time—about an hour a week of daily, or at least weekly, brushing with a stiff bristle brush, plus three or four times as much during the massive twice-yearly molt. If this task is neglected, the coat tangles and mats and may need to be clipped off.

HOW suitable are they as family dogs?
Keeshonds are great family dogs, very people oriented, good with children, and delighted to be involved in family activities. They are best suited to calm, stable families, where they can develop the sensible side of their characters.

● *Keeshond puppies look like cuddly toys, but socialization is needed to make the most of their sweet natures.*

A Keeshond in a rowdy family is likely to become overexcitable and rowdy himself.

WHAT type of home?
This adaptable breed will be happy in a city or the country as long as he has his family's attention and a reasonable amount of exercise. He will be happier with access to a yard, and is not suited to an overheated home because of his heavy coat. A home with tolerant neighbors is recommended as Keeshonds tend to bark.

WHAT type of owner?
This active and affectionate dog needs a reasonably active and certainly affectionate owner and one who has plenty of time for him. Keeshonds need company and are not happy left alone for long periods. Potential owners should be committed to regular grooming and prepared to cope with a coat that carries in mud and dirt and molts heavily.

HOW compatible with other pets?
Keeshonds are friendly creatures who are normally good with other pets in the same household and with strange dogs as long as puppy socialization is not neglected.

HOW much exercise?
Moderate. Keeshonds are active dogs who like to be on the go, but they don't need to walk marathons—two half-hour walks a day plus some free running will keep them fit. Most Keeshonds love their food and can easily become obese if denied exercise.

Character Trait	Poor	Average	Good	Excellent
Attitude to other dogs			▓	
Quietness	▓			
Not destructive		▓		
Protective behavior			▓	
Not likely to stray		▓		
Good with children				▓
Ease of training			▓	

Place of origin: **Holland**

Original purpose: Companion and watchdog
Male height: 17–18.5 in. (43–47 cm)
Female height: 16–17.5 in. (41–44.5 cm)
Weight: 35–41 lb. (16–20.4 kg)
Life span: 12–14 years

HOW easy to train?

Much depends on the approach. Like other Spitz breeds, Keeshonds are intelligent but have a mind of their own rather than an inclination to follow orders. On the other hand, they enjoy activities with their owners and respond well as long as training is made fun, with a positive, reward-based approach and no boring repetition by rote.

● *Sturdy yet glamorous, the Keeshond is one of the prettiest of the Spitzes.*

WHAT good points?

Affectionate, playful, friendly, intelligent, sweet natured, bold, alert, fun loving, lively, gentle, good watch dog, entertaining company.

Medium dogs

WHAT to be aware of?

Tends to be a great barker and can be excitable. Above-average grooming needs and heavy molt twice a year.

WHAT medical problems?

Generally a healthy breed; reported problems include hip malformation (dysplasia), heart disorders, von Willebrand's disease (a blood disorder), epilepsy, and skin allergies. Keeshonds are prone to flea allergies, so it is important to not allow an infestation.

American Staffordshire Terrier _Other names: American Pit Bull Terrier_

19th-century dog-fighting men combined Bulldog and terrier blood to produce the ideal dog for their savage sport. Their "bull-and-terrier" creation developed in different directions in different continents. In Britain, it became the foundation of the Staffordshire Bull Terrier. Stock exported to the US around 1870 developed into a larger, heavier breed recognized by the AKC in 1936 as the American Staffordshire Terrier.

The AmStaff is a wonderful dog in the right hands: intelligent, good humored and keen to please. He makes a devoted companion, a versatile worker, and an outstanding protection dog. However, his fighting ancestry, strong will, powerful build, and potential for aggression make good socialization and expert training essential. This is not a suitable choice for novices or for anyone who cannot earn his respect. Indeed the breed is now banned in Britain simply because some are owned by would-be macho types who are unable to control them.

WHAT colors?
Any color, solid, parti, or patched is permissible; but all white, more than 80 percent white, black and tan, and liver are not encouraged.

WHAT grooming does the coat need?
The short coat requires minimal care. Weekly brushing with a firm bristle brush to remove dead hairs will keep it in perfect condition.

HOW suitable are they as family dogs?
A well-bred, well-socialized AmStaff is a great family dog and trustworthy with children. However, only breeders who place a high priority on good temperament should be considered, and only owners who are already experienced with this breed should consider an AmStaff when looking for a family dog.

WHAT type of home?
This active breed is best suited to a country home but will adapt to city life as long as he has enough exercise. Secure fencing is a must.

WHAT type of owner?
Only confident, strong-minded, and experienced owners who are thoroughly committed to a proper regime of socialization, training, and exercise should consider this breed. Potential owners should also consider the serious impact of breed-specific legislation. AmStaffs are banned in some countries and subject to draconian controls in others.

HOW compatible with other pets?
Be very careful. Thorough socialization is essential to ensure that an AmStaff does not become aggressive toward other dogs. He should be supervised with other animals at all times—if another dog provokes him, he will not take it lying down. In ideal circumstances, he will be trustworthy with cats in his own household. In general, he is not recommended for a home with other pets.

HOW much exercise?
This powerful and active breed needs plenty of regular exercise. However, he should be kept leashed in public to avoid any risk of a fight, to reassure passersby in view of the breed's poor public image, and in many areas as a legal requirement.

HOW easy to train?
Experienced handlers will find the AmStaff a joy to work with, eager to perform whatever task is set him. However, he needs firm,

Character Trait	Poor	Average	Good	Excellent
Attitude to other dogs	■			
Quietness		■		
Not destructive			■	
Protective behavior				■
Not likely to stray			■	
Good with children			■	
Ease of training			■	

Original purpose: Fighting
Male height: 18–19 in. (46–48 cm)
Female height: 17–18 in. (43–46 cm)
Weight: 57–67 lb. (26–30 kg)
Life span: 12–14 years

confident leadership, as he is strong willed and has a mind of his own. It is a mistake to imagine that tough dogs need tough treatment. The AmStaff responds to praise and motivational training far better than to a domineering approach.

WHAT good points?
In the right hands, the AmStaff is a dog of many virtues: brave, loyal, affectionate, intelligent, responsive, and good natured.

WHAT to be aware of?
In the wrong hands, the AmStaff is potentially a dangerous dog. Be aware of breed-specific legislation and its implications, including poor public image and refusal of many insurers to consider this breed.

WHAT medical problems?
Generally a healthy breed, the AmStaff may suffer from hip malformation (dysplasia), hereditary cataracts, heart problems, skin disorders, and ataxia (an inherited disorder of the nervous system).

● *The ears are often cropped in the US and some other countries, but this is illegal in the UK. Uncropped ears are smallish and semierect or folded over and backward.*

Medium dogs

Soft Coated Wheaten Terrier _Other names: Irish Soft-Coated Wheaten Terrier_

Combining a perennial shaggy-dog appeal with the game terrier spirit, the Wheaten is a merry, active, medium-sized dog who makes an excellent pet. His ancestors were Irish farm dogs, so he is somewhat steadier and less aggressive than some terrier breeds though as energetic, enthusiastic, and self-opinionated as any. Bouncy and sociable, he enjoys a close involvement in family life and needs time, attention, and exercise for mind and body to keep him out of mischief. The silky coat, which adds so much to his appeal, does take considerable, regular maintenance, so this is not a breed for busy owners.

Wheatens were part of Irish family life for many years before the breed achieved recognition—in 1937 in its native land, nine years later in the UK, and not until 1950 in the US. Still not a breed that everyone recognizes in the street, they are deservedly growing in popularity, both as family companions and as show dogs.

WHAT colors?

Clear light wheat—the shade of ripening wheat. Dark shading on ears not uncommon. Puppies are born dark, lightening gradually, and may not clear to the correct color until 18–24 months old.

WHAT grooming does the coat need?

The coat is soft, silky, and abundant; loosely waved or curly, and does not shed. If neglected, it mats and tangles. Regular (ideally daily) grooming down to the skin is essential, using a pin brush followed by a metal comb to ensure that no tangles are left. Show dogs are trimmed to create a tidy outline; pet owners often clip some of the hair covering the eyes to improve the dog's vision.

HOW suitable are they as family dogs?

This is a great dog for a lively family willing to include him in all their activities. Wheatens are very good with sensible children. Their sense of fun and abundant energy making them great playmates, although like most terriers they can be too excitable to be recommended for households with very young children.

WHAT type of home?

Wheatens are just as happy in the city as in the country as long as they have reasonable exercise and plenty to do. They will appreciate a yard, which needs to be securely fenced—otherwise they are very likely to disappear over or under inadequate barriers in pursuit of trespassing cats.

WHAT type of owner?

This is a breed for an active, strong willed owner who appreciates an exuberant and extroverted dog and has plenty of time for socialization, exercise, play, training, and grooming. Wheatens are not part-time dogs but require a lot of commitment—which they will repay in full.

HOW compatible with other pets?

Early socialization is essential to ensure that terrier bossiness does not become aggression. If accustomed to other dogs in puppyhood, the Wheaten will be friendly and playful—though if he meets with aggression, he won't

● _This Wheaten has received a fairly close clip._

Character Trait	Poor	Average	Good	Excellent
Attitude to other dogs		■		
Quietness		■		
Not destructive	■			
Protective behavior			■	
Not likely to stray		■		
Good with children			■	
Ease of training	■			

Original purpose: Vermin hunter and farm dog
Male height: 18–19 in. (46–49.5 cm)
Female height: 17–18 in. (44–46 cm)
Weight: 35–45 lb. (16–20.5 kg)
Life span: 13–14 years

back down. He is fine with cats in his own household if raised with them but generally not to be trusted with strange cats or small pets.

HOW much exercise?

Plenty. This active breed will take all the exercise he can get, at the least two half-hour walks a day plus playtime. Be careful when he is off leash as he has a strong chase instinct and will disappear over the horizon after rabbits, squirrels, or any other temptation. That beautiful coat will need considerable attention after a muddy country walk.

HOW easy to train?

Difficult. He is a terrier, a bossy dog who needs to be persuaded kindly but firmly that he is not the pack leader. He can be trained, but it takes time and dedication. He is never likely to excel at formal obedience. Keep training sessions short, reward based, and above all fun to get his attention.

Medium dogs

WHAT good points?

Happy, good tempered, confident, spirited, game, exuberant, affectionate, lively, inquisitive, good watchdog.

WHAT to be aware of?

Highly boisterous and bouncy. Early socialization needed to prevent aggression toward strange dogs. Heavy commitment to coat care required.

WHAT medical problems?

The main problem with this breed is a tendency to kidney disorders (renal dysplasia), with some occurrence of hip deformity (dysplasia) and sensitivity to anesthesia.

Chinese Shar-Pei *Other names: Chinese Fighting Dog*

A striking-looking breed, the Chinese Shar-Pei has a hippo's head, dramatically wrinkled skin, and the bristly fur that gave him his name (literally "sandpaper skin"). Despite his scowling expression, he is a calm, good-natured dog who makes a great companion. Though, like other Oriental breeds, he is quite independent and needs to establish a relationship of mutual respect with his owner. Excessive skin folds cause skin and eye disorders, so look for responsible breeders producing unexaggerated stock.

From near-extinction in the 1960s to fashion icon today, the dog with a skin several sizes too large has come a long way. Dating back to at least the 13th century, the Chinese Shar-Pei was the all-purpose dog of Chinese peasant farmers, used for hunting, guarding, herding, and dog-fighting contests. The breed nearly died out under Communist rule in China, but was revived by dedicated breeders in Hong Kong, reaching the West in the 1970s.

WHAT colors?

Black, red, fawn, cream, chocolate, blue, apricot; may have dark mask and often has darker shading down back and ears with lighter shading on underparts. Parti-color ("flowered") dogs are unacceptable by AKC standards, but some breeders consider them an authentic breed color.

WHAT grooming does the coat need?

Low maintenance. Groom once a week with a hound glove or bristle brush to maintain healthy skin. The tiny ears need regular cleaning with cotton swabs.

HOW suitable are they as family dogs?

Very. This is a breed that is happiest as a family dog and is particularly good with children. Early socialization is important to ensure that his natural aloofness with strangers does not develop into suspicion, and new owners should research the breed to familiarize themselves with its health needs.

WHAT type of home?

The Chinese Shar-Pei is happy in city or country as long as he is part of the family. He can adapt to apartment living if he has enough daily exercise. He does appreciate a large yard where he can play and space to run.

WHAT type of owner?

This is a dog for owners looking for calm companionship; capable of firm, sensitive leadership, and who have time for training, exercise, mental stimulation, and affection. Chinese Shar-Peis need company and are not suitable for owners who are out all day, leaving them alone. They may be too strong minded for novices.

HOW compatible with other pets?

Early socialization is important, as with all guard breeds. A properly socialized Chinese Shar-Pei will be good with other dogs, although there is always the possibility of intermale aggression. He is OK with his own cats but has strong chase instincts and should not be trusted with strange cats or with farm livestock.

HOW much exercise?

This is an adaptable breed that will be happy with as much or as little exercise as is offered. If given a large yard, they will exercise themselves quite well with active play. However regular walks are much enjoyed and beneficial to their health. Think in terms of two brisk daily walks, but avoid exercise in hot weather as this breed overheats easily.

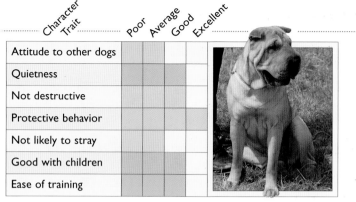

Character Trait	Poor	Average	Good	Excellent
Attitude to other dogs		▦		
Quietness			▦	
Not destructive			▦	
Protective behavior				▦
Not likely to stray			▦	
Good with children		▦		
Ease of training		▦		

Original purpose: Guarding, hunting
Male height: 18–20 in. (46–51 cm)
Female height: 18–20 in. (46–51 cm)
Weight: 45–60 lb. (20.4–27.2 kg)
Life span: 8–10 years

HOW easy to train?

Given confident leadership and firm but gentle training, this intelligent breed can be trained to a high standard. Strong minded and independent, they will obey only when a mutual respect has developed. They are quick to learn but easily bored with constant repetition. Keep training sessions varied to maintain interest.

WHAT good points?

Calm, independent, good-natured, affectionate, devoted to owners, playful, intelligent, excellent watchdog

WHAT to be aware of?

Fashionable breeds attract commercial breeders producing unhealthy stock. Avoid puppies whose parents have excessive wrinkles and skin folds. Bristly coat can cause a rash in some people. Loud snoring. May need special care with diet.

WHAT medical problems?

A range of skin disorders, inward-turning eyelids (entropion) and drooping lower lids (ectropion), lens dislocation, blocked tear ducts, lack of thyroid hormone (hypothyroidism), kidney problems, "swollen hock syndrome" or "familial Shar-Pei fever" (inherited condition leading to bouts of joint swelling and fever), gastric torsion (bloat), some hip deformity (dysplasia).

Medium dogs

Whippet

A small but workmanlike sighthound, the Whippet was developed as "the poor man's greyhound," providing rabbits for the pot and entertainment in the form of coursing and racing.

Although he retains his hunting and running instincts, he makes an ideal pet, quiet, very affectionate, and home loving. His convenient size, easy-care coat and gentle disposition make him an undemanding companion. All he needs is love, exercise and a cozy bed. This racing dog can reach 35 mph (56 km/h) in 15 seconds and loves to run, but he is a sprinter, not a marathon runner. He needs only moderate exercise—at home, he is a regular couch potato who loves his comfort.

Whippet-type dogs have been known since ancient times, but the modern Whippet was probably the creation of 19th-century miners in the north of England. KC recognition (AKC 1890; KC 1888) gave him social acceptability as show dog and smart companion.

WHAT colors?

Any color or mixture of colors, including black, blue, brindle, cream, red, fawn, white, and parti-color.

WHAT grooming does the coat need?

The fine short coat is very low maintenance. A weekly brushing with a rubber hound glove, followed by a polish with a scrap of silk or chamois leather, will keep his coat in perfect condition.

HOW suitable are they as family dogs?

Highly suitable. This is one of the best family dogs, gentle, affectionate, responsive, and with a natural affinity for children. He fits into most lifestyles and is very adaptable in terms of exercise. Families should be prepared for the fact that before growing up into sensible dogs, Whippet puppies are mischievous whirlwinds who need lots of attention.

● *Graceful and elegant, the Whippet is nonetheless a highly functional worker who retains his hunting instincts.*

WHAT type of home?

Happy to live wherever his owners choose, the Whippet makes a great sporting dog in the country or a smart dog about town. Provided he has his regular walks, he will live happily in an apartment. He enjoys a yard and should have access to a park or other area where he can safely enjoy running off leash.

WHAT type of owner?

The Whippet is a great choice for a gentle, easygoing, and reasonably active owner who wants loving companionship and has access to a secure park or paddock where this little sighthound can run safely. His calmness and quietness at home make him suitable for a single elderly owner, but he is just as well suited to family life with children for playmates.

HOW compatible with other pets?

Whippets are generally friendly with other dogs and with cats in the same household. They are bred to chase, so they should not be trusted with small pets such as rabbits or guinea pigs, and nextdoor's cat is likely to be viewed as fair game.

HOW much exercise?

Medium—think in terms of 2 miles (3 km) a day plus 20 minutes' free

Character Trait	Poor	Average	Good	Excellent
Attitude to other dogs				
Quietness				
Not destructive				
Protective behavior				
Not likely to stray				
Good with children				
Ease of training				

Place of origin: **Britain**

Original purpose: Rabbiting, racing
Male height: 19–22 in. (48–56 cm)
Female height: 18–21 in. (46–53 cm)
Weight: 27–30 lb. (12.5–13.5 kg)
Life span: 12–15 years

running in a secure place, although your Whippet will enjoy a great deal more exercise if that suits your lifestyle. As a sighthound, he must be kept on a leash near traffic or livestock. This breed thoroughly enjoys activities such as lure coursing, whippet racing, agility, and flyball.

HOW easy to train?

Fairly easy. Whippets are not as obedience geared as some breeds but more trainable than most sighthounds. Alert, intelligent, and eager to please, they respond to positive training methods with plenty of encouragement and rewards. A heavy-handed approach will only upset this sensitive breed. Because of the Whippet's strong chase instinct, a lot of work needs to be put in on the recall.

WHAT good points?

Gentle, affectionate, adaptable, good-natured, loyal, clean, quiet, very good with children, low maintenance.

WHAT to be aware of?

Strong chasing instinct. Feels the cold. No sense of heights— beware open windows. Puppies are real live wires (and take two to four years to grow up).

WHAT medical problems?

This very healthy breed is largely free from genetic problems, although progressive retinal atrophy (degeneration of the light receptor cells in the eyes) occurs in some bloodlines. Thin skin prone to damage from brambles, barbed wire, and so on.

Medium dogs

● *Typical of sighthounds, the Whippet loves to run but also revels in a couch potato lifestyle between bouts of exercise.*

Border Collie

Often considered the canine Einstein, the Border Collie is highly intelligent and highly trainable, excelling not only at sheepdog trials but at competitive obedience, agility, flyball, search and rescue, and as a sniffer dog. This is a dog that could be described as a workaholic. He lives for work in one form or another and becomes highly frustrated if not kept occupied. Suited to highly dog-oriented homes only, he needs early socialization, sensitive handling, and a major commitment of time and attention. Given plenty of stimulation, exercise, and employment, he is a loyal, affectionate, highly responsive, and rewarding companion—but not a dog to take on lightly.

Developed in the hills of the English, Scottish, and Welsh borders, the breed was famous worldwide as a worker long before receiving belated AKC recognition in the 1990s. Today it has added success in the show ring to its many achievements.

WHAT colors?

Black and white is the most common variety, but other accepted colors include tricolor, brown and white, and red or blue merle (a sort of marbled effect distinguished by the presence of irregular dark blotches against a lighter background of the same basic pigment).

WHAT grooming does the coat need?

Two coat types are recognized, smooth and long coated. Smooth coats need only a weekly grooming with stiff bristle or slicker brush to remove dead hairs. Long coats should be groomed daily, paying particular attention to the areas behind the ears and under the tail.

HOW suitable are they as family dogs?

The question is rather how suitable is a particular family for a Border Collie? For those with the time and inclination to keep him happy and occupied, the Border can be a great family member. Many families cannot commit enough time and effort, and a frustrated Border is a major liability. Not recommended with young children: Borders can be hyperactive and overexcitable, and their innate herding instincts can lead to nipping.

WHAT type of home?

This highly active breed really needs a country home and certainly a fair-sized yard with a very secure fence.

WHAT type of owner?

Only energetic people who can provide companionship and have a keen interest in training should consider this breed. He needs to be kept busy and is emphatically not a dog for couch potatoes. He is not an ideal first dog.

HOW compatible with other pets?

Generally good with other animals, but they do need sensible early socialization to prevent nervous aggression. The strong herding instinct may be a problem with other pets.

HOW much exercise?

Probably the most active breed of dog, the Border Collie needs a great deal of exercise and is absolutely tireless. However, physical exercise alone will simply keep him on his toes and must be balanced by mental stimulation to avoid frustration and hyperactivity. Activities such as agility and flyball are a great way to combine exercise for body and mind.

HOW easy to train?

Highly intelligent, exceptionally sensitive, and a quick learner, the Border is very trainable in the right

Character Trait	Poor	Average	Good	Excellent
Attitude to other dogs				
Quietness				
Not destructive				
Protective behavior				
Not likely to stray				
Good with children				
Ease of training				

Original purpose: Sheepdog
Male height: 20–23 in. (51–58.5 cm)
Female height: 18–21 in. (46–53 cm)
Weight: 30–49 lb. (14–22 kg)
Life span: 10–14 years

hands. With unfocused or inconsistent handling, he will learn bad habits just as easily. His incredibly quick responses mean that his handler needs to be equally quick to keep one step ahead. Lessons need to be challenging and stimulating to keep his interest.

WHAT good points?

Keen, alert, responsive, highly intelligent, sensitive, loyal, faithful, energetic, good watchdog.

WHAT to be aware of?

One of the most demanding breeds, he needs work or can be destructive, often developing stereotypic behavior (repeated meaningless actions such as tail chasing) if frustrated. Good socialization essential.

WHAT medical problems?

This is generally a hardy breed, but it can suffer from inherited eye disorders (collie eye anomaly, progressive retinal atrophy) and joint problems. Breeding stock should be eye tested and hip scored and puppies should be hearing tested.

Medium dogs

● *Always alert, this working dog has unlimited resources of energy.*

Bull Terrier *Other names: English Bull Terrier*

A powerful dog with a uniquely egg-shaped head, the Bull Terrier originated as a 19th-century fighting breed combining Bulldog and terrier blood, but by the 1860s a more elegant show strain had developed. Despite his ancestry, the modern Bully is first and foremost a cheerful companion, enthusiastic, fun loving, and with a great sense of humor. He loves human company and is generally good tempered, although early socialization is vital to ensure that he is safe with strange dogs.

The Bully is a lovable clown who can be gentle and reliable, but he is not a dog for the novice owner. Strong willed and physically powerful, he needs firm, patient handling. He can be hard to live with, being boisterous, destructive if bored, and often keener on playing the fool than on obedience. Potential owners should also think about public perception of bull breeds and breed-specific legislation.

WHAT colors?
Pure white, white with colored patches on head, brindle, black, red, and tricolor. Colored dogs may have white markings on chest, under-belly, tail tip, socks, and facial blaze.

WHAT grooming does the coat need?
Mimimal. Daily to weekly brushing with a hound glove or hard-bristled brush will keep the coat healthy.

HOW suitable are they as family dogs?
In the right hands the Bully is an outstanding family dog, affectionate, stable, and gentle with sensible children. He is not recommended for households with very young children, as he does not tolerate teasing very well, can be possessive with food, and as a youngster (up to three years old) can be too rough and rowdy for the safety of little ones.

WHAT type of home?
This people-oriented breed can thrive in city or country, but city dogs need a secure yard with strong fencing—Bullies can and will barge through flimsy barriers. Owners should have access to areas where a Bully can be exercised safely off lead to burn off energy.

WHAT type of owner?
This energetic, stubborn, powerful breed needs an active, experienced owner, assertive enough to cope with a dominant breed but kind and affectionate, ready to appreciate a dog with personality plus, and possessed of a strong sense of humor. Owners must also have plenty of time for training, exercise, play, and company—Bullies are miserable if left alone.

HOW compatible with other pets?
Given plenty of early socialization and training, many Bullies live happily and lovingly with cats and other dogs; others are best as sole pets. A great deal of planning and care is important when introducing a Bull Terrier to other animals. His ancestors were bred to kill animals, and he often still has a strong prey drive. Males can be dominant with other males, and although not quarrelsome, this breed will never back down from a challenge.

HOW much exercise?
This active breed needs plenty of exercise, although not all Bullies will agree with you on this point. They are often quite content to be couch potatoes and have to be persuaded of the importance of keeping fit. Be careful where you

Character Trait	Poor	Average	Good	Excellent
Attitude to other dogs	▧			
Quietness		▧		
Not destructive	▧			
Protective behavior			▧	
Not likely to stray		▧		
Good with children			▧	
Ease of training		▧		

Original purpose: Fighting and ratting
Male height: 18–24 in. (46–61 cm)
Female height: 18–24 in. (46–61 cm)
Weight: 52–62 lb. (24–28 kg)
Life span: 11–13 years

let a Bull Terrier off the lead. If he meets a badly behaved dog, there could be trouble.

HOW easy to train?

Moderate to difficult. Bullies are not naturals for the obedience ring, although it is essential that they be trained to an acceptable standard of behavior. A firm, patient approach with plenty of positive reinforcement in the form of food rewards or toys will achieve the best results.

WHAT good points?

Cheerful, affectionate, friendly, active, courageous, protective, entertaining, extroverted, stable and reliable in the right hands, great sense of humor.

WHAT to be aware of?

Not for owners who work full-time. Not the easiest breed to train. Enjoys chewing and has powerful jaws. Provide tough chew toys to deflect his interest away from furniture. Tendency to believe that, given enough determination, anything from shoes to trash cans is edible.

Medium dogs

WHAT medical problems?

Some Bull Terriers suffer from kidney disease (familial nephropathy), heart defects, kneecap dislocation (patellar luxation), skin problems, and (especially whites) inherited deafness. Behavioral problems such as compulsive tail chasing do also occur.

● *Once known as the "Gladiator," the Bully is no longer required to be aggressive—but he still needs watching with other dogs.*

Brittany
Other names: Brittany Spaniel

France's favorite pointing dog, the Brittany is the smallest and perhaps most enthusiastic of the Continental all-around gundogs bred to hunt, point, and retrieve game. He is keen, energetic, and tireless, very much a working dog who needs plenty of exercise for body and mind. He is also sweet natured and affectionate, and makes a wonderful companion and family dog—provided he has suitable outlets for his abundant energy such as fieldwork, obedience, or agility.

The Brittany resulted from a happy combination of French and English breeds. Workmanlike Breton spaniels, dating back to at least the 1700s and known as Fougeres ("high spirited"), were crossed in the 19th century with setters and pointers brought over by British sportsmen, resulting in a superb gundog which achieved breed recognition in the early 1900s. Having reached the US in the 1920s and the UK not until the 1970s, the Brittany is now deservedly popular worldwide.

WHAT colors?
Brittanys come in a rainbow spectrum of orange and white, liver and white, black and white, roan, or tricolor (liver; white and orange; or black, white, and orange), with spots, ticking, or flecking—no two dogs are identically colored.

WHAT grooming does the coat need?
The flat, medium-length coat is moderately low maintenance, needing little more than 10 minutes brushing and combing twice a week. Some individuals have more feathering on ears and legs, which will need extra attention. Check the ears and any feathering for burrs and twigs after country walks.

HOW suitable are they as family dogs?
If he has plenty of stimulation, exercise, and employment, the Brittany is a wonderful family dog who loves attention. He is excellent with children—owners often comment that he will cooperate with the children of the family better than with his master! However, if he has no job to do, he may be too hyperactive to make a good family pet and as a youngster is often too exuberant for the comfort of small children.

● Very appealing—but too energetic for some.

WHAT type of home?
Better suited to country than city life, the Brittany needs access to land where he can enjoy long, interesting walks and off-leash gallops. He is very active indoors and needs a fair-sized, securely fenced yard where he can burn off some energy.

WHAT type of owner?
The Brittany is not for couch potatoes. Only active people who enjoy long country walks in all weather and have time for training and stimulating canine activities should consider this high-energy breed. This is a dog that can be spoiled by insensitive handling and needs a gentle owner who can be firm and consistent without being tough.

HOW compatible with other pets?
If properly socialized in puppyhood, the Brittany is generally friendly with other dogs and good with cats in his own household—though strange cats had better be careful. This is a hunting breed with an innate chase instinct, so small pets such as rabbits are best kept out of harm's way.

Character Trait	Poor	Average	Good	Excellent
Attitude to other dogs			●	
Quietness			●	
Not destructive		●		
Protective behavior		●		
Not likely to stray	●			
Good with children			●	
Ease of training				●

Original purpose: Hunting, pointing and retrieving game
Male height: 19–20 in. (48–51 cm)
Female height: 18–19 in. (46–48 cm)
Weight: 30–40 lb. (13.5–18 kg)
Life span: 13–15 years

HOW much exercise?

This very active dog needs long, interesting walks plus one or two hours' free running every day. Mental exercise is just as important. If he is not working as a gundog, owners should consider agility, competitive obedience, or working trials to keep him happy and occupied. He is not suited to unemployment!

HOW easy to train?

Eager to please and a quick learner, the Brittany is highly trainable, although some individuals can be stubborn and need gentle but firm direction. Stick to a calm, consistent, reward-based approach. This is a very sensitive dog that reacts badly to rough handling but responds well to encouragement.

WHAT good points?

Affectionate, sensitive, responsive, eager to please, intelligent, enthusiastic, energetic, good-natured, gentle.

WHAT to be aware of?

High working drive and energy, frustrated if unemployed. Needs a lot of attention and may suffer from separation anxiety.

WHAT medical problems?

Some hip malformation (dysplasia) reported; also occasional progressive retinal atrophy (degeneration of the light receptor cells in the eyes), epilepsy, hemophilia, and some skin disorders.

Medium dogs

● A great gundog and a wonderful companion in the right hands.

English Springer Spaniel

One of the larger spaniels, the handsome and versatile English Springer is popular as a working gundog, a family pet, and as a sniffer dog, detecting anything from drugs to illegal immigrants. Extroverted and enthusiastic, he has endless vitality and stamina and really loves to work—and to play. This is not a dog for anyone seeking a placid companion, as he is strong willed, active, and excitable. His good humor, sociable nature, and willingness to learn make him a wonderful companion for active owners who can provide the mental and physical exercise he needs.

Spaniels developed to assist falconers and later shooters by finding, flushing, and retrieving game. The tallest of the land spaniels, the Springer was recognized as a separate breed in 1902. Today show and working strains have diverged, the latter, which are smaller and stockier, being unsuited for pet life because of their strong working drive.

WHAT colors?
Liver and white, black and white, or either of these with tan markings

WHAT grooming does the coat need?
The Springer's coat is easy to keep in good condition with a brisk daily brushing and combing. Ears need particular attention after meals and after foraging in the yard. On country walks the coat will pick up an astonishing amount of mud and foliage, which need to be cleaned out promptly before mats and tangles can form.

HOW suitable are they as family dogs?
An ideal family dog who loves children and is always ready for play but patient and tolerant with the very young. As a puppy (and there are those who would say he never really leaves puppyhood behind), the Springer can be a whirlwind of energy needing a lot of time and attention from all family members—not an ideal choice for families with a hectic lifestyle.

WHAT type of home?
Essentially a country dog, the Springer is too active and energetic to be happy cooped up in an apartment. A yard is a must—along with tolerant owners who can cope with the Springer's passion for digging holes.

WHAT type of owner?
This ebullient breed needs an owner who enjoys long walks—Springers are great companions for joggers, though generally too lively for the elderly. Patience and gentleness are also needed when training this sensitive character—and a sense of humour is vital, especially during the puppy stage when Springers can be quite wild.

HOW compatible with other pets?
Like most spaniels, this is a friendly breed and good with other dogs if sensibly socialized when young. Springers are generally good with other pets in the home, but exercise caution with regard to strange cats—chasing is such a temptation,

HOW much exercise?
Regular long walks and free-running exercise are essential for such an active breed. Fair-weather walkers should not consider a Springer—he needs his walks every day, rain or shine.

Character Trait	Poor	Average	Good	Excellent
Attitude to other dogs				
Quietness				
Not destructive				
Protective behavior				
Not likely to stray				
Good with children				
Ease of training				

Original purpose: Finding and retrieving game
Male height: 19–21 in. (48–53 cm)
Female height: 18–20 in. (46–51 cm)
Weight: 49–53 lb. (22–24 kg)
Life span: 10–14 years

HOW easy to train?

Intelligent, quick to learn, and eager to please, the Springer is a rewarding dog to train, but it is vital to start his education early. Puppies left to their own devices become pests. Springers need to be motivated and respond well to praise; harsh training methods are counterproductive.

WHAT good points?

Friendly, happy disposition, docile, nonaggressive, active, devoted to his owner, willing, intelligent, tireless.

WHAT to be aware of?

A demanding breed in terms of exercise and attention. Not for the house proud. They love muddy walks, and their coats carry in astonishing amounts of mud and vegetation.

WHAT medical problems?

Springers are generally a healthy breed. However, all breeding stock should be eye tested for defects such as progressive retinal atrophy (degeneration of the light receptors in the eyes). This is one of the few breeds affected by fucosidosis, a disease of the nervous system, but this is rare and affected stock can be identified by blood tests. As with all drop-eared breeds, ear infections are not uncommon.

Medium dogs

● *Working Springers don't have the heavy ear fringes that are required in the show ring—they leave them behind on brambles.*

Norwegian Elkhound

This handsome silver-gray Spitz is a robust outdoors type, developed to hunt game and especially moose (elk) in the Norwegian forests. This role demanded an active, energetic, and strong-willed dog with a keen hunting drive. Friendly and people oriented, the Elkhound makes a great companion for adults and older children but is never a "yes dog." He likes to make his own decisions and needs firm but kindly handling. His friendly disposition makes him a great companion, loyal, affectionate, and intelligent. He is a great playmate for older children, protective with little ones, and a sensible watchdog who knows when to take action.

Long held to be the direct descendant of Viking farm dogs, the Elkhound is now known via unromantic genetic research to be a more modern creation. First officially recognized in its native Norway in 1877, this attractive breed was soon adopted elsewhere as show dog and companion.

WHAT colors?

Various shades of gray, with black tips to the outer coat and distinctive darker "harness marks" from shoulder to elbow, lighter coat on chest and underparts.

WHAT grooming does the coat need?

The dense coat is moderately easy care, needing only weekly brushing and combing—plus daily grooming during the twice-yearly heavy molt. He is a naturally clean dog with little "doggy" smell, but he does shed quite a bit throughout the year—a good vacuum cleaner will be needed.

HOW suitable are they as family dogs?

This is a great family dog provided he is sensibly socialized and trained. He is very people oriented and likes to be involved in family activities. He is generally very good with children, patient, tolerant, and protective, especially when raised with them.

WHAT type of home?

The Elkhound's ideal home would be in the country or at least the suburbs, and he needs a reasonably large (and well-fenced) yard, but he will adapt to city life if sufficient exercise can be provided. This breed tends to be noisy, so a home with tolerant neighbors is recommended.

WHAT type of owner?

This people-loving but tough-minded dog needs an affectionate, strong-willed owner who can provide firm but sensitive discipline. He is best suited to outdoor types who enjoy country walks, as his exercise needs are high. He is not a dog for owners who expect to leave him alone a great deal nor the ideal choice for obedience fanatics.

HOW compatible with other pets?

Most Elkhounds will accept other dogs and cats in the same household if they are properly socialized, but some tend to be aggressive with other dogs of the same sex. As a hunting breed, they are generally not to be trusted with small pets such as rabbits and hamsters.

HOW much exercise?

Elkhounds have a lot of energy and need vigorous daily walks—at least an hour a day, plus the opportunity for free running and active play. This is a dog with a strong hunting instinct, so care needs to be taken when exercising him off leash. If he picks up an interesting scent, he may disappear over the horizon.

HOW easy to train?

Moderately difficult. Elkhounds are intelligent but have been bred to

Character Trait	Poor	Average	Good	Excellent
Attitude to other dogs				
Quietness				
Not destructive				
Protective behavior				
Not likely to stray				
Good with children				
Ease of training				

Original purpose: Hunter and companion
Male height: 19–21 in. (48–53 cm)
Female height: 19–21 in. (48–53 cm)
Weight: 48–55 lb. (21.8–25 kg)
Life span: 10–12 years

work independently rather than to follow orders. Training needs to start early and to be firm but kindly—this dog's respect has to be earned. He has a low boredom threshold and high energy level, so keep training sessions short, fun, and reward based to maintain his interest and enthusiasm.

Medium dogs

WHAT good points?
Friendly, intelligent, loving, good-natured, independent, hardy, bold, energetic, dignified, clean, good watch dog.

WHAT to be aware of?
May bark a great deal. Probably too strong willed for the novice. Needs a great deal of exercise.

● *Elkhounds come in only one color—gray—but many shades of it.*

WHAT medical problems?
Generally a healthy breed, but some hip deformity (dysplasia), kidney disease, eye problems (lens dislocation, glaucoma), and a tendency to sebaceous cysts in some bloodlines.

Chow Chow

He looks like a very dignified teddy bear, but the Chow is far from being a cuddly toy. A highly civilized dog with many virtues, he is nonetheless not suited to everyone's tastes. He is independent, aloof, and reserved by nature, very strong willed and often stubborn and dominant—not an easy dog for a first-time owner. His devotion to his family is absolute, and he is highly protective. Given an owner who understands Chow nature and is prepared to work at socialization, he is a loyal companion, peaceful and mannerly about the house. Early socialization is vital with this breed, otherwise his innate suspicion of strangers and highly territorial nature can lead to aggression.

This ancient Chinese breed first reached England in 1760—as zoo animals rather than pets. Modern Chows are burlier, thicker coated, and shorter faced than the original breed, developments that have led to a number of health problems.

WHAT colors?

Black, red, blue, fawn, cream, or white, frequently shaded but not in patches or parti-colored. Underpart of tail and back of thighs frequently a lighter color.

WHAT grooming does the coat need?

Two coat varieties. The rough-coated variety (more common) has very dense fur that mats if neglected. A short daily brushing plus weekly grooming down to the skin will keep it in good condition, with extra care when the puppy coat is shed and during the twice-yearly molt. The upstanding plush coat of the rarer smooth coats is less work but still needs regular grooming.

HOW suitable are they as family dogs?

A lot depends on the individual dog, the individual family, and the quality of puppy socialization. Some Chows are wonderful family dogs and great with children; others are

● Chows were once believed to be related to bears.

not. This breed also has a natural tendency to become a one-person dog, not the obvious choice unless you are already attuned to the Chow temperament.

WHAT type of home?

Quiet and mannerly himself, this dog is most comfortable in an orderly household with set routines. Although he enjoys country life, he will adapt to living in a city, even in an apartment as long as enough exercise is provided.

WHAT type of owner?

This is a dog for those who appreciate the independent character typical of Oriental breeds. He needs an experienced, confident owner who is assertive enough to demand respect and patient enough to earn it. Owners should also be prepared to spend a lot of time on socialization, training, and grooming.

HOW compatible with other pets?

Again, socialization is the key. If sensibly introduced to other animals at a young age, Chows generally get along well with other household pets. They tend to show little interest in dogs outside the family and may be aggressive toward dogs of the same sex. Many have strong hunting instincts, so smaller animals should be introduced with care.

HOW much exercise?

The Chow's exercise needs are moderate for his size—a mile's walk twice a day is recommended. He

Character Trait	Poor	Average	Good	Excellent
Attitude to other dogs				
Quietness				
Not destructive				
Protective behavior				
Not likely to stray				
Good with children				
Ease of training				

Original purpose: Hunting, guarding, herding
Male height: 19–22 in. (48–56 cm)
Female height: 18–20 in. (46–51 cm)
Weight: 46–70 lb. (20–32 kg)
Life span: 8–12 years

will enjoy long walks, but great care has to be taken in hot weather to prevent overheating. Not a dog for joggers or hill walkers.

HOW easy to train?

Difficult. Chows are independent, dominant dogs who will cooperate when it suits them but have no inbuilt tendency to obedience. They will respond in their own time to firm, patient, and consistent training. Because Chow puppies tend to be naturally well behaved, many owners neglect early training and end up with behavior problems.

WHAT good points?

Intelligent, intensely loyal, dignified, independent, protective, very individual character, quiet, naturally clean, and well behaved.

WHAT to be aware of?

Demanding breed in terms of socialization, training, and grooming. Seek a reputable breeder: poor temperament in some bloodlines. Health problems in the breed. Poor public perception of the breed: may be included in breed-specific dog control legislation.

WHAT medical problems?

This breed is prone to a number of inherited ailments, including entropion (inturned eyelids, often requiring surgical correction), skin problems, thyroid disease, and hip malformation (dysplasia). Heart problems and cancer are also noted. Its heavy build and short muzzle make it extremely vulnerable to heatstroke.

Medium dogs

● *The cuddly look is misleading—Chows tend to be aloof and rather undemonstrative in nature.*

Samoyed

With his sparkling white coat and characteristic smiling face, the Samoyed is an eye-catching beauty, and in temperament he is friendliness personified. This is a dog who really wants to be part of the family. Happy, sweet-natured, and loving a fuss, he makes a great companion. However, keep in mind that this is a working breed and consequently needs to keep busy. He wants plenty of exercise and play but also benefits from activities such as agility, tracking, sledding, or therapy work. If denied a proper outlet for his energy, he can be noisy and destructive. He also needs a lot of coat care—so don't consider a Samoyed unless you are prepared to make the commitment.

In his native Siberia, the Samoyed served the Samoyede tribes as reindeer herder, draft animal, and bed warmer. Introduced to the West in 1889, he is now employed largely as a companion—a role at which he excels.

WHAT colors?

Typically thought of as white, but cream and biscuit shaded also acceptable. The breed originally included a wide range of colors including black, brown, and spotted. After its introduction to the West, white came to predominate.

WHAT grooming does the coat need?

This is a dense coat requiring daily brushing plus a weekly thorough combing down to the skin. If neglected, it mats and tangles into an unmanageable mass. Extra work is needed during the heavy molt once or twice a year, when mounds of fur are shed—many owners collect bags of combings, which can be spun into a high-quality soft wool.

HOW suitable are they as family dogs?

Samoyeds make wonderful family pets as long as they can be in the heart of the family—they don't cope well with being ignored and demand attention. They love human company and are generally good with children. A busy family without time for exercising, grooming, and cuddling would not find a Samoyed a suitable choice.

WHAT type of home?

The Samoyed needs space and a well-fenced yard—many of this breed are escape artists. Essentially a country breed, he will adapt to city life only if sufficient exercise can be provided.

WHAT type of owner?

Samoyeds thrive with affectionate, energetic owners who enjoy long walks and grooming sessions, are prepared to spend plenty of time with their dogs, and are laid-back about dog hair on furniture. This breed wants to be the center of attention and may be too demanding for some. Not recommended for the frail, as Samoyeds are strong dogs who tend to pull on the lead.

HOW compatible with other pets?

This friendly dog usually gets along well with pets in his own home. However, he has a strong chase instinct; most will chase small animals like rabbits when on walks and should not be expected to ignore the nextdoor cat. Most are good with other dogs, although some males may be rather dominant.

HOW much exercise?

The Samoyed needs plenty of vigorous outdoor exercise, including free running in a safe, open space. It is almost impossible to tire him out. Joggers and hikers will find him a great companion. Alternatively, sports such as sledding, carting, or agility are a great way to satisfy his need for lots of action.

Character Trait	Poor	Average	Good	Excellent
Attitude to other dogs				
Quietness				
Not destructive				
Protective behavior				
Not likely to stray				
Good with children				
Ease of training				

Original purpose: Reindeer herd and sled dog
Male height: 21–23.5 in. (53-60 cm)
Female height: 19–21 in. (48–53 cm)
Weight: 50–66 lb. (23–30 kg)
Life span: 10–12 years

HOW easy to train?

Not the easiest breed to train, although individuals vary considerably. This is a strong-willed breed with a sense of humor and little natural tendency toward obedience, so training has to be patient, persistent, and consistent.

Medium dogs

WHAT good points?

Friendly, happy, intelligent, gentle, active, sensitive, affectionate, full of fun, energetic, good-natured.

WHAT to be aware of?

Needs lots of attention. Heavy molt once or twice a year. Can be very destructive if bored, and generally very vocal.

WHAT medical problems?

Generally healthy. Occasional hip deformity (dysplasia) and some tendency to diabetes. Other problems include kidney failure, glaucoma (increased pressure in the eyeball), abnormal development of the retina (retinal dysplasia), and heart conditions.

● The characteristic Samoyed smile reflects a happy nature.

Australian Shepherd

Confusingly, the Australian Shepherd is an American creation. His ancestors arrived in the US in the 1900s, the herding dogs of emigrant Spanish Basque shepherds accompanying imported Australian sheep. It was in the US that these "little blue dogs" established themselves as a proficient working breed. They achieved AKC recognition as recently as 1993 and since then have become widely known and appreciated.

To a casual glance the Aussie resembles a burlier Border Collie, often strikingly colored in marbled and pastel shades. He has the sheepdog virtues of intelligence, tenacity, and versatility, with strong herding and guarding instincts and abundant energy. Very much a working dog, he needs a job to do and excels at activities such as agility, flyball, and obedience. This is a demanding breed, strong minded, protective, and often territorial—not the ideal choice for a novice but a rewarding and devoted companion when properly socialized and trained.

WHAT colors?
A spectacular range of blue merle (a kind of marbled effect), black, red merle, and red, with or without white markings and/or tan to copper points. Eyes may be blue, brown, or bicolored.

WHAT grooming does the coat need?
The dense coat needs brushing down to the skin with a stiff bristle brush two or three times a week to remove dead hair.

HOW suitable are they as family dogs?
Provided he has enough physical and mental exercise to keep him happy, the Aussie makes a great family dog, devoted and protective. However, busy families with demanding jobs and young children are unlikely to have enough time to keep him appropriately occupied. He is not recommended for homes with small children as he may be tempted to play too roughly for their comfort.

WHAT type of home?
This is a dog with high energy levels better suited for a country home with a fair-sized yard and access to suitable land for exercise. City life is unlikely to provide enough activity for him.

WHAT type of owner?
The Aussie needs an active, experienced owner with plenty of time, who can provide socialization and appropriate employment, whether this be herding sheep or racing around an agility ring. He is not suitable for owners who go out to work and expect to leave him alone. A bored Aussie is likely to express his unhappiness through destructive behavior.

HOW compatible with other pets?
Good early socialization is important to ensure that the Aussie gets along

Aussies excel at obedience and other activities like agility.

Character Trait	Poor	Average	Good	Excellent
Attitude to other dogs		●		
Quietness		●		
Not destructive			●	
Protective behavior			●	
Not likely to stray			●	
Good with children			●	
Ease of training				●

Original purpose: Sheepdog
Male height: 20–23 in. (51–58 cm)
Female height: 18–21 in. (46–53 cm)
Weight: 40–65 lb. (18.2–29.5 kg)
Life span: 12–15 years

well with other animals. He does have strong chasing instincts, so watch out for small pets and neighbors' cats. Some individuals are very dominant with other dogs and need careful supervision.

HOW much exercise?

A great deal. This is a very active breed and virtually tireless—a great companion for joggers. He needs at least an hour's vigorous walking a day plus active play and mental stimulation.

HOW easy to train?

This intelligent breed can be trained to a very high standard but needs a slow and steady approach. Aussies are slow to mature, and a lot of patience is required. They are willing to please but need to understand fully what they are doing and why, rather than learning by rote, and need encouragement rather than pressure.

WHAT good points?

Intelligent, loyal, affectionate, responsive, attentive, enthusiastic, energetic, protective, versatile, highly trainable.

WHAT to be aware of?

Challenging breed that needs something to do. Different bloodlines very different in temperament (some highly reactive and energetic, some calmer). To ensure the right choice, meet the family before choosing a pup.

WHAT medical problems?

Most Aussies are sound, but hereditary problems include hip deformity (dysplasia), dislocating kneecaps (patellar luxation), skin disorders and eye defects (juvenile cataracts, collie eye anomaly, progressive retinal atrophy, glaucoma, lens dislocation). Breeding stock should be hip scored and eye tested. Merles should not be mated together as this can produce white puppies that are often deaf and/or blind.

Medium dogs

● *This handsome dog is strikingly colored in various merle shades.*

Siberian Husky

The Siberian Husky was born to run. Beautiful and stylish enough to grace a cat walk, he is an athletic working dog who needs mental and physical stimuli. He loves to race, to pull sleds or carts, or to go backpacking. Since he also loves people, in between these activities he makes an affectionate, gentle, and playful companion who enjoys being part of the family. Don't consider this active and intelligent breed unless you can provide the exercise and company he needs. A bored Siberian is destructive indoors and a great escapologist outside. He is also strong willed, with an intense hunting drive—not an ideal choice for the novice.

Developed by the Chukchi people of Siberia as a sled dog, the breed was introduced to the US in the 1900s for sled racing. It achieved AKC recognition in 1930 and was taken up by UK breeders in the early 1970s, becoming increasingly popular.

WHAT colors?

All colors, including black, white, tan, gray, red brown, and sable, often with striking head markings and beautiful coat patterns. Coat color and pattern change over time, so puppies may look quite different as adults. Eyes may be a gleaming ice blue, brown, parti-color, or even one blue and one brown.

WHAT grooming does the coat need?

The weatherproof coat is relatively easy care; a weekly thorough brushing with a pin-wire brush to remove dead hair will keep it healthy. This breed molts heavily twice a year, when more vigorous grooming is required.

HOW suitable are they as family dogs?

Provided he has an appropriate occupation, the Siberian's friendly nature makes him a good family pet—though youngsters (up to two years) are likely to be too rough for small children. In any case, most families with young children will not have sufficient time to keep him suitably occupied.

WHAT type of home?

Huskies are not city dogs. They need space. They should have a large yard or paddock with room to run and very secure fencing—this breed can jump, chew through or dig under most fences—and with access to countryside where they can burn off energy. Their intense hunting drive means they are unlikely to be popular in areas where they may encounter livestock.

WHAT type of owner?

The Siberian Husky is a dog for active outdoor types who can provide firm, competent leadership and who will enjoy canine activities. He is not suited to anyone who wants a dog that can run free in the park and will return on command. However, he is a great companion for hikers and backpackers and for those who live in areas where there are sled-racing clubs and the like.

HOW compatible with other pets?

Huskies get along well with other well-adjusted dogs but will take up a challenge if one is offered. As regards other species, they have a very strong hunting drive and will chase anything that moves. They usually accept cats in the same household if brought up with them but should never be regarded as safe with livestock.

Character Trait	Poor	Average	Good	Excellent
Attitude to other dogs			■	
Quietness	■			
Not destructive		■		
Protective behavior	■			
Not likely to stray	■			
Good with children			■	
Ease of training		■		

Original purpose: Hauling sleds, carrying packs, hunting
Male height: 21–23.5 in. (53–60 cm)
Female height: 20–22 in. (51–56 cm)
Weight: 35–60 lb. (16–27 kg)
Life span: 12–15 years

HOW much exercise?

An adult Husky needs a 4 mile (6–7 km) brisk walk every day at the minimum, with no maximum. It is impossible to tire him out. Most Siberians must be exercised on a lead because of their urges to roam and to hunt. Puppies should have limited exercise to prevent damage to growing bones. Build up gradually from about six months until 18 months, when they are full grown.

HOW easy to train?

Moderately difficult. Siberians are intelligent but independent minded and not programmed for obedience. They need and will respond to training, but patience is essential—and don't expect too much. Early socialization is a must, and training needs to start early and to be very patient.

WHAT good points?

Affectionate, playful, active, gentle, friendly, alert, outgoing, intelligent, clean, tireless, minimal "doggy" smell.

WHAT to be aware of?

For experienced owners only. Strong inbuilt urge to run and may never be trustworthy off lead; champion escapologist; strong hunting drive and unsafe with livestock. Can be destructive and noisy if left alone. Sheds hair heavily.

WHAT medical problems?

Generally a healthy breed, but some occurrence of eye problems (juvenile cataracts, corneal defects, and progressive retinal atrophy) and occasional hip deformity (dysplasia)—breeding stock should be hip scored and eye tested. Huskies are sensitive to some drugs, particularly anesthetics and sedatives.

Medium dogs

● *Despite the languid pose, he is almost inexhaustible!*

Large Dogs

Big dogs often suffer the misfortune of being purchased as image builders. They deserve better. Some wonderful breeds are in this group, but think before you buy. Their upkeep needs a major commitment of time, space, and money, and training is essential when you own a dog of this size.

Bearded Collie

This is the ultimate "shaggy dog." His winsome appearance, undoubted intelligence, and good temper make him an ideal family dog—for the right family. However, this is essentially a working breed. He excels at obedience, agility, working trials, herding, mountain rescue, and therapy work. As a pet, he excels only if provided with appropriate outlets for his abundant mental and physical energy. This is a bouncy, boisterous, fun-loving breed, strong minded like most working dogs but also sensitive and responsive—not the ideal dog for a novice. He also represents a major time commitment in terms of grooming, training, and exercising.

The Beardie is Scotland's native herder and drover, probably of considerable antiquity although the breed was not granted Kennel Club recognition until 1944 in the UK and 1977 in the US. Today show and working strains have diverged, the latter being less glamorous, tougher, and less suited to pet life.

● *The owner of a Beardie must be prepared to groom its coat daily.*

WHAT colors?
Slate gray, reddish-fawn, black, blue, all shades of gray, brown and sandy with or without white markings (foreface, facial blaze, tail tip, chest, legs, feet, or collar); slight tan markings acceptable. Some bloodlines possess a "fading gene" that makes coat color fade from about eight weeks to about one year of age before darkening again.

WHAT grooming does the coat need?
The long, thick coat is high maintenance. It needs daily grooming with a slicker brush and metal comb to prevent matting, paying particular attention to the areas behind the ears and under the arms, the bib, neck, and hindquarters. Neutered dogs may develop a softer, woollier coat that requires extra work.

HOW suitable are they as family dogs?
The Beardie is an ideal pet for an active family with plenty of time for him. He needs human company and likes to share in family activities—if left alone he can be destructive and noisy. He is generally very good with sensible, older children. However, he may be too excitable and boisterous for the safety of small children, who are easily bowled over by a speeding dog.

WHAT type of home?
This active breed is best suited to country life, although he can cope with apartment living if he has plenty of daily exercise. Ideally he needs a large yard with a secure fence.

WHAT type of owner?
A Beardie needs an owner who has time (and inclination) for grooming, training, exercise—and play. He is not recommended for owners who are out at work most of the day since he needs company, nor for the house proud since his heavy coat spreads hair and mud. Not an ideal first dog. Sensitive, experienced owners will get the best out of this exuberant breed.

HOW compatible with other pets?
Beardies are generally good with other animals if properly socialized in puppyhood. However, they may be too bouncy for the safety of smaller pets, and owners should

Character Trait	Poor	Average	Good	Excellent
Attitude to other dogs				
Quietness				
Not destructive				
Protective behavior				
Not likely to stray				
Good with children				
Ease of training				

Original purpose: Herding
Male height: 21–22 in. (53-56 cm)
Female height: 20–21 in. (51–53 cm)
Weight: 40–60 lb. (18–27 kg)
Life span: c.12 years

monitor their innate herding and chasing reactions on first introductions.

HOW much exercise?
A great deal. Adult Beardies need at least one long walk each day and plenty of free running and active play.

HOW easy to train?
Much depends on the handler. These are smart dogs who can be trained to a very high standard using firm but gentle reward-based methods. They are also independent minded, stubborn, quickly bored by repetitive exercises, and easily upset by harsh treatment.

Some strains are harder to train than others.

WHAT good points?
Happy, good tempered, intelligent, responsive, sensitive, lively, self-confident, friendly, affectionate, nonaggressive.

WHAT to be aware of?
Can be oversensitive to loud noises such as thunder and fireworks. Some are enthusiastic barkers.

WHAT medical problems?
Beardies are generally a healthy breed, but occasional hip malformation (dysplasia), eye problems (including cataracts), lack of thyroid hormone (hypothyroidism), allergies, and autoimmune disorders are reported.

Large dogs

● *At rest now, but the Beardie needs lots of exercise.*

Golden Retriever

This handsome and kindly gundog is an all-around dog, a great working dog and family pet but also widely used as guide dog for the blind, service dog for the disabled, therapy dog, and sniffer dog. Intelligent, friendly, and cheerful, he is ideal for anyone who enjoys long walks and wants a loving companion to share in activities. He needs plenty of regular exercise and mental stimulation.

Owners should be prepared for an exuberant dog with a sense of humor who loves retrieving, can't resist splashing about in water, and carpets the house with mud and golden hairs.

The Goldie originated in the 1860s from yellow pups that cropped up accidentally in black retriever strains, receiving a breed standard in 1931. Since then he has become hugely popular—too much so, as puppy mills churn out stock with uncharacteristically aggressive temperaments, so it is essential to buy from responsible breeders.

WHAT colors?

Any shade of gold or cream. Originally Goldies were required to be the exact shade of a gold British guinea coin. The standard was altered in 1920 to include lighter shades.

WHAT grooming does the coat need?

Coats vary in length and thickness, but all need at least a weekly brushing down to the skin with a hard brush and combing through the feathers. A quick daily combing will remove dead hairs and reduce the amount of hair shed in the house. The coat will also need cleaning and tidying after muddy walks—and if there is mud anywhere, a Goldie will find it.

HOW suitable are they as family dogs?

The Goldie's kind, affectionate temperament and love of children make him an ideal family dog provided he has enough exercise. He needs to be part of the family and fully involved in their activities.

Time must be spent on his training, as he is a big, heavy, energetic dog who can bowl children over if he has not been taught good manners.

WHAT type of home?

The Goldie would prefer a country home but can be just as happy with city life provided he has enough exercise and mental stimulation. He needs a well-fenced yard and access to a park where he can burn off energy, and is generally too active to be confined to an apartment.

WHAT type of owner?

This is a great dog for active, affectionate owners who enjoy long daily walks and seek a kind, easygoing companion that is reliable with children. Owners should enjoy training to channel a dog's intelligence and physical energy in acceptable directions— and be prepared to cope with a mischievous, high-energy puppy who turns into an exuberant adolescent. They also need a relaxed attitude to dog hairs and mud on carpets and clothes.

HOW compatible with other pets?

The Goldie's friendly nature extends to other pets as well as people. As a youngster he can be too bouncy for the safety of small pets. He may have a tendency to carry them around—his soft mouth won't hurt them, but they may not care for the experience. He is fine with cats in his own household but may well chase strange cats just for the fun of it.

HOW much exercise?

Gundogs like the Goldie were bred

Character Trait	Poor	Average	Good	Excellent
Attitude to other dogs				
Quietness				
Not destructive				
Protective behavior				
Not likely to stray				
Good with children				
Ease of training				

Place of origin: **Britain**

Original purpose: Retrieving shot game
Male height: 22–24 in. (56–61 cm)
Female height: 20–22 in. (51–56 cm)
Weight: 55–75 lb. (25–34.1 kg)
Life span: 10–13 years

to work all day in the field and have endless energy and stamina, so they need a lot of outdoor exercise daily, in all weather. Puppies under nine months need limited exercise to prevent damage to growing bones but have endless energy for play—and mischief.

HOW easy to train?
Goldies are intelligent, quick to learn, eager to please, and highly trainable, though handlers need patience with exuberant youngsters and need to allow for a tendency to stubbornness and a sense of humor. Start training early and keep training sessions fun and reward based to maintain their interest.

WHAT good points?
Friendly, outgoing, loyal, stable, affectionate, intelligent, docile, kindly, confident, active, sensitive, full of fun.

WHAT to be aware of?
Buy only from responsible breeders to be sure of good temperament. Not a part-time dog—he needs a lot of commitment and can be clingy.

Large dogs

WHAT medical problems?
Hip malformation (dysplasia) and cataracts are serious problems in this breed, all breeding stock must have hips and eyes screened. Some epilepsy and a tendency to skin problems (eczema, allergies).

● *A pair of high-energy Goldies take a break.*

Rough Collie

The attractive and intelligent collie of northern Britain first came into the limelight in the 19th century when it took the fancy of Queen Victoria. The breed was smartened up for the show ring, and the modern "Lassie" is a glamorized version of his tough herding ancestors, taller, more elegant, and with a glorious, richly colored coat. Today, the Rough Collie has lost much of his intense working drive while retaining the intelligence and loyalty of his ancestors. This is a very handsome dog, indeed loving, sweet natured, and a wonderful family pet—in the right hands.

This is not, however, a breed suitable for everyone. Collies are very demanding dogs in terms of time and attention. They need company, extensive socialization, and mental stimulation. They are highly sensitive and can become neurotic in a stressful environment. The coat, which is the breed's crowning glory, requires hours of work.

WHAT colors?

Three recognized colors: sable and white (any shade from gold to mahogany); tricolor (black with white collar and tan markings over eyes, inside legs, and under tail); and blue merle (a sort of marbled effect distinguished by the presence of irregular dark blotches against a lighter back-ground of the same basic pigment), with or without white and/or tan markings. In the US, white is also an accepted color variety.

WHAT grooming does the coat need?

This is a maximum-maintenance coat that needs frequent, regular brushing—at least every other day—to prevent mats and tangles. It is essential to brush right down to the skin to work through the dense undercoat. A de-matting rake is useful to reduce the undercoat to manageable levels.

HOW suitable are they as family dogs?

For the family that has time for him, the Rough Collie is hard to beat as a companion. Given a well-balanced family life, he is a loyal, devoted, and well-mannered pet, particularly fond of and good with children.

However, his high sensitivity makes him react badly to stress and family tensions, so he is not the best choice for a home with a hectic lifestyle.

WHAT type of home?

This breed is essentially a country dog needing access to the outdoors, although he will adapt to city life given sympathetic owners. He needs company and involvement in family activities and, if left alone, may become noisy and destructive through boredom. Not the ideal dog for the house proud as he molts heavily and his coat carries in mud and muck.

WHAT type of owner?

A calm and patient personality is required to get the best out of this breed—a sensitive dog needs a sensitive owner. This is emphatically not a breed that can be left alone at home all day while his owner goes out to work. Rough Collie owners should also be prepared to commit time to socializing, grooming, and training.

HOW compatible with other pets?

His kind, tolerant nature makes the Rough Collie generally excellent with other household pets. Some collies retain a strong herding instinct that they may attempt to employ upon other pets, circling and nipping in a manner that is

Character Trait	Poor	Average	Good	Excellent
Attitude to other dogs			●	
Quietness		●		
Not destructive			●	
Protective behavior			●	
Not likely to stray				●
Good with children			●	
Ease of training			●	

Place of origin: **Scotland**

Original purpose: Herder
Male height: 22–24 in. (56–61 cm)
Female height: 20–22 in. (51–56 cm)
Weight: 51–75 lb. (23–34 kg)
Life span: 12–15 years

unlikely to be appreciated. Providing other activities should keep this instinct under control.

HOW much exercise?

The Rough Collie's exercise needs are surprisingly moderate for his size. He will keep fit with a daily walk of an hour or so, ensuring that he has time for free running off lead—and taking care to ensure that his herding instinct does not lead him to chase other dogs, joggers, children, and bicycles.

HOW easy to train?

Intelligent, eager to please, and quick to learn, this breed is easy to train provided his sensitive nature is recognized. Gentle, consistent, reward-based training is required. Harsh scolding or physical punishment will only make the dog nervous and uncooperative. This is a breed that needs the mental stimulation and reassurance of training sessions to build confidence.

WHAT good points?

Friendly, intelligent, loyal, affectionate, protective, sensitive, sweet natured, nonaggressive, polite with strangers and other pets.

WHAT to be aware of?

Tendency to separation anxiety when left alone. Highly reactive to loud noises. Some strains may be very highly strung and neurotic.

Large dogs

WHAT medical problems?

Generally a healthy breed with few problems. However, all puppies should be screened for eye problems (collie eye anomaly). Epilepsy, inward-turning eyelids (entropion), and collie nose (nasal solar dermatitis) characterized by skin lesions around the nose also occur. The breed is susceptible to skin complaints.

Labrador Retriever

This versatile gundog stars not only in the shooting field but as guide dog for the blind, sniffer dog detecting anything from drugs to gas leaks, life-saving search and rescue dog, service dog for the disabled—and one of the most popular family dogs. However, these achievements don't happen by magic: they depend on good breeding and excellent training. Reputable breeders aim to produce a good temperament as well as a good physique. Even the best-bred Labs can be real hooligans if left to their own devices. These are powerful, energetic dogs whose intelligence needs channeling. Given sensible owners, Labs are great companions and reliable family dogs, eminently trainable and adaptable.

The breed originated in Canada as a water dog, but it was in 19th-century Britain that its retrieving skills made it the sportsman's favorite. Today show and working strains have diverged, the latter being lighter in build.

WHAT colors?

Black, yellow (ranging from cream to fox red but never termed golden in this breed), or chocolate.

WHAT grooming does the coat need?

This is an easy-care coat but does benefit from weekly grooming with slicker or stiff bristle brush to remove dead hair and massage the skin. Tends to molt year-round—get the vacuum cleaner ready.

HOW suitable are they as family dogs?

This good-natured dog is ideal for an active family prepared to spend plenty of time on exercise and training and with someone at home most of the time. These very sociable dogs need company and can be destructive and noisy if left alone too long. Labs are generally very good with children but may be too big and boisterous for the comfort of little ones as well as tending to mouth hands in play—gently, but sometimes too much for youngsters.

● *Dark or light, the versatile Lab is a worker as well as a loving companion.*

WHAT type of home?

A country home is best, but a Lab will be just as happy with city life provided they have enough exercise and mental stimulation. He does need a well-fenced yard and access to a park where he can burn off energy. Not an ideal apartment dog because of his size and bounciness—nor suited to homes with low coffee tables and fragile ornaments for the same reason.

WHAT type of owner?

Labradors need owners who enjoy long walks every day, regardless of the weather, who are prepared for a mischievous puppy that grows into an exuberant adult, and who enjoy training a responsive dog. They are not the best choice for the house proud. Labradors mean mess, with muddy footprints, slobber, tail marks on the walls, and a fair amount of chewing.

HOW compatible with other pets?

Friendly and kind, Labradors are generally good with other dogs and household pets, although as with all breeds early socialization is important. Their innate retrieving instinct means that small pets like rabbits and guinea pigs may find themselves being carried around, unharmed but soggy. Some males may be rather dominant with other male dogs they encounter.

Character Trait	Poor	Average	Good	Excellent
Attitude to other dogs				
Quietness				
Not destructive				
Protective behavior				
Not likely to stray				
Good with children				
Ease of training				

Original purpose: Retrieving game
Male height: 22–24.5 in. (56–62 cm)
Female height: 21–23.5 in. (54–60 cm)
Weight: 55–75 lb. (25–34 kg)
Life span: c.12 years

HOW much exercise?

Lots. Think in terms of at least two hours' walking a day—more will be appreciated. This breed has a tendency to be lazy and greedy, so it is easy to turn a Labrador into an obese couch potato who will trudge round the block once a day—but a dreadful waste of all that Labrador delight in life.

HOW easy to train?

Labradors are eminently trainable. They like to please and enjoy the mental and physical exercise of training sessions. Young Labradors do enjoy playing the fool, and it takes patience and persistence to get through this stage. Keep training sessions fun and reward based to maintain their interest.

WHAT good points?

Cheerful, loving, energetic, trustworthy, good with children, patient, eager to please, nonaggressive, intelligent, highly trainable.

WHAT to be aware of?

High exercise needs. Watch out for puppy mills producing dogs with poor temperament and health problems.

WHAT medical problems?

Labs are generally healthy, but hip and elbow malformation (dysplasia), weakness of the muscle that propels food down the gullet (megaoesophagus), degeneration of receptor cells in the eye (progressive retinal atrophy), muscle weakness (myopathy), and lack of thyroid hormone occur. All breeding stock should have hips and eyes screened.

Large dogs

Ibizan Hound *Other names: Podenco Ibicenco*

This graceful Mediterranean sighthound is the rabbiting dog of Ibiza and other Balearic Islands. First formally recognized in Spain in 1922, the breed gradually attracted interest worldwide. This is a dog of striking appearance, resembling the hounds depicted in ancient Egyptian paintings and sculptures. His gentle, affectionate, and playful nature makes him an excellent companion for owners who appreciate that he is not just a decorative pet but a natural athlete with a strong hunting drive, who loves to run and, like most hounds, can be difficult to recall as a consequence. He is also a high-jump champion who can clear fences with ease and leap up onto kitchen surfaces for self-service snacks.

The Ibizan's energy and athleticism suit him well for sports such as agility, lure coursing, and tracking. given appropriate physical and mental exercise, he is a sweet and reliable family dog but may be too demanding for the novice.

WHAT colors?

Red and white, all white or all red, the red varying in depth from a light yellowish red ("lion") to dark chestnut or mahogany. The nose is always flesh colored, not dark.

WHAT grooming does the coat need?

Ibizans come in two coat varieties, rough and smooth. Both are easy care, a brief daily grooming with a soft bristle brush serving to remove dead hairs and keep the skin healthy. Note that they may prove sensitive to flea sprays.

HOW suitable are they as family dogs?

Given a family that can provide an appropriate lifestyle with plenty of exercise, the Ibizan makes an excellent family pet, good with children, and remaining very playful throughout his life. He loves human company and wants to be part of the family—not a part-time dog.

WHAT type of home?

Ideally this is a dog for a country home, as it will be harder for city dwellers to provide him with sufficient exercise and freedom to gallop. He needs a securely fenced yard of reasonable size and access to land where he can run free without running risks from traffic or causing risks to livestock. This breed is not suited to kennel life but needs to live as part of his family.

WHAT type of owner?

This breed needs an active owner who appreciates hound nature, who enjoys walking and playing with a dog, and who is gentle and affectionate like the Ibizan himself. Not a dog for busy owners who are out at work all day, as he needs company and supervision, and not an ideal first dog, as he needs careful socialization and training.

HOW compatible with other pets?

Ibizans are generally friendly with other dogs and good with cats in the same household if raised with them. However, they have a strong chasing instinct and should not be expected to resist the temptation to pursue strange cats or be trusted with small pets like rabbits and hamsters.

HOW much exercise?

A great deal. Ibizans need at least an hour's walk every day plus free running. However, their strong hunting drive and tendency to ignore a recall mean that care

Character Trait	Poor	Average	Good	Excellent
Attitude to other dogs				
Quietness				
Not destructive				
Protective behavior				
Not likely to stray				
Good with children				
Ease of training				

Original purpose: Rabbit hunting
Male height: 23–27.5 in. (58.5–70 cm)
Female height: 22.5–26 in. (57–66 cm)
Weight: 42–55 lb. (19–25 kg)
Life span: 12–14 years

should be taken in choosing areas where they can be trusted off leash. They will also benefit from active play and enjoy retrieving.

HOW easy to train?

Like most hounds, the Ibizan is trainable but needs an experienced handler, as he is easily bored, distractible, and can be willful. This is a sensitive breed that can be put off by harsh handling. He needs gentle, calm and consistent training starting at an early age. Early socialization is important to bring out the best in him.

WHAT good points?

Kind, sensitive, loyal, affectionate, non-aggressive, versatile, energetic, athletic, alert, protective.

WHAT to be aware of?

Can be timid and suspicious of strangers if not properly socialized. Demanding in terms of exercise. Strong chase instinct, needs considerable training to run near livestock.

WHAT medical problems?

Generally a healthy breed; some nerve and muscle disorders reported. Sensitive to some drugs including insecticides and flea sprays.

● *The elegant lines of the Ibizan are reminiscent of ancient Egypt.*

Large dogs

● *Not just a sighthound, the Ibizan was developed as an all-purpose hunting dog who works by sight, hearing, and smell and can point and retrieve game as well as run it down. Quiet, playful, and loving, he makes a great pet for an owner who appreciates his strong hunting drive.*

Boxer

The Boxer is a loving clown, bursting with energy and retaining a puppyish playfulness often well into old age. He is a fun dog but one who requires a major commitment. He needs a lot of exercise, a lot of training, a lot of affection—and a lot of patience. For those who want a high-energy dog, this most exuberant of breeds makes a wonderful companion, but he is usually too boisterous for anyone who prefers peace and quiet. Very much a people dog, he adores his family and needs them to adore him—Boxers don't thrive without plenty of human companionship.

The Boxer developed in the 1880s from the German Bullenbeisser ("bull biter," originally a hunting mastiff) and English Bulldog. Early Boxers served nobly in World War I as scouts, messengers, and guards. Today the breed is a popular companion—and one whose undoubted intelligence and ability are often underused.

WHAT colors?

Dark red to fawn, or brindle, with or without white markings not exceeding one-third of ground color. White boxers occur quite frequently but are not accepted by the AKC because a high percentage are born deaf.

WHAT grooming does the coat need?

The Boxer's short, dense coat is very low maintenance, needing only a quick brushing from time to time to remove dead hairs.

HOW suitable are they as family dogs?

Loving, playful, and protective, the Boxer is a wonderful dog for an energetic, experienced family with older children—and a sense of humor. He is a great playmate for children who are used to dogs and too big to be bowled over by a running Boxer but is too boisterous for tots or the frail elderly. He needs a sensible, orderly home where he can learn good manners. In a rowdy, chaotic household, his exuberance will often make him unmanageable.

WHAT type of home?

A Boxer can be a city dog or a country dog as long as he has plenty of exercise, but this energetic dog needs space and is not suited to life in an apartment. He should have access to a yard, as large as possible, and with a high fence—Boxers are great jumpers and often great escapologists.

WHAT type of owner?

Boxers do best with experienced, active, affectionate owners who appreciate their sense of fun and have time, energy, and a sense of humor. Although powerful and strong willed, they are sensitive dogs who need kindness. They are not recommended for novices, the physically frail, or anyone whose lifestyle cannot accommodate a whirlwind of energy.

HOW compatible with other pets?

Most Boxers are good-natured and friendly with other animals, although some can be dominant with other dogs of the same sex. They can be too boisterous for the comfort of smaller animals—a playful pounce from a Boxer can hurt a little dog and won't do much for the health of a hamster.

Character Trait	Poor	Average	Good	Excellent
Attitude to other dogs				
Quietness				
Not destructive				
Protective behavior				
Not likely to stray				
Good with children				
Ease of training				

Original purpose: Guard and companion
Male height: 22.5–25 in. (57–63.5 cm)
Female height: 21–23 in. (53–59 cm)
Weight: 50–80 lb. (22.7–36.4 kg)
Life span: 8–10 years

HOW much exercise?

As much as possible, as often as possible! Think in terms of a minimum of one to two hours' walking a day, but remember that Boxers are poorly suited to extremes of temperature. Like other short-faced breeds, they can over-heat easily, and they also feel the cold. Active sports like agility and flyball provide mental stimulation as well as exercise.

HOW easy to train?

Boxers are a challenging breed to train: strong minded, stubborn, but also sensitive. In the right hands they are very capable dogs, but they need an owner they can respect as well as love. Training should start early and be firm but kind, consistent, and patient. This breed is slow to mature and would rather play the fool than work unless persuaded that lessons are fun too.

WHAT good points?

Cheerful, lively, strong, loyal to owner, affectionate, equable, fearless, self-assured, playful, brave, intelligent, outgoing, energetic.

WHAT to be aware of?

Large dogs

A demanding breed. Boxers bounce. They also snore, slobber, and break wind. Some Boxers have a strong guard instinct; others don't.

WHAT medical problems?

Boxers have a high incidence of heart defects and also of cancer. They are also prone to bloat (gastric torsion); hip malformation (dysplasia) and lack of thyroid hormone (hypothyroidism) also occur. Progressive axonopathy (affecting the nervous system and leading to paralysis) was a major problem, now largely under control.

● Boxers have lots of "bounce," and need a firm hand in training.

Vizsla

The Vizsla is a working multi-purpose gundog bred to hunt, point, and retrieve game. His roots go back to the Middle Ages, when he was developed as the favorite sporting dog of the Hungarian nobility. Today he is still very much a working dog, but his beauty and people-oriented nature have made him increasingly popular as a companion breed. Affectionate, outgoing, and friendly, he makes a delightful family member for those who can satisfy his needs for loads of exercise, stimulation, and social life. He wants to be with his family the whole time and is not a dog who can be content when left alone. His working talents suit him for activities such as competitive obedience, agility, tracking, and so on.

His cousin the Wirehaired Vizsla is classed as a separate breed and was created in the 1930s by introducing German Wirehaired Pointer blood to give a more protective coat.

WHAT colors?
Russet gold. Small white marks on chest and feet are acceptable though not desirable.

WHAT grooming does the coat need?
Minimal. The short, smooth coat needs little more than a weekly brushing with a firm bristle brush to remove dead hairs.

HOW suitable are they as family dogs?
A poor choice for a family wanting a placid, undemanding pet, the Vizsla is a wonderful dog for families who recognize the needs of a working dog. He is devoted to his owners, keen to please, protective without being aggressive, and reliable with children. If denied exercise and attention, he will become frustrated and may turn mischievous.

WHAT type of home?
A country home with plenty of space for exercise is the ideal home

● *The short, smooth coat of the Vizsla requires only minimal upkeep.*

for a Vizsla. His people come first with him, and he will adapt to city life as long as he has plenty of regular activity and is allowed to participate fully in family life. He needs a secure yard. If bored, he can easily clear a 6-foot (2 m) fence in his quest for something to do.

WHAT type of owner?
Vizslas need active owners, preferably with an interest in canine activities whether sporting or obedience oriented and a sensitive approach to training. This is not a part-time pet but one who needs to be part of the family. Don't consider a Vizsla unless you appreciate an affectionate, demanding, tactile, and talkative relationship with your dog.

HOW compatible with other pets?
If appropriately socialized in puppyhood, Vizslas get along well with other animals. However, remember that they are hunting dogs with an innate chasing instinct, so don't expose small pets such as rabbits to their attentions or expect them to ignore next door's cat without proper training.

HOW much exercise?
A great deal, every day, including plenty of free galloping. This is not a breed for the sedentary owner! Puppies under nine months should be limited to short walks and backyard play to prevent damage to growing bones.

Character Trait	Poor	Average	Good	Excellent
Attitude to other dogs		●	●	
Quietness	●	●		
Not destructive		●	●	
Protective behavior		●	●	
Not likely to stray		●		
Good with children		●	●	
Ease of training		●	●	

Original purpose: Hunting, pointing, and retrieving game
Male height: 22.5–25 in. (57–63.5 cm)
Female height: 21–23.5 in. (53–60 cm)
Weight: 44–66 lb. (20–30 kg)
Life span: 12 years or more

HOW easy to train?

This breed is eager to please and responds well to firm, patient training but it may take time, as Vizslas can be late developers. They are highly sensitive dogs, sometimes willful and easily distracted and do not take well to rough handling.

WHAT good points?

Lively, intelligent, obedient, sensitive, affectionate, loyal, responsive, gentle mannered, versatile, protective, easy-care coat, and little "doggy" smell.

WHAT to be aware of?

A delightful but demanding breed that may be too clingy for some. His habits include a tendency to mouth hands or arms, which may be off-putting to the unprepared, but this is a gesture of friendship, not an attempt to bite! Vizslas are also a highly vocal breed given to "talking."

WHAT medical problems?

Generally a healthy breed. Conditions known to occur include hip malformation (dysplasia,) blood disorders including von Willebrand's disease and hemophilia, epilepsy, tail defects and sensitivity to anesthesia. Recent concerns about osteochondritis dissecans (OCD), which affects cartilage in the joints of the limbs.

Large dogs

● Although a working dog, the Vizsla is a gentle and sensitive animal. As a companion, he demands lots of attention and plenty of exercise.

Airedale Terrier

The "King of the Terriers" deserves his title not just for his size (he is the biggest of all terrier breeds) but for his versatility. Airedales have shone as police dogs, search and rescue dogs, therapy dogs, and hunters of anything from rats to grizzly bears as well as serving heroically in World War I as sentry, messenger, and ambulance dogs. Above all, this handsome dog excels as a loyal companion and home guard. Affectionate but independent, he is a strong-willed character who needs occupation for mind and body. Otherwise he can be a bit too much of a live wire for the average family.

The Airedale developed in northern England as a hunting dog and, despite his classic terrier appearance, probably has otterhound ancestry. Officially recognized in the UK in 1886, by the 1920s he was one of the most popular breeds in both the UK and the US.

WHAT colors?

Black and tan or grizzle and tan. The body saddle, top of the neck, and top surface of tail are black or grizzle and the rest of the dog tan. Pups are born black, gradually developing the tan coloring from about ten weeks old.

WHAT grooming does the coat need?

The dense, wiry coat benefits from daily combing and also needs hand stripping at least twice a year—a skilled task that many owners prefer to leave to a professional. Clipping achieves the same effect of tidying the outline but spoils the texture and color. Left to its own devices, the nonshedding coat grows into a thick, unruly fleece that is hard work to comb.

HOW suitable are they as family dogs?

The Airedale is a great companion and protector for an active family who have time to satisfy his needs for mental and physical exercise. Properly trained and exercised, he is great with children. However, Airedale puppies (up to at least two years old) may be too boisterous for the very young. Busy families should be aware that a young Airedale is a full-time job.

WHAT type of home?

Airedales have endless energy and need space for exercise and play. They are ideal dogs for country dwellers but will adapt to city life with a sufficiently committed owner. A well-fenced yard is a must. Don't imagine you can just leave your Airedale there to exercise himself—while happy to play in the yard, he will also require full participation from his owner.

WHAT type of owner?

Airedales are powerful as well as energetic, and owners need to be physically strong and active, with a taste for long walks. This breed needs considerable time and attention from its owner as well as firm, patient training and mental stimulation. A sense of humor is also a must. Many Airedales have a strong streak of mischief and can be rowdy and disruptive.

HOW compatible with other pets?

Good if brought up with them—early socialization, as always, is the key. However, this is a boisterous breed that may be too rough for the health of small pets and that also has strong chasing instincts. Some males can be aggressive with other dogs.

Character Trait	Poor	Average	Good	Excellent
Attitude to other dogs		■		
Quietness	■			
Not destructive	■			
Protective behavior			■	
Not likely to stray		■		
Good with children			■	
Ease of training		■		

Original purpose: Hunting
Male height: 23–24 in. (58–61 cm)
Female height: 22–23 in. (56–58 cm)
Weight: 44–50 lb. (20–23 kg)
Life span: 12–13 years

HOW much exercise?

Plenty. The Airedale has boundless energy to burn off. He needs space to play and regular long walks. A great dog for joggers, backpackers, and hikers (but remember that puppies should not be encouraged to walk too far until they are physically mature).

HOW easy to train?

Moderate. Much depends on the trainer: in the right hands, the Airedale can achieve a great deal, but he has no predisposition to slavish obedience. Training must be fun and stimulating to capture his interest, as he is easily bored with repetitive exercises. Owners need to be patient and flexible—and to retain a sense of humor.

WHAT good points?

Loyal, affectionate, protective, intelligent, sensitive, humorous, adventurous, fun loving. Non-molting coat suits many allergy sufferers.

WHAT to be aware of?

High maintenance in terms of grooming, exercise, and attention. Very active, sometimes to the point of rowdiness. Strong willed and stubborn. Can be noisy and destructive. Early socialization essential to control protective and chasing instincts.

WHAT medical problems?

Generally a hardy and healthy breed. Problems that occur include hip deformity (dysplasia)—parents should have hip certificates—and skin problems.

Large dogs

● *Largest of the terriers, the Airedale has loads of energy and makes a great companion for an active owner.*

Dalmatian

Instantly recognizable with his distinctive spotted coat, the Dalmatian is a dog for the energetic owner. In the 18th century he was employed as a fashionable carriage dog, escorting horse-drawn carriages for 20 miles (30 km) or more. Today his outgoing, friendly character and striking good looks have made him popular as a family companion, but he still retains his love of exercise and his affinity with horses. Recently the *101 Dalmatians* films have inspired many to acquire Dalmatian puppies without considering whether a dog bred to run marathons will fit into their lifestyle—don't make this mistake! This is a great dog for the right home, loving, intelligent, good-natured, and playful, but quite unsuitable for couch potatoes.

The Dalmatian's origins are obscure. There is no evidence to connect the breed with Dalmatia (part of former Yugoslavia). Its present type probably was actually established in 18th-century England.

WHAT colors?

Best known is the classic white with black spots, but liver (brown) spots are also acceptable. Show dogs require well-rounded, evenly distributed spots; mismarked dogs cannot be shown but make just as good pets. Puppies are born pure white, developing their spots from about ten days old.

WHAT grooming does the coat need?

The short sleek coat is low maintenance, needing only regular brushing to remove loose hair. Prospective owners should be aware that this breed does shed, and white hairs show up on clothes and furniture.

HOW suitable are they as family dogs?

For an active family, the Dalmatian makes a great family dog. He is good with children and loves to play. However, he is probably not a good choice for households with children under the age of ten as he is boisterous and powerful and can be very hard work before he matures.

WHAT type of home?

The Dalmatian needs a home with access to suitable exercise areas, but this doesn't mean he has to live in the country. He is an adaptable dog who will readily adapt to city life as long as he has enough company and enough exercise. Ideally he should have a large, securely fenced yard where he can work off some of his energy.

WHAT type of owner?

These energetic dogs need energetic owners who like long walks and have time for lively ball games. Dalmatians also need company and tend to express loneliness loudly and destructively. Although a well-reared adult Dalmatian is a delightful companion, adolescent Dallies are often boisterous hooligans who are likely to be too much for young children or the frail elderly.

HOW compatible with other pets?

Dalmatians have an innate affinity with horses and are usually good with other pets in general. They are, however, big bouncy dogs who may play too enthusiastically for smaller breeds to enjoy their company.

HOW much exercise?

The Dalmatian was bred to run marathons, and adults need plenty of exercise—at least an hour's brisk walk a day. (Pups under a year old should have exercise limited to

Character Trait	Poor	Average	Good	Excellent
Attitude to other dogs			■	
Quietness	■			
Not destructive		■		
Protective behavior			■	
Not likely to stray			■	
Good with children			■	
Ease of training			■	

Original purpose: Carriage dog
Male height: 23–24 in. (58.5–61 cm)
Female height: 22–23 in. (56–58.5 cm)
Weight: 40–60 lb. (18.2–27.3 kg)
Life span: 12–14 years

prevent damage to growing bones.) If deprived of exercise, he will have to work off his surplus energy somehow, probably at the cost of household furnishings.

HOW easy to train?

This intelligent breed learns easily and can be trained to a high standard, but training can be an uphill struggle. They are strong-minded dogs who can be very stubborn. It takes patience, persistence, and absolute consistency to get them into the habit of obedience.

WHAT good points?

Loyal, intelligent, easygoing, friendly, tireless, protective, outgoing, a great companion for long walks.

WHAT to be aware of?

Exercise and training essential to prevent hooligan behavior. A heavy shedder. Choose your breeder with care as some puppy mills have produced strains with atypically poor temperament.

WHAT medical problems?

Inherited deafness (responsible breeders test puppies' hearing at six weeks— ask for a certificate). Predisposition to form dangerous kidney stones, especially on high-protein diet. Some skin problems.

● *These Dalmatian puppies will grow up to be big, boisterous, and bouncy dogs.*

Large dogs

Flat-Coated Retriever

Less well-known than the Labrador and Golden Retrievers, the Flat-Coat is slightly taller and more elegant but has comparable virtues—plus a more mischievous sense of humor. This is a working gundog breed, energetic, intelligent, people loving, and in need of employment—not a dog for couch potatoes but a great family dog for those who can meet his needs for exercise and company. Lively and extroverted, he is often known as the "Peter Pan" among gundogs who never really grows up. He craves human company and attention and can be destructive and noisy if bored and lonely. In the right hands, his delightful personality and versatility make him a wonderful companion.

The Flat-Coat shares a common ancestry with the Newfoundland and Labrador Retriever, developing as a separate breed in the late 19th century. Overshadowed in the past by the other, more amenable, retriever breeds, it is now increasing in popularity as show dog and companion.

WHAT colors?
Black or liver only.

WHAT grooming does the coat need?
The medium-length, weatherproof coat is easy care, with a brush and comb through two or three times a week. The coat should be brushed right down to the skin and a comb used for the feathering and longer hair. The comb will also be needed to strip out dead hair during the molt.

HOW suitable are they as family dogs?
The Flat-Coat is a wonderful dog for an active, country-living family with older children. He loves children but can be too boisterous for little ones. His ever-wagging tail can land quite a painful blow on a small child. He needs to be fully involved in activities and is unsuited to any household where he cannot be at the center of the family lifestyle.

WHAT type of home?
This is really not a city dog. He thrives in a country lifestyle where he can have long, interesting walks and employ his highly developed nose. He needs a home with a fair-sized yard, which must be securely fenced.

WHAT type of owner?
The Flat-Coat is a dog for active outdoor types who will provide firm but sensitive training and can find employment to keep him busy and happy. Owners need to be patient and have a sense of humor in order to enjoy a dog who can be something of a clown. This breed is emphatically not for an owner who goes out to work all day, leaving him alone.

HOW compatible with other pets?
This breed is generally good with other dogs if properly socialized in puppyhood and with cats in the same household if brought up with them. With training and supervision, he can be brought to accept other small pets in the home, though his boisterous nature should always be borne in mind. However, strange cats are likely to be considered fair game.

HOW much exercise?
The adult Flat-Coat needs a great deal of exercise: several daily walks plus a period of free galloping. If given the opportunity, he will also enjoy swimming. He is a great companion for country walks, as he likes to stay within sight of his owner

Character Trait	Poor	Average	Good	Excellent
Attitude to other dogs				
Quietness				
Not destructive				
Protective behavior				
Not likely to stray				
Good with children				
Ease of training				

Original purpose: Retrieving shot game
Male height: 23–24 in. (58.5–61 cm)
Female height: 22–23.5 in. (55–60 cm)
Weight: 60–70 lb. (27.3–31.8 kg)
Life span: 12–14 years

rather than disappearing over the horizon. Immature puppies must not be overexercised because of the risk of damage to growing bones.

HOW easy to train?

Like most retrievers, this is a highly trainable breed, perhaps a little slower to learn than some, with a tendency to be the "class clown."

Harsh treatment will ruin this sensitive dog, but handlers need to be firm and consistent or he will seize the opportunity to play the fool. Training is a must for the Flat-Coat, otherwise he will use his considerable intelligence for his own ends.

WHAT good points?

Devoted, enthusiastic, energetic, friendly, affectionate, playful, even tempered, loyal.

WHAT to be aware of?

Needs lots of exercise and lots of attention.

Large dogs

Likely to be destructive if bored or lonely. Often greedy—don't let him become overweight. Exercise will help.

WHAT medical problems?

Generally robust and healthy, but some hip malformation (dysplasia), epilepsy, diabetes, glaucoma (increased pressure in the fluid of the eyeball), eyelid malformation, and dislocation of the kneecap (patellar luxation) as well as a higher-than-average incidence of bone cancer, typically arising in middle age.

● *This robust and well-muscled working gundog is also an absolute gem as a family companion, as he has a loving, cheerful, and friendly nature.*

German Shorthaired Pointer

This is a working, multipurpose gundog bred to hunt, point, and retrieve game. He was developed between the 17th and 19th centuries by crossing slow, heavy German pointers with other breeds for improved performance and a more stylish appearance. The result is a top-notch, versatile gundog who has also achieved renown as search and rescue dog, sniffer dog, therapy dog and even sled dog. Affectionate, sociable, and well tempered, he makes a great family companion as long as his needs for physical and mental exercise are satisfied and he has plenty of human companionship and supervision. A bored, lonely GSP can be a one-dog wrecking machine.

Introduced to the US in 1925, the GSP soon found admirers and was recognized by the AKC in 1930. British sportsmen were slower to take up the breed, and KC recognition was not granted until 1954. Today the virtues of the GSP are recognized and appreciated worldwide.

WHAT colors?

Solid liver, liver and white (spotted, ticked, or both), solid black, or black and white (spotted, ticked, or both).

WHAT grooming does the coat need?

The short dense coat is easy care, needing only weekly brushing (twice a week during the molt) to remove dead hair.

HOW suitable are they as family dogs?

The GSP is a wonderful dog for families who can provide employment for this intelligent and energetic breed. He is devoted to his owners, keen to please, and generally good with children. However, he is a disastrous choice for a family who cannot keep him busy. As a youngster he is normally too exuberant and demanding to suit a household with very young children.

WHAT type of home?

More suited to country than city life, the GSP needs at the very least to live within easy reach of the countryside or a large park where he can enjoy a gallop. He needs a secure yard, although keen gardeners may not need him—he is a great digger and no respecter of plants. He can live in an outdoor kennel as long as he has enough time with his family but prefers indoor life.

WHAT type of owner?

These active dogs need active owners who enjoy walking in all weather and can provide them with a job to do—if not as gundogs then in activities such as agility or working trials. They are not part-time pets but need to be part of the family. Not recommended for the elderly or for homes with young children because of their high energy level.

HOW compatible with other pets?

If properly socialized in puppyhood, the GSD is generally friendly with other dogs and good with cats in his own household. Some males can be aggressive with strange dogs, and some are enthusiastic cat chasers. This is a hunting breed with an innate chase instinct, so small pets such as rabbits are best kept out of harm's way.

HOW much exercise?

A great deal—at least two hours' free running a day. The GSD was bred to work all day, and he needs

Character Trait	Poor	Average	Good	Excellent
Attitude to other dogs				
Quietness				
Not destructive				
Protective behavior				
Not likely to stray				
Good with children				
Ease of training				

Place of origin: **Germany**

Original purpose: Hunting, pointing and retrieving game
Male height: 23–25 in. (58.5–63.5 cm)
Female height: 21–23 in. (53–58.5 cm)
Weight: 45–70 lb. (20.5–31.8 kg)
Life span: 12–14 years

● GSPs need minimal grooming but must be given plenty to do.

plenty of varied exercise and occupation, including the opportunity for off-leash galloping. Agility, competitive obedience, or working trials will provide appropriate mental stimulation. Puppies under nine months should not be overexercised to prevent damage to growing bones.

HOW easy to train?

Intelligent and eager to please, the GSP is highly trainable. Indeed, training is a must for this active dog, who will channel his energy into misbehaving if not properly directed. Youngsters can be easily distracted and slow to mature, but persistence pays off. Stick to a calm, consistent, reward-based approach. This is a sensitive dog that reacts badly to rough handling.

Large dogs

WHAT good points?

Gentle, affectionate, even tempered, alert, intelligent, docile, very loyal, sociable, tireless, easy-care coat.

WHAT to be aware of?

High maintenance in terms of exercise and training. Needs a lot of input from owners. Tendency to separation anxiety.

WHAT medical problems?

Generally healthy, but hip and elbow malformation (dysplasia) and cataracts have been reported.

Chesapeake Bay Retriever

This powerfully built retriever is an individualist. Physically and mentally adapted for the tough work of retrieving shot wildfowl from icy water, he has a dense, water-repellent coat, webbed feet, and a great deal of determination. A superb hunting dog, he also excels as guard, sniffer dog, service dog for the handicapped, and even livestock dog and makes a great companion as long as his working drive is satisfied. He is more serious and strong willed than most retrievers and tends to be a one-person dog, devoted to his owner and his owner's family but aloof with strangers. Socialization is essential to prevent this from becoming shyness or aggression.

Said to originate from two Newfoundland dogs shipwrecked off Chesapeake Bay on the east coast of America in 1807, the Chesapeake was first registered with the AKC in 1878 and was declared the official state dog of Maryland in 1964.

WHAT colors?
Various shades of brown, including the attractively named dead grass (straw to bracken) and sedge (red gold to strawberry blond). White spots on chest, toes, and belly are permitted.

WHAT grooming does the coat need?
The dense, springy, oily coat needs minimal maintenance. Weekly grooming with a rubber brush will remove dead hairs and help to distribute the natural oil evenly through the coat. Overgrooming can damage the coat, making it less waterproof.

HOW suitable are they as family dogs?
Provided his working drive is satisfied, the Chesapeake is a great family dog, intensely loyal to his people, and usually very tolerant and protective with children.

● A working dog, the Chesapeake is happiest in a country home.

As a youngster he is likely to be too bouncy for the comfort of small children and like most retrievers has a tendency to mouth hands. So he is better suited to families with older children.

WHAT type of home?
As an energetic working breed, the Chesapeake is best suited to a country home. He can cope with city life if he has plenty of exercise and attention and a securely fenced yard, but is not suitable for an apartment.

WHAT type of owner?
A strong-willed dog with a powerful working drive, the Chesapeake is not recommended for novices or couch potatoes. He needs an active owner who can keep him employed, who enjoys outdoor exercise in all weather, and who has some experience of socializing and training an assertive breed. This is not a part-time breed but one that needs plenty of companionship and should not be left alone for long periods.

HOW compatible with other pets?
Socialization is essential if a Chesapeake is to get along well with other animals. They tend to be dominant, and males in particular may be intolerant of other dogs

Character Trait	Poor	Average	Good	Excellent
Attitude to other dogs	▨			
Quietness		▨		
Not destructive			▨	
Protective behavior				▨
Not likely to stray			▨	
Good with children			▨	
Ease of training			▨	

Original purpose: Retrieving waterfowl
Male height: 23–26 in. (58.5–66 cm)
Female height: 21–24 in. (53–61 cm)
Weight: 55–80 lb. (25–36 kg)
Life span: 10–13 years

of the same sex and may display territorial aggression toward other animals. They have a strong hunting drive and tend to see small animals—sometimes including cats—as prey to be chased.

HOW much exercise?

This breed needs a great deal of vigorous, athletic exercise, preferably including swimming. Walking alone is not enough, mental exercise is also important. If deprived of exercise, the Chesapeake is likely to turn his energy toward mischief. Puppies under a year old should not be overexercised as this may damage growing bones.

HOW easy to train?

Chesapeakes are intelligent and attentive and respond well to firm, fair, consistent training. Rules need to be established in puppyhood. If this is neglected, this strong-minded and independent dog is likely to take over. Training sessions

need to be made fun. Boring repetition and a heavy-handed approach are likely to make the Chesapeake "switch off."

● *Chesapeakes need both mental and physical stimulation.*

WHAT good points?

Loyal, protective, hard working, calm, confident, devoted, intelligent, sensitive, serious.

WHAT to be aware of?

A working breed that needs employment. Can be prone to dominance problems if not properly socialized and trained.

WHAT medical problems?

Generally a healthy breed; some incidence of hip and elbow malformation (dysplasia), progressive retinal atrophy (degeneration of the light receptor cells in the eyes), and cataracts.

Large dogs

Standard Poodle

There is a great deal more to the Standard Poodle than a fancy haircut. Although today usually regarded as a companion breed, he was originally a functional water retriever and still makes a highly efficient gundog. Indeed, he excels at a range of tasks, from service dog for the disabled to sledding, and is a popular choice for competitive obedience and agility. As a companion, he is well tempered, responsive, and sensitive to his owner's moods—and also a fun dog with abundant energy and a notable sense of humor. He is one of the few larger breeds suitable for novice owners, although he does need quite a bit of exercise and a great deal of coat care.

Poodles date back to at least the 15th century, achieving KC recognition in 1875. The oldest and largest of the three Poodle breeds, the Standard was bred down to produce Miniatures and Toys.

WHAT colors?

Any solid color, including white, cream, brown, apricot, black, silver and blue. Parti-colors occur but are not recognized by the AKC.

WHAT grooming does the coat need?

The thick curly coat does not molt and keeps growing if not clipped. Daily grooming with a slicker brush and wide-toothed comb is essential to prevent the coat from matting. It needs clipping every six to eight weeks. Show dogs are presented in an elaborate lion clip that requires a great deal of maintenance; pets are usually more comfortable with a practical short trim (sporting or puppy clip).

HOW suitable are they as family dogs?

The Standard Poodle makes a great family dog as long as he is treated as a member of the family and not denied attention. Most Standards love children, make great playmates,

● Standard Poodles need lots of grooming, whatever the clip.

and are often very protective. They are, however, demanding dogs who need company and stimulating activities, and they do not do well in stressful surroundings.

WHAT type of home?

This is an adaptable breed, equally well suited to city or country. For his size, the Standard Poodle takes up surprisingly little space and can even thrive in an apartment if he has enough attention and exercise. In the country, he can happily walk his owners off their feet.

WHAT type of owner?

Poodles need loving owners who can give them loads of attention. They are ideal for anyone who wants an entertaining and responsive companion, has a lively sense of humor, and is committed to grooming. The Standard Poodle is a good choice for people who enjoy long, energetic walks and for those who enjoy canine activities such as agility, which exercise both mind and body.

HOW compatible with other pets?

This friendly dog is generally excellent with other animals, although he will find it amusing to chase strange cats, squirrels, or anything else that can run unless he is taught not to do so.

HOW much exercise?

Standard Poodles need a fair amount of exercise, at least two brisk walks a day plus active playtime—and at most as much as their owners can take. A team

Character Trait	Poor	Average	Good	Excellent
Attitude to other dogs				
Quietness				
Not destructive				
Protective behavior				
Not likely to stray				
Good with children				
Ease of training				

Original purpose: Wildfowlers' dog
Male height: 23–26 in. (58–66 cm)
Female height: 21–24 in. (53–61 cm)
Weight: 45–70 lb. (20–32 kg)
Life span: 11–13 years

of Standards has completed the gruelling 1,158-mile (1,865-km) Iditarod sled race in Alaska! Mental exercise is equally important, whether in the form of games or formal obedience training.

HOW easy to train?

The intelligent Poodle is one of the most trainable of breeds. He is eager to learn, quick to respond, and very capable. He needs sensible and sensitive handling and a handler with a sense of humor. Poodles are easily bored by repetition and often have a creative approach to obedience.

WHAT good points?

Intelligent, well tempered, obedient, eager to learn, affectionate, reliable, lively, sensitive, adaptable, fun loving, nonaggressive.

WHAT to be aware of?

High coat care and exercise requirements. Can be noisy; some lines oversensitive, needing gentle handling. Youngsters often rowdy and mischievous.

● As a companion, the Poodle is generally most comfortable with his coat in the practical short trim seen here.

WHAT medical problems?

Inherited disorders include hip malformation (dysplasia), eye problems (cataracts and progressive retinal atrophy), and von Willebrand's disease (a hereditary bleeding disorder). Standard Poodles are also vulnerable to bloat (gastric torsion) and ear infections.

Large dogs

Saluki

Other names: Persian Greyhound, Gazelle Hound

This beautiful eastern sighthound is a dog with a mind of his own—a companion rather than a pet. Graceful and aristocratic, he is nonetheless essentially a working dog, bred for speed, endurance, and a powerful hunting drive. He was developed by nomadic Arab tribes to course hare and gazelle in harsh desert conditions, and his working instincts remain intact. He was born to run, he will chase anything that moves, and he is not programmed for obedience. He has a catlike self-sufficiency and independence—and, like a cat, he tends to choose where he will give his affection.

When given enough exercise and an owner who appreciates sighthound nature, he is a sweet-natured gentle, undemanding, and faithful companion. However, too many Salukis end up in rescue because they have been bought by people attracted to their beauty but unable to cope with their needs. A neglected Saluki becomes a liability!

WHAT colors?

Any color except brindle is acceptable. Colors include white, cream, fawn, golden red, grizzle, tricolor (white, black, and tan), black, and tan.

WHAT grooming does the coat need?

This is an easy-care coat, requiring weekly brushing. There are two coat varieties, smooth and feathered, the latter having fringes on ears, tail, and legs that need combing. Ear fringes may become fouled if they dangle in the Saluki's dinner. Either hold them back in a headband at mealtimes or clean after every meal.

HOW suitable are they as family dogs?

The Saluki is not the ideal pet for the average family because of his high exercise needs, strong hunting instinct, and highly strung, sensitive nature. He is good with sensible children if raised with them, but he does not enjoy roughhousing or conventional canine games such as chasing sticks or retrieving toys.

WHAT type of home?

A Saluki needs space, so a home with a large, secure yard is best. He can cope with city life if enough exercise is provided, although he is unsuited to apartment living. He does need access to areas where he can run free without danger to himself (i.e., no dashes across busy roads) or to local livestock. Farmers will not welcome unleashed Salukis near their animals.

WHAT type of owner?

This is a breed for an active person with access to land where a Saluki can run free, who will respond to this sensitive dog, and is not looking for formal obedience but is prepared to spend time and effort on training.

HOW compatible with other pets?

Salukis are generally friendly with other dogs, especially other sighthounds. They can be good with cats within their own household if raised with them. However, their natural instinct is to chase and kill anything that looks like prey, so they should not be

● *Graceful and highly sensitive, the Saluki needs a caring owner.*

Character Trait	Poor	Average	Good	Excellent
Attitude to other dogs				
Quietness				
Not destructive				
Protective behavior				
Not likely to stray				
Good with children				
Ease of training				

Place of origin: **Middle East**

Original purpose: Hunting
Male height: 23–28 in. (58.5–71 cm)
Female height: 23–28 in. (58.5–71 cm)
Weight: 40–60 lb. (18.2–27.3 kg)
Life span: 12–14 years

trusted with small pets or livestock.

HOW much exercise?

A great deal. Salukis need at least an hour's walk every day, plus free running. However, their strong hunting drive and deafness to the recall mean that areas where they can be trusted off leash are hard to find. Many owners find that the answer is to join a lure coursing club, where hounds like the Saluki pursue an artificial hare.

HOW easy to train?

Difficult. The Saluki is wayward, independent, and not remotely docile—not a dog for obedience enthusiasts. Nonetheless, careful socialization and training are essential to make him a pleasant companion.

● *The Saluki's coat needs only weekly grooming, but more frequent care must be taken of the ear fringes.*

Training must be gentle, patient and consistent: Salukis are slow maturing, sensitive, and respond badly to harsh treatment.

WHAT good points?

Dignified, intelligent, independent, affectionate, good-natured, faithful, gentle, fun loving, and an excellent watchdog.

WHAT to be aware of?

Strong hunting drive; hard to recall when off leash. Highly strung and does not react well to stress. Early socialization vital to prevent shyness.

Large dogs

WHAT medical problems?

Salukis are generally a healthy breed, although congenital heart problems, autoimmune diseases, and thyroid problems have been reported. Sensitive to anesthesia. Some occurrence of "sudden death syndrome," unexplained deaths of dogs usually while they are under five years of age.

Dogue de Bordeaux

This burly French mastiff is the descendant of medieval war dogs and hunting dogs, developing over the centuries into an all-purpose working dog used for herding, guarding, hunting, hauling carts—and for the bloody sports of bull baiting and dog fighting. Some-times described as France's answer to England's Bullmastiff, the breed was little known outside France until 1988, when the comedy film *Turner and Hooch* brought it into the limelight.

Since then, this magnificent dog with his striking red color and quizzically wrinkled face has won many fans—perhaps too many for his own good, for this is not a breed for the novice. Dignified, gentle, and loyal with his own family, he is a powerful and strong-willed dog who takes his guard role seriously and needs early socialization and training to prevent aggression to strangers. This is a lovable dog in the right hands—a liability in the wrong ones.

WHAT colors?

All shades of red and fawn; may have white patches on chest and toes, and red or black facial mask.

WHAT grooming does the coat need?

The short coat is easily maintained by weekly brushing with a slicker brush. However, the facial wrinkles may need daily wiping to avoid soreness, especially in heavily wrinkled specimens.

HOW suitable are they as family dogs?

For a family experienced with giant breeds and who have older children, the Dogue can be an excellent family dog. As an adult, he is calm and gentle with children. His size and strength make him unsuitable for a home with small children—a half-grown puppy can knock over an adult with one bounce, and young Dogues (under three years old) are great bouncers. They are also very loving and like to sit on people, not realizing their own weight.

● *The massive and powerful Dogue de Bordeaux needs a strong and confident owner whose will and determination match his own.*

WHAT type of home?

A large country house with a securely fenced yard is best. These big dogs need space and are not suitable for an apartment. Playful and clumsy, they can send furniture flying, so small or cluttered rooms are not a safe environment. The short muzzle means that they are prone to over-heating, so they need somewhere cool to relax in hot weather.

WHAT type of owner?

The Dogue needs a strong, confident, and experienced owner who has time to train and socialize him and to provide the company he craves. If left alone too much, he will be miserable and probably destructive. Not a breed for the fastidious: snoring, snorting, drooling, and flatulence are part of the package.

HOW compatible with other pets?

Be careful. With training, he will accept other pets in the household, though smaller animals run the risk of being trampled. Early socialization with other dogs is essential, as this breed tends to be dominant and can be dog aggressive, especially with dogs of the same sex. Some have strong chasing instincts, so watch out for next door's cat.

HOW much exercise?

Moderate. An adult Dogue needs daily walks to build up and maintain good muscle but should not be

Character Trait	Poor	Average	Good	Excellent
Attitude to other dogs		■		
Quietness	■			
Not destructive			■	
Protective behavior				■
Not likely to stray			■	
Good with children			■	
Ease of training		■		

Place of origin: France

Original purpose: Guarding, hunting
Male height: 23.5–26.5 in. (60–68 cm)
Female height: 22.5–26 in. (58–66 cm)
Weight: 99–110 lb. (45–50 kg) or over
Life span: 8–9 years

allowed to overheat. Puppies under two years must not be over-exercised, which is likely to damage growing bones.

HOW easy to train?

Moderately difficult: early, firm, and consistent training is essential. Dogues are stubborn, strong willed, and often dominant. However, a dog of this size absolutely must be under control. This is an intelligent breed that responds well to training once persuaded that it wishes to do so. Praise and food rewards are more motivating than force, which is usually counter-productive.

WHAT good points?

Loyal, affectionate, vigilant, courageous, even tempered, protective, a devoted family dog.

WHAT to be aware of?

Needs socialization and training to control his protective and territorial instincts. Puppies are powerful and boisterous. Not a dog to take on lightly.

Large dogs

WHAT medical problems?

Hip and elbow malformation (dysplasia), some heart murmurs, cancer. Loose skin on face can lead to eyelid problems (entropion and ectropion).

Spinone Italiano

He looks like a shaggy hound, but the Spinone is a versatile gundog bred to hunt, point and retrieve game. Like most gundogs, he also makes a great family dog provided his needs for exercise and company are met. Intelligent, playful, and easygoing, he is nonetheless not a dog who will suit everyone. He is certainly not a part-time commitment, but needs to be fully involved in family life. Neither is he the best choice for the house proud. He tends to drool, while that attractively scruffy coat carries in a lot of dirt and often betrays a distinct doggy smell. Highly sensitive, he needs early socialization and sympathetic training. In the right environment, however, he will blossom into a devoted and very individual member of the household.

The Spinone is said to be one of the oldest gundog breeds but has only recently become popular outside his native Italy.

WHAT colors?

White, white with orange or brown markings, or brown roan (white flecked with brown, with or without large brown markings).

WHAT grooming does the coat need?

A thorough weekly or twice-weekly brushing with a wire slicker brush will keep the oily weatherproof coat in good condition, with some stripping of dead hair during the molt. The beard and pendulous ears collect food and mud. They need washing daily to prevent a buildup of dirt, which could lead to infections.

HOW suitable are they as family dogs?

Gentle, laid back, and affectionate, the Spinone is an excellent dog for an active country-dwelling family who can meet his needs for exercise and attention. He has a great affinity with children, with whom he is patient, playful, and dependable—although in puppy-

● *This Spinone appears to have had all the exercise he craves!*

hood he may be too boisterous for the comfort of toddlers.

WHAT type of home?

A country home with plenty of space for exercise is the ideal home for a Spinone. His people come first with him. He will adapt to city life as long as he has plenty of regular activity and is allowed to participate fully in family life. Not recommended for apartment life.

WHAT type of owner?

A patient, gentle owner who wants a dog as a constant companion, enjoys country walks and other canine activities, and who is not excessively house proud will find the Spinone a rewarding choice. This dog needs a good deal of company, physical activity, and mental stimulation. He is not suitable for treating as a part-time pet but has to be fully involved in his owner's life.

HOW compatible with other pets?

The sociable Spinone gets along well with other animals and enjoys the company of other dogs, although as with all breeds early socialization is important. However, this is a hunting dog with an innate chasing instinct, so introduce other pets with care and don't expect him to ignore next door's cat without proper training.

HOW much exercise?

A great deal. The adult Spinone needs at least 60–90 minutes of walking every day, including plenty

Character Trait	Poor	Average	Good	Excellent
Attitude to other dogs			■	
Quietness	■			
Not destructive		■		
Protective behavior		■		
Not likely to stray			■	
Good with children				■
Ease of training			■	

Original purpose: Pointing and retrieving game
Male height: 23.5–27.5 in. (60–70 cm)
Female height: 23–25.5 in. (58–65 cm)
Weight: 64–86 lb. (29–39 kg)
Life span: 12–14 years

of free galloping. This is not a breed for the sedentary owner! Puppies under nine months should be limited to short walks and yard play to prevent damage to growing bones.

HOW easy to train?
This highly intelligent breed responds well to training provided the approach is patient, gentle, and consistent. The Spinone is highly sensitive and usually quite submissive, and does not take well to rough handling. He is also a slow-maturing breed, so training takes time on a "little and often" principle.

WHAT good points?
Faithful, intelligent, patient, affectionate, docile (as an adult!), nonaggressive, easygoing, playful.

WHAT to be aware of?
A demanding breed that can be destructive when bored. Timid if not socialized. Definitely not for the house proud. Highly vocal breed, given to "talking." Most are confirmed scavengers and food stealers.

WHAT medical problems?
Usually a healthy breed; occasional hip malformation (dysplasia)—breeding stock should be hip scored, ectropion, and entropion (malformed eyelids). Some lines carry cerebellar ataxia, a hereditary condition in which affected puppies lose control of their limbs and rarely survive their first year.

Large dogs

● *The oily coat of the Spinone does not need much grooming, but the beard and ears require daily attention.*

Belgian Sheepdog

This is a very handsome dog–or rather four handsome dogs, since it comes in four varieties, differing only in coat. The Laekenois is wirehaired, the Malinois short coated, and the Groenendael and Tervueren are both long-coated but different in color. Once a farm herder and guard, today the intelligent and versatile Belgian Sheepdog is used for military and police work; stars at agility, herding, or tracking, and makes a great companion dog in the right hands. However, he is very much a working dog who needs both physical and mental exercise and is unsuited to any home that cannot provide him with appropriate activity.

Affectionate (and demanding) with his own family, he is naturally reserved with strangers and needs a lot of early socialization so that this trait is not over-developed. This is not a dog to take on lightly, but he unquestionably makes a superb working companion for an experienced owner.

WHAT colors?

Laekenois: reddish fawn with black shading. Malinois: all shades of red, fawn, gray with black overlay. Groenendael: black. Tervueren: all shades of red, fawn, gray with black overlay. On Malinois, Groenedael and Tervueren, white on chest and tips of hind toes acceptable.

WHAT grooming does the coat need?

Brush at least twice a week to keep the coat healthy, working right down to the skin. Long-haired varieties will develop mats and tangles if grooming is neglected. Belgians shed copiously once or twice a year, when the dead under-coat needs stripping out with a comb.

HOW suitable are they as family dogs?

This is a fine dog for a family that has time for training and exercise, can keep him occupied, and has someone at home most of the day. He is good with children if raised with them, and his strong protective instincts make him a superb watch-dog and family guardian. He is highly unsuitable for any family unprepared or unable to give him the commitment he needs.

WHAT type of home?

The Belgian will be happiest in the country, but will adapt to city life as long as he has enough exercise. He needs a well-fenced yard and access to areas where he can enjoy long walks.

WHAT type of owner?

Belgians need owners who appreciate the high energy level and drive of a working breed and who can provide company and mental stimulation. They are best for confident and sensitive owners, as they are strong willed yet easily put off by aggressive training methods.

HOW compatible with other pets?

This depends very much on the quality of early socialization. Generally good with other dogs and with pets in the same household if raised with them. However, he has a strong chase instinct as well as a tendency to herd other animals by nipping and shoving, so smaller pets should be carefully introduced and first encounters supervised.

HOW much exercise?

A great deal. Belgians need daily long walks plus active training sessions to keep them healthy and happy. Off-leash running is essential for fitness, but ensure that the recall is properly taught

Character Trait	Poor	Average	Good	Excellent
Attitude to other dogs				
Quietness				
Not destructive				
Protective behavior				
Not likely to stray				
Good with children				
Ease of training				

Original purpose: Herder and guard
Male height: 24–26 in. (61–66 cm)
Female height: 22–24 in. (56–61 cm)
Weight: 61–63 lb. (27.5–28.5 kg)
Life span: 12–13 years

first, as the chase instinct will send this dog racing off after joggers or livestock unless he is under control.

HOW easy to train?

This is a highly trainable breed but needs sympathetic handling as it is so sensitive.

Positive, reward-based training is the way. Forceful or bullying tactics will simply break down his trust.

WHAT good points?

Active, alert, athletic, intelligent, affectionate, loyal, willing to please, easily trained, protective, adaptable

WHAT to be aware of?

Very high energy level—needs to be kept occupied. Needs more socialization than most breeds, otherwise can be shy or aggressive.

Large dogs

WHAT medical problems?

Generally a healthy breed, but inherited problems include eye disorders (progressive retinal atrophy and cataracts), hip malformation (dysplasia), lack of thyroid hormone (hypothyroidism), and epilepsy. Breeding stock should be tested and certified clear by a veterinarian.

● *Long-coated Belgians like the Tervueren and Groenendael will develop mats and tangles if grooming is neglected.*

German Shepherd Dog *Other names: Alsatian*

One of the world's most popular dogs, the German Shepherd's virtues are legion. Intelligent and adaptable, it makes an ideal working companion, helping to rescue people in distress, assisting people with disabilities, working alongside the police and military, and proving itself a vigilant guard dog. Beneath the proud, courageous exterior lies an even-tempered character that makes the German Shepherd an alert, loyal and devoted family dog. Athletic and tireless, it needs plenty of exercise and stimulation to flourish—owners must have sufficient time and vitality to devote to this splendid dog.

The German Shepherd derives from old breed of herding and working dog that flourished in Germany many centuries ago. First exhibited at a show in Hanover in 1882, it was introduced into the UK and the US after World War I. Also known for a time as the Alsatian, from 1971 its official AKC designation has been German Shepherd Dog.

What colors?
All black, bicolor (mostly black with some gold on legs), black and gold, gray, gold, sable. Whites, albinos, blues, and livers are not accepted in the breed standard and do not make show dogs.

What grooming does the coat need?
Weatherproof, straight, harsh outer coat with thick undercoat. Though attractive, a long coat is not accepted in the show ring. Short-coated German Shepherds need only one good brushing a week; long-coated dogs need vigorous grooming daily.

How suitable are they as family dogs?
When properly trained, German Shepherds are ideal family dogs, loyal, obedient, and protective of family members. They are vigorous and strong animals that need plenty of exercise and so are not suitable for the elderly or infirm who might have trouble exercising and controlling such an athletic companion.

What type of home?
These are essentially working dogs, so they need a home environment that will allow ample opportunity for exercise, activity, and tasks to perform. Ideal dogs for country dwellers; city owners should really have a reasonably sized yard and/or convenient access to a park for long walks. Not a dog to coop up behind four walls all day long.

What type of owner?
An owner of this intelligent breed must be prepared to devote considerable time and attention to the dog every day. It needs physical activity and mental stimulation. If you cannot spend quality time daily with your dog, do not consider a German Shepherd. It is unfair to subject the breed to a life of boredom and solitude if you are out at work all day.

How compatible with other pets?
Normally gets along well with other dogs and cats in the home, but be careful about the introductions—a boisterous new puppy can overwhelm and irritate existing pets, which can cause friction.

How much exercise?
An adult dog needs at least one

Character Trait	Poor	Average	Good	Excellent
Attitude to other dogs				
Quietness				
Not destructive				
Protective behavior				
Not likely to stray				
Good with children				
Ease of training				

Original purpose: Herder and guard
Male height: 24–26 in. (61–66 cm)
Female height: 22–24 in. (56–61 cm)
Weight: 75–95 lb (34–43 kg)
Life span: 12–13 years

good walk a day lasting around an hour, ideally with time spent running safely off the lead. The German Shepherd thrives on exercise.

How easy to train?
This breed is highly intelligent, has excellent working ability, and loves a challenge. Dogs are generally very responsive to training and highly suitable for advanced training disciplines, like agility and competitive obedience.

What good points?
Reliable, self-confident, athletic, bold, obedient, loyal, even tempered, immensely willing, good guard dog.

What to be aware of?
Shy or nervous dogs should be avoided because they may exhibit aggressive tendencies when unsettled. Dogs left alone for long periods or that lack mental stimulation may become destructive or start to bark excessively.

What medical problems?
This breed can suffer from allergies, epilepsy, malformation of the hip joint (dysplasia), inflammation of the cornea, lameness (panosteitis), chronic degenerative radiculomyelopathy (gradual loss of use of hind legs), anal furunculosis (ulcerated anal tissue), and skin problems.

Large dogs

● Intelligent and loyal—rightfully one of the world's favorites.

Old English Sheepdog *Other names: Bobtail*

The ultimate shaggy dog, the Old English Sheepdog is big, boisterous, and very hairy indeed. He is often born tailless (and sometimes docked), hence his popular nickname of the "Bobtail." He is a good-natured, happy, playful dog who likes to have something to do. He is also a very high-maintenance breed, needing a lot of physical and mental exercise, company, attention, and hours of grooming—hard work but a great companion in the right hands. Sheepdogs are sociable creatures who need to be involved in family activities and, like most working breeds, can be destructive if bored.

The Sheepdog originated as a tough shepherd's and drover's dog but today has become a glamorous show dog and lovable companion. In recent years, media exposure has made the breed too popular for its own good—many end up in rescue as impulse buyers discover cute puppies become demanding and labor-intensive dogs.

WHAT colors?
Body and hindquarters any shade of gray, grizzle, or blue, with or without white socks; head, neck, forequarters, and underbelly white.

WHAT grooming does the coat need?
A lot ... and then some more. A big coat on a big dog, it needs three or four hours a week with brush and comb (for a pet)—up to 15 hours for a show dog. If dead hair is not combed out frequently, it mats into lumps. Expect a massive cleanup job after walks in the rain and regular cleaning of the rear and legs—an unpleasant task if the dog has an upset stomach. Professional grooming recommended; pet owners often prefer to have the coat clipped down to a puppy trim for ease of care.

HOW suitable are they as family dogs?
Sheepdogs thrive as family dogs and are great playmates for older children, gentle by nature though physically heavy and rather clumsy. However, they are too big and bouncy to be recommended to households with toddlers or frail, elderly people.

WHAT type of home?
This is a country dog who needs space. He is not suitable for an apartment, or for a home without a yard. He is not recommended for homes where everything is kept immaculate. Big, hairy dogs can make a great deal of mess, especially after a rainy and muddy walk.

WHAT type of owner?
Sheepdogs need active owners who enjoy long walks, have plenty of time for exercise and training, and are committed to grooming or to frequent trips to a professional groomer. This is not a dog for people who are out all day, as he needs company, and definitely not one for the house-proud.

HOW compatible with other pets?
Sheepdogs are generally good with other dogs if well socialized in puppyhood, though they can be suspicious of strange dogs. They will be friendly with cats in their own household but are likely to chase others. Small pets are at risk of being squashed.

HOW much exercise?
Adults will enjoy as much exercise as you can give and should have at least two hours' daily exercise plus playtime in the garden. Avoid walks in hot weather, as the heavy coat

Character Trait	Poor	Average	Good	Excellent
Attitude to other dogs		X		
Quietness		X		
Not destructive		X		
Protective behavior			X	
Not likely to stray			X	
Good with children				X
Ease of training		X		

Original purpose: Droving and herding
Male height: 24–26 in (61–66 cm)
Female height: 22–24 in. (56–61 cm)
Weight: 60–90 lb. (27.3–40.9 kg)
Life span: 10–12 years

easily leads to overheating. Puppies should not be overwalked, to prevent damage to growing bones, but have endless energy that needs to burned off in play.

● *The Sheepdog needs an owner prepared to make considerable commitments to both grooming and daily exercise.*

HOW easy to train?

Moderate. Sheepdogs are intelligent and quick learners who are always interested in something new to do. They are also strong willed and stubborn and can be very unco-operative if their

interest is not captured, so make training sessions fun for best results. This breed needs mental stimulus and is capable of a range of activities, from agility to herding.

WHAT good points?

Even tempered, bold, faithful, trustworthy, nonaggressive, intelligent, playful, loyal, affectionate, outgoing, people oriented.

WHAT to be aware of?

Massive grooming commitment. Can be overterritorial and possessive of toys or food.

Large dogs

WHAT medical problems?

Hip and elbow malformation (dysplasia), osteochondritis (joint disease), eye disorders including cataracts and progressive retinal atrophy (degeneration of the light receptor cells in the eyes), thyroid disorders, hemophilia, heart problems. Breeding stock should have hips and eyes checked.

Briard *Other names: Berger de Brie*

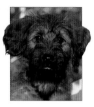

This shaggy French farm dog takes its name from the province of Brie. Said to date back to medieval times, the Briard has a long history as herder and guard as well as a noble record with the army (notably in World War I), police, and search and rescue teams. Formally recognized in the US as early as 1920, the breed did not reach the UK until the late 1960s.

Still very much a working dog, the Briard is strong willed, often dominant, and needs a lot of socialization and training to channel his innate herding and guarding instincts. If under exercised mentally or physically, he can be destructive or even aggressive. In the right hands he makes a loyal, intelligent, and versatile companion, devoted to his family, highly trainable, and bursting with energy. This challenging breed is not one to take on lightly nor an ideal choice for a novice. Briards demand an active and confident owner.

WHAT colors?

Black (with or without a sprinkling of white hairs), slate gray, or any shade of fawn (from cream to rich gold) with dark ears, muzzle, back, and tail. Puppies may change color—indeed, fawns may continue to change shade until they are several years old.

WHAT grooming does the coat need?

The long, wavy coat needs daily grooming with a slicker brush and metal comb—a minimum of one to two hours a week, more for an adolescent changing coat. Pay particular attention to the dense hair of neck, chest, and hindquarters and behind the ears. If neglected, the coat will mat heavily.

HOW suitable are they as family dogs?

With appropriate exercise and mental stimulation, the Briard makes a great family dog, protective, eager to share in family activities, and a fun playmate for older, sensible children. Generally too energetic and exuberant to be recommended for households with small children, he can also be overprotective and needs to understand his role in the household.

WHAT type of home?

His high energy levels suit the Briard for a country home, and he needs a reasonably-sized yard. This is a dog who will not thrive kept in a kennel but needs to live in the home with his family.

WHAT type of owner?

This breed is strong minded enough to walk all over an easygoing owner yet too sensitive to react well to harsh discipline. The ideal Briard owner would be experienced, active, and able to provide calm, confident leadership as well as have time for socializing, training, exercise, grooming, and companionship. Not one for the house proud. Shaggy dogs carry in dirt and mud.

HOW compatible with other pets?

Intensive socialization is important to ensure that the Briard is good with other dogs and with pets within his household generally. Without proper training he can be aggressive with other dogs and is naturally predisposed to chase (and nip) anything that moves. If sensibly raised and trained, however, he will normally be fine with other pets.

HOW much exercise?

This is a high-energy breed with vigorous exercise requirements—at least two hours a day plus active play and plenty of mental stimulation.

Character Trait	Poor	Average	Good	Excellent
Attitude to other dogs				
Quietness				
Not destructive				
Protective behavior				
Not likely to stray				
Good with children				
Ease of training				

Original purpose: Herding and guarding
Male height: 23–27 in. (58.5–68.5 cm)
Female height: 22–25.5 in (56–65 cm)
Weight: 75–100 lb. (34.1–45.5 kg)
Life span: 10–12 years

HOW easy to train?

Moderate. The Briard has a mind of his own and can be very stubborn. He is intelligent and eminently trainable but needs a handler who understands the independent mind-set of a working breed and can earn his respect. Training needs to start early, and sessions should be kept short and exciting to hold his interest. Briards are quick learners but get bored equally quickly.

WHAT good points?

Sensible, lively, intelligent, kind, devoted, sensitive, playful, protective, plenty of initiative.

WHAT to be aware of?

Shaggy coat needs lots of grooming and creates mess. Intensive socialization and training necessary. High exercise needs.

WHAT medical problems?

Generally a healthy and long-lived breed. Known problems include hip malformation (dysplasia), eye problems, lack of thyroid hormone (hypothyroidism), von Willebrand's disease (an inherited condition that prevents blood from clotting), tendency to gastric torsion (bloat).

Large dogs

● Plenty of grooming and exercise are demanded of a Briard's owner.

Weimaraner *Other names: Weimar Pointer*

The "Gray Ghost" is one of the most striking gundog breeds, with his metallic gray coat and light eyes. A superb and versatile working dog, he is intelligent, keen, and devoted to his owner. He is also a high-powered dog with abundant energy and a dominant character who needs extensive socialization, training, attention, and affection from an experienced and equally strong-willed handler. In the right hands, he is a marvelous dog; but he must have employment. A bored, underexercised Weimaraner can be a nightmare—possessive, over-protective, restless, noisy, and destructive.

German hunters employed dogs of Weimaraner type as early as the 17th century, but by the 19th century the Weimaraner was kept exclusively at the German court of Weimar. Introduced to the US in 1929 and to the UK in 1952, it is now renowned worldwide as a working gundog. A long-haired variety appeared in 1973 but remains uncommon.

WHAT grooming does the coat need?

This is an easy-care coat: brush about twice a week to remove dead hairs and daily during the molt. Long-haired Weimaraners need the feathering behind ears and legs and on the tail combing through regularly.

HOW suitable are they as family dogs?

So long as he has the opportunity to employ his working abilities to the full, the Weimaraner is an admirable family dog, generally gentle and reliable with children. However, he is a powerful, boisterous dog, not recommended for families with small children or frail elderly people and generally too head-strong for the average household.

WHAT type of home?

This is a country dog who needs a well-fenced yard and access to suitable land for exercise. He is not suited for confined small spaces such as apartments or homes with tiny yards.

WHAT type of owner?

Weimaraner owners need to be physically strong and mentally tough, capable of the firm but kind leadership that this breed needs. Ideally they should be looking for a working companion and will need plenty of time for training and exercising. This is a breed for out-door types who enjoy a great deal of exercise—not a dog for novices nor for couch potatoes or the frail.

HOW compatible with other pets?

If well socialized in puppyhood, the Weimaraner is generally good with other dogs but tends to be dominant and will not back down if challenged. He is fine with cats in his own household if raised with them, but he is a hunting dog with an innate chasing instinct who should not be trusted with small pets such as rabbits—or next door's cat.

HOW much exercise?

Adults need a great deal of exercise every day, including the opportunity for off-leash galloping. Puppies under

WHAT colors?

Ideally silver gray, but mouse gray or roe gray acceptable, with a metallic sheen. May have dark eel stripe down back, and small white mark permissible on chest. Eye color amber or blue gray, never dark. Puppies are born with stripes, which disappear before they leave the nest.

Place of origin: **Germany**

Character Trait	Poor	Average	Good	Excellent
Attitude to other dogs				
Quietness				
Not destructive				
Protective behavior				
Not likely to stray				
Good with children				
Ease of training				

Original purpose: Hunting, pointing, and retrieving game
Male height: 24–27 in. (61–68.5 cm)
Female height: 22–25 in. (56–63.5 cm)
Weight: 65–75 lb. (29.5–34.1 kg)
Life span: 10–13 years

nine months should be limited to short walks and yard play to prevent damage to growing bones.

HOW easy to train?
Depends on the owner. This is a challenging breed, willful and easily bored. He can be trained to a very high standard by an owner who can establish firm but kind leadership right at the start but may be too much of a handful for most novices. Training should be firm, patient, and gentle, keeping lessons short and interesting.

WHAT good points?
Intelligent, friendly, outgoing, fearless, devoted, protective, sensitive, powerful, versatile.

WHAT to be aware of?
Very strong-willed, dominant dog who needs work to do. Potential aggression to other dogs if not properly socialized.

Large dogs

WHAT medical problems?
Generally a healthy breed; some problems with entropion (inverted eyelids), cataracts, hip malformation (dysplasia), bloat (gastric torsion), and heart defects. Over rapid growth in puppies is also a problem in the breed.

Bullmastiff

This impressively powerful dog was developed in 19th-century England, using a blend of Mastiff and Bulldog to create the "Gamekeeper's Night Dog" to tackle violent poaching gangs. Today his career in protection work has been taken over by more versatile and trainable breeds, and his main role is as companion and home guard. Dignified, loyal, and affectionate, he is gentle with his own family but retains all the guarding instincts of his ancestors. With proper socialization and training to ensure that his protective drive does not veer toward aggression, he is a lovable family companion, but this strong and stubborn dog is not a suitable choice for the inexperienced. He needs space and supervision. His sheer size can be a problem, especially since he often fancies himself as a lapdog.

Modern Bullmastiffs vary in type. Beware stock with overheavy bone and foreshortened faces, which may have health problems.

WHAT colors?

Any shade of brindle, fawn, or red, with black muzzle, dark markings around the eyes, and dark ears. A little white on the chest is acceptable, but white markings elsewhere are undesirable.

WHAT grooming does the coat need?

This is a low-maintenance coat, needing only regular brushing (say ten minutes twice a week) with a firm bristle brush. Grooming should include checking the feet, because they carry a lot of weight.

HOW suitable are they as family dogs?

In the right home and with the right upbringing, the Bullmastiff can be an excellent family dog. However, his size and strong guarding instincts make him unsuitable for most families with small children. He may be over-protective, putting visiting children at risk if he misinterprets rough play. As a youngster (up to about three years old) he tends to be quite rowdy and liable to knock small people flying.

WHAT type of home?

Big dogs take up a lot of space, so this is not the ideal breed for a small house. A large country house with a strongly fenced yard (Bullmastiffs can walk through lightweight fences if they feel the need) is more suitable. This breed does not tolerate extremes of temperature, so they need somewhere cool to relax in hot weather.

WHAT type of owner?

This is a dog for a strong, easy-going, confident, and experienced owner who has the time to train and socialize him and to provide the company this breed craves. Bullmastiff owners should also be prepared to put up with snoring, snorting, slobbering, and flatulence.

HOW compatible with other pets?

Be careful. Adult Bullmastiffs can be aggressive with other dogs of the same sex, and early socialization is important. They are usually good with the family cat if raised together but should not be trusted with strange animals. Smaller pets may be at risk of being trodden on.

HOW much exercise?

The Bullmastiff's exercise needs are moderate, but he does need daily walks. This breed tends to be lazy and should be encouraged to exercise, as they tend to put on

Character Trait	Poor	Average	Good	Excellent
Attitude to other dogs		■		
Quietness			■	
Not destructive			■	
Protective behavior				■
Not likely to stray			■	
Good with children			■	
Ease of training		■		

Original purpose: Protection
Male height: 25–27 in. (63.5–69 cm)
Female height: 24–26 in. (61–66 cm)
Weight: 100–133 lb. (45–60 kg)
Life span: 8–10 years

weight. Puppies under two years must not be overexercised, which is likely to cause damage to growing bones.

HOW easy to train?

Moderately difficult. Strong and stubborn, the Bullmastiff needs to be persuaded that he is not the leader of the family. Training should start early and be firm, patient, and consistent, keeping sessions short and interesting. Bullying tactics will get you nowhere with this breed. Praise and food rewards are more effective.

WHAT good points?

Fearless, loyal, protective, alert yet calm, high spirited, active, reliable, tolerant, stoical, courageous, powerful.

WHAT to be aware of?

Not a dog for the novice. Although adults are generally calm and sensible, puppies are hard work. Guard instincts mean this breed can be a real liability if not properly trained and socialized.

Large dogs

WHAT medical problems?

This breed has a short life span and serious problems with bone and joint problems such as hip malformation (dysplasia); eyelid problems (entropion) may also occur. Bullmastiffs are also prone to cancer and susceptible to bloat.

● This is a guard breed, and puppy socialization is vital to ensure that your pet accepts visitors to the home. Training is essential for such a large dog.

Rhodesian Ridgeback

Originally developed to track lions and hold them at bay until the hunters arrived, the Rhodesian Ridgeback nowadays employs his courage, loyalty, and protective instincts in the role of companion and house guard. He is a handsome dog who is built to combine speed, agility, and stamina with muscular power and who owes his name to the distinctive ridge of hair down his spine. He is also a strong-willed dog who needs an equally strong-minded owner who can provide early socialization, appropriate training and a heavy investment of time. In the right hands, he is an excellent companion, very much a "people dog" with strong but discriminating guard instincts.

The Ridgeback was developed in South Africa from a mixture of ridge-backed Hottentot dogs and European settlers' sporting breeds, achieving formal recognition in Africa in 1922 and reaching the UK shortly thereafter. The breed was recognized by the AKC in 1955.

WHAT colors?

Light wheat to red wheat; may have dark muzzle and ears, and a little white on chest and toes is permissible.

WHAT grooming does the coat need?

The short, sleek coat requires little maintenance. A weekly brushing with a hound glove will keep it in good condition.

HOW suitable are they as family dogs?

With careful early socialization and in the right hands, the Ridgeback can be a great family dog. He is an excellent and good-tempered companion for older children who treat him with respect. Although as with all powerful guard breeds, supervision is advisable. Not a good choice for households with preschool children, particularly as puppies (under two years) are very exuberant and quite likely to send toddlers flying.

WHAT type of home?

The Ridgeback is best suited to a country home with a well-fenced yard. This very athletic dog can clear quite high fences and will be tempted to do so if bored. He can cope with apartment living only if provided with plenty of exercise and attention, and indeed should be considered as a city dog only if there is easy access to suitable exercise areas for free running.

WHAT type of owner?

This rewarding but demanding breed needs a strong, confident, and experienced owner who is able to establish leadership and who has plenty of time and energy for training, exercise, and companionship. Ridgebacks are not suited to homes where they will be left alone for long periods as they can be very destructive indeed if neglected. Not one for dedicated gardeners. They dig with enthusiasm and are likely to regard treasured shrubs as chew toys.

HOW compatible with other pets?

Be careful. If properly socialized, Ridgebacks are not quarrelsome with other dogs, but they are very dominant. Some may display aggression toward dogs of the same sex. Cats in the same household will usually be accepted, but strange cats are just asking to be chased. This hunting breed has a very high prey drive, and small pets are at serious risk from them.

Character Trait	Poor	Average	Good	Excellent
Attitude to other dogs		▨		
Quietness			▨	
Not destructive		▨		
Protective behavior				▨
Not likely to stray		▨		
Good with children			▨	
Ease of training		▨		

Original purpose: Big-game hunting
Male height: 25–27 in. (63.5–68.5 cm)
Female height: 24–26 in. (61–66 cm)
Weight: 70–85 lb. (31.8–38.5 kg)
Life span: 10–12 years

HOW much exercise?

Above average—several brisk daily walks (at least 2 miles/3 km a day) and the opportunity for free running. Ridgebacks are natural chasers and need training not to pursue joggers, other dogs, or livestock when off leash. Activities such as lure coursing and agility are a great way for them to burn off excess energy. Puppies under six months should not be overexercised.

HOW easy to train?

These strong-willed, independent dogs can be extremely stubborn, and novices are likely to find them difficult. Training needs to start early, while a puppy is young enough to be manageable, and to be firm, fair, and consistent. Reward-based methods (especially food rewards) work best. A heavy-handed approach is usually counterproductive.

WHAT good points?

Dignified, intelligent, affectionate, loyal, powerful, active, protective, nonaggressive, independent.

WHAT to be aware of?

Early socialization essential to avoid dominance aggression. Puppies (and adults) can be very destructive. Can be dog aggressive and overprotective.

WHAT medical problems?

Generally a healthy breed, but inherited defects include hip and elbow malformation (dysplasia), thyroid problems, and cataracts. All puppies should be screened for dermoid sinus (abnormal tissue on back or neck.)

Large dogs

● *Once known as the "African lion dog," the Ridgeback was employed in his native land to hunt, retrieve, take care of children, and guard property, tasks he can still perform.*

Rottweiler

Rottweilers have suffered from bad press in recent years, largely because these powerful, imposing dogs have too often attracted unsuitable owners. Like any natural guard breed, Rotties need proper socialization and expert training. They are suited only to strong-minded, experienced handlers who can provide firm leadership. Essentially working dogs, they have brains as well as brawn and in the right hands can be trained to a very high standard. They have served as police and military dogs, guide dogs for the blind, search and rescue dogs, and therapy dogs. This is not a breed to take on lightly. With sensible discipline and plenty of love and attention, the Rottie is an admirable companion and reliable family dog.

The Rottweiler takes its name from Rottweil in southern Germany, where it was renowned as a drovers' dog and guard. Today it is one of the world's best-known protection dog breeds.

WHAT colors?

Black with rich tan markings on chest, legs, under tail, and face; facial markings to include cheeks, muzzle, and spots above eyes.

WHAT grooming does the coat need?

This is an easy-care coat, needing little more than a good brushing twice a week to remove dead hairs and keep a good shine on the coat.

HOW suitable are they as family dogs?

This is a superb family dog for experienced owners who can provide suitable training. A family environment suits the Rottie, who needs human contact if he is to be happy and well balanced. Not recommended with young children because, although generally reliable, there is always an element of risk with powerful guard breeds. Older, sensible children will find the Rottie a good friend but should not be allowed to take him out unsupervised.

WHAT type of home?

This is a big dog who needs plenty of space. Given enough exercise, he can be equally happy in the city or country but is not suited to apartment living. He needs a securely fenced yard.

WHAT type of owner?

Rottweiler owners should be calm but assertive, able to provide confident leadership and also plenty of affection, as well as having time for training, exercise, and play. This is not a breed for novices nor for couch potatoes. The Rottie is a working dog who needs a great deal of physical and mental exercise.

HOW compatible with other pets?

Be careful. A properly socialized Rottweiler will accept other animals in the same household as members of his family. However, Rotties are highly dominant and can often be intolerant of dogs of the same sex. Some have a strong chasing instinct that may put cats and other small pets at risk.

HOW much exercise?

The Rottweiler's forebears were expected to drive herds of cattle perhaps 40 miles (65 km) a day. Although few modern owners can offer this level of activity, the breed

Character Trait	Poor	Average	Good	Excellent
Attitude to other dogs		■		
Quietness			■	
Not destructive			■	
Protective behavior				■
Not likely to stray		■		
Good with children			■	
Ease of training				■

Original purpose: Guarding and herding
Male height: 24–27 in. (61–68.5 cm)
Female height: 22–25 in. (56–63.5 cm)
Weight: 80–135 lb. (36.4–61.4 kg)
Life span: 8–11 years

does need plenty of exercise. Puppies under a year old must have their exercise limited to prevent damage to growing bones.

HOW easy to train?

Highly trainable but need calm, confident handling. Early socialization and training are essential for this powerful and strong-willed breed. The Rottie is quick to learn—and will learn bad behavior unless corrected kindly but consistently. A confrontational approach will lead to problems. Owners need to earn respect with a firm but sympathetic approach, using reward-based training to motivate the dog to want to learn.

WHAT good points?

Courageous, intelligent, loyal, versatile, confident, affectionate, protective, self-assured, good-natured.

Large dogs

WHAT to be aware of?

Can be very dominant, especially adolescent males, and also territorial. Youngsters should never be allowed to develop bad habits that are difficult to break in maturity. Buy only from responsible breeders who make good temperament a priority.

WHAT medical problems?

Hip malformation (dysplasia), cruciate ligament problems can affect the knees, cancer, heart disease, eye disease.

● *Rottweiler puppies are as appealing as any breed, but remember that they grow up to be big, powerful dogs and need sensible training.*

Bloodhound

Bred for centuries for an incredible sense of smell, the Bloodhound is renowned as the greatest tracker dog of them all, tracing criminals and finding lost people. His name signifies noble breeding (as in "bloodstock") rather than savagery, and he is generally good-natured and affectionate. However, he will not suit most pet homes. This is a powerful dog with minimal predisposition to obedience who eats hugely, can be destructive, bays like the Hound of the Baskervilles, and slobbers profusely. He needs a lot of exercise, but a big dog who is ruled by his nose is not easy to walk. It takes considerable strength to haul him off the trail, and off leash he is deaf to the recall once he has picked up a scent.

Today famous worldwide, the Bloodhound is said to have originated in Belgium and to have been introduced to Britain by William the Conqueror in 1066.

WHAT colors?

Black and tan, liver and tan (red and tan), and red. A small amount of white on chest, feet, or tip of tail is permissible.

WHAT grooming does the coat need?

The short coat is easy care, needing only a weekly rubbing with a hound glove to remove dead hairs. However, the heavy, hanging ears regularly pick up muck and slobber, and frequent cleaning is needed to prevent ear infections.

HOW suitable are they as family dogs?

Despite his gentle nature and affection for children, the Bloodhound is not the ideal family dog. He is big and clumsy and may well bowl over or trample small children or the frail elderly. He can also be food possessive. Children too young to understand this could be at risk. By nature he is often more suited to be a one-person dog rather than a family member.

WHAT type of home?

This is definitely not a city dog. Bloodhounds need a lot of space and require a home with a large yard or extensive grounds. Secure fencing is a must, or they will disappear after a scent. Though hound aficionados describe the Bloodhound's baying as melodious, a home with deaf or highly tolerant neighbors is recommended.

WHAT type of owner?

This specialist breed is best suited to an owner who has an interest in tracking. Owners also need to be physically fit and strong enough to handle a powerful dog. Bloodhounds are certainly not the breed for anyone who wants to enjoy relaxing country walks. They need a major commitment of time, plenty of company (they dislike being left alone), and firm but sensitive handling.

HOW compatible with other pets?

The good-natured Bloodhound is generally good with other animals, although he is clumsy and small pets run the risk of being squashed. Some bloodlines may tend toward aggression to other dogs of the same sex.

HOW much exercise?

A great deal. Puppies should have limited exercise to prevent damage to growing bones, but adults need long walks daily. Bloodhounds will not ignore a scent, so they are

Character Trait	Poor	Average	Good	Excellent
Attitude to other dogs				
Quietness				
Not destructive				
Protective behavior				
Not likely to stray				
Good with children				
Ease of training				

Original purpose: Tracking
Male height: 25–27 in. (63.5–68.5 cm)
Female height: 23–25 in. (58.5–63.5 cm)
Weight: 80–110 lb. (36–50 kg)
Life span: 7–10 years

normally walked on a long leash to prevent them from disappearing over the horizon. Off-leash exercise is safe only in totally secure areas.

HOW easy to train?

Difficult. Bloodhounds are stubborn, independent, and willful, but they are also highly sensitive and can be ruined by harsh treatment. Training needs to be firm but gentle, endlessly patient, and realistic—don't expect collie-style obedience. Adolescent males can be a real handful and need sensible, consistent leadership before they settle down.

WHAT good points?

Affectionate, sensitive, not quarrelsome, dignified, gentle, good-natured, loyal, a superb tracker.

WHAT to be aware of?

Excessive drooling—a shake of the head can send slobber flying 20 feet (600 cm). Strong "doggy" smell. Food thief. Highly vocal.

Avoid specimens with excessive skin wrinkles and obscured or discharging eyes.

WHAT medical problems?

Bloodhounds are prone to ear infections, inward-turning eyelids (entropion), hip malformation (dysplasia), and skin allergies and are highly vulnerable to gastric torsion (bloat).

Large dogs

● *This is a high-maintenance breed that demands serious commitment from an owner.*

Bernese Mountain Dog *Other names: Berner Sennenhund*

Striking good looks and a calm, friendly, people-oriented nature give the Bernese considerable appeal as a family dog. He developed in the Swiss mountains as an all-purpose farm dog, herding, guarding, and hauling carts, and remains a versatile worker who enjoys obedience, agility, tracking, herding, and carting. Given the attention he requires, he is a lovable companion, gentle, and tolerant. However, this is a demanding breed and not for the inexperienced. He is big, powerful, and strong willed. He needs occupation for his working intelligence, and he is a highly sociable creature who needs human company. He does not cope well with boredom or loneliness. He also needs a fair amount of exercise and grooming.

The Bernese is the most popular of the four Swiss Mountain breeds developed for work on Alpine farms. The breed was rescued from near extinction in the late 19th century and has now achieved world-wide popularity.

WHAT colors?

Jet black with rich tan on all four legs, cheeks, chest, and over eyes, and white facial blaze and chest marking. White paws and white tail tip are desirable but not essential.

WHAT grooming does the coat need?

The long, thick coat needs regular (twice weekly) brushing and combing, with extra attention during the molt. It is important to groom right down to the skin. Combing the topcoat only will look good on the surface but will leave dead hair clogging the undercoat and eventually matting. This breed sheds heavily—you will need a good vacuum cleaner.

HOW suitable are they as family dogs?

The Bernese is an ideal family dog for an experienced family with plenty of time for him. He likes to

be involved in family activities and to be the center of attention. He is generally good with children, although as a youngster he may be too rough for young children and needs sensible supervision.

WHAT type of home?

As a large working breed, the Bernese is not ideally suited to city life and is certainly not a dog to keep in an apartment. He needs human company and should not be confined to an outdoor kennel. He will not be comfortable in a very warm house or, indeed, in an unshaded yard in hot weather as his heavy coat makes him susceptible to overheating.

WHAT type of owner?

Best for experienced owners who have the time and patience to train a strong-minded, powerful dog and enjoy activities such as carting or agility. Owners should also expect to give and receive a great deal of affectionate attention and appreciate a dog who needs to be a full-time family member.

HOW compatible with other pets?

Most Bernese are good with other animals if raised with them and sensibly socialized. They are big dogs and boisterous in puppyhood, so care needs to be taken to protect smaller pets from accidental injury.

Character Trait	Poor	Average	Good	Excellent
Attitude to other dogs			▨	
Quietness			▨	
Not destructive			▨	
Protective behavior				▨
Not likely to stray			▨	
Good with children				▨
Ease of training		▨		

Original purpose: Herding, guarding, carting
Male height: 25–27.5 in. (63.5–70 cm)
Female height: 23–26 in. (58.5–66 cm)
Weight: 87–90 lb. (40–41 kg)
Life span: 6–9 years

HOW much exercise?

This breed has only moderate exercise requirements for its size. Adults are quite adaptable and will thrive on a minimum of half an hour's walk a day or alternatively will enjoy a great deal more, depending on your lifestyle and their level of fitness. Puppies under twelve months should not be overexercised, which is likely to cause damage to growing bones.

HOW easy to train?

Moderate. Bernese are generally willing to please, but they do have a mind of their own and a sense of humor. So training needs to be firm, patient and consistent, keeping sessions short and interesting. Some males can be dominant and require an experienced handler. Training should start early. If left to his own devices, boisterous youngsters can become uncontrollable.

WHAT good points?

Good-natured, friendly, confident, protective, intelligent, versatile, affectionate, loyal, active, non-aggressive.

WHAT to be aware of?

A demanding breed, highly rewarding in the right hands but needing a lot of commitment. Sadly, this breed tends to have a very short life span.

WHAT medical problems?

Hip and elbow malformation (dysplasia), osteochondritis (a disease affecting developing bone, causing foreleg lameness), and a high incidence of cancer. This breed has a notably short average life expectancy, although individuals do reach their teens.

Large dogs

Alaskan Malamute

This magnificent Arctic sled dog was not designed to be a pet. He has a friendly nature, impressive personality, and great natural dignity, but he is essentially a working dog. The "cart horse of the North" was bred to pull heavy loads long distances and is among the most powerful of dog breeds. He needs the stimulus of activities such as backpacking, draft work (pulling a sled or, lacking snow, a wheeled rig), or weight pulling. Given this activity, he can make a great companion, though not for novices as he is powerful, stubborn, and has a strong hunting drive.

Originally developed by the Mahlemiut Inuit of Alaska to haul sleds and carry packs, the breed nearly died out in the 1920s. Preserved by a few dedicated breeders, it achieved AKC recognition in 1935, was introduced into the UK in 1959, and is now a star of the show ring.

WHAT colors?

Any shade of gray through to black, or shades of red through to liver, always with white markings on underbody, legs, feet, and face. Characteristic facial markings in the form of dark cap or mask. The only solid color allowed is white.

WHAT grooming does the coat need?

The dense coat needs regular deep combing to remove dead hair, say three or four times a week. This breed molts hugely once a year, when hair comes out in clumps and extra grooming is required.

HOW suitable are they as family dogs?

Provided he has appropriate occupation, the Malamute's love of people makes him a great family pet. Although he is generally patient with children, he is not recommended for homes with small children simply because he is so powerful and can cause accidental injury to little ones.

WHAT type of home?

Malamutes are totally unsuited to city life. They need space. An ideal home would have plenty of acreage and opportunities for this dog to enjoy the work at which he excels. A home without neighbors nearby may be best as, although Malamutes don't bark much, they enjoy a good howl sometimes.

WHAT type of owner?

Malamute owners need to be energetic outdoor types who enjoy being out in all weather. They should be strong willed and dedicated to working their dogs as well as having time for grooming and enjoying their dogs' company.

This breed is a great companion for hikers and backpackers and for those who live in areas where there are sled-racing clubs and the like.

HOW compatible with other pets?

Individuals vary, but be cautious! Malamutes have a very strong prey drive and will chase anything that moves. They will usually accept cats in the same household if brought up with them but should never be regarded as safe with livestock. They can be aggressive toward dogs of the same sex, and early socialization is essential to prevent problems.

HOW much exercise?

An adult Malamute needs a brisk, 4-mile (6-km) walk a day at the minimum, with no maximum. It is impossible to tire him out. Care must be taken when walking in the vicinity of livestock: don't trust him! Puppies should have limited exercise to prevent damage to growing bones. Build up gradually from about six months until 18 months, when they are full grown.

Character Trait	Poor	Average	Good	Excellent
Attitude to other dogs	■			
Quietness			■	
Not destructive		■		
Protective behavior	■			
Not likely to stray	■			
Good with children			■	
Ease of training	■			

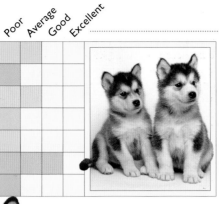

Original purpose: Hauling sleds, carrying packs, hunting
Male height: 25–28 in. (63.5–71 cm)
Female height: 23–26 in. (58.5–66 cm)
Weight: up to 85 lb. (38.6 kg)
Life span: 10–12 years

HOW easy to train?

Difficult. Malamutes are intelligent but not programmed for obedience. They learn quickly but are equally quick to grow bored with training sessions and are quite likely to ignore commands. Training needs to start early and to be very, very patient. This is a strong-willed breed that needs an equally strong-willed (but never aggressive) owner.

WHAT good points?

Intelligent, hard working, tireless, affectionate, good with children, loyal, dignified, people friendly, clean, little "doggy" smell.

WHAT to be aware of?

A demanding, dominant dog, not for novices. Large, powerful, and stubborn, needing a great deal of exercise. Strong chase instinct and can be aggressive toward other dogs. Very heavy molt.

WHAT medical problems?

Known problems include hip malformation (dysplasia), cataracts, thyroid problems, bloat, and skin irritations. Responsible breeders will have their stock hip scored and eye tested.

Large dogs

● *Brawn, brains, and beauty in one dog— but not an easy pet.*

English Setter *Other names: Llewellin Setter (working type)*

The beauty and friendly temperament of this most elegant of gundogs have made him more popular today as a show dog and companion than as a worker. Gentler than the other setter breeds, he does indeed make a wonderful companion dog, provided he has plenty of exercise (including free galloping) and plenty of company. He is a sociable creature who is devoted to his family and does not like being left alone for long periods. He is also highly energetic and fun loving. He can be quite demanding, especially as a youngster— not a dog for the inactive nor for house-proud owner who cannot cope with mud, molt, and mischief.

Setters developed in the age of falconry to find and mark the position of game birds, performing the same task later as gundogs. Today they are popular companions, but avoid pups from working bloodlines, which are usually too active for pet homes.

WHAT colors?

The white coat is ticked with color to create a marbled effect known as belton. Color varieties are blue belton (black and white), orange belton (orange and white), lemon belton (lemon and white), and tri-color (blue or liver belton with tan). Puppies are born white, gradually developing color after the first week.

WHAT grooming does the coat need?

The long, silky, slightly wavy coat needs regular brushing and combing to remove dead hair and prevent tangles. It is important to comb out mud, grass seeds, and other debris after country walks. Show dogs are also trimmed to achieve a tidier effect. Neutering can cause coat changes, leading to a thicker, woollier coat that needs more grooming.

HOW suitable are they as family dogs?

English Setters enjoy the company of children and want to share fully in family life. They make wonderful family pets for the right family, provided they have enough space and plenty of exercise. Young children could be a problem as this is a big, bouncy breed, especially in youth, which can all too easily knock over toddlers.

WHAT type of home?

This is essentially an outdoor dog that needs plenty of space and is best suited to a country home. He will adapt to city life if enough exercise is provided but is not recommended for an apartment. He needs a secure yard with a high fence to prevent escapes.

WHAT type of owner?

Only those who enjoy regular long walks in all weather need apply! The English Setter needs a patient owner who will persist with training and can provide plenty of company for this sociable breed. A large, active family with time for exercise, play, and training will suit this dog best.

HOW compatible with other pets?

Generally the English Setter is very good with other pets, although he needs to learn in puppyhood that cats are not for chasing. He may also be rather too bouncy and eager for the safety and comfort of smaller animals.

Character Trait	Poor	Average	Good	Excellent
Attitude to other dogs				
Quietness				
Not destructive				
Protective behavior				
Not likely to stray				
Good with children				
Ease of training				

Original purpose: Gundog (bird dog)
Male height: 25.5–27 in. (65–69 cm)
Female height: 24–25.5 in. (61–65 cm)
Weight: 55–66 lb. (25–30 kg)
Life span: c. 12 years

HOW much exercise?

Setters were bred to run for miles and still need plenty of free running exercise. Puppies must not be overexercised as this will damage young joints. Build up the length of walks gradually from six months onward. This period is the time to teach the recall, as without proper training English Setters tend to suffer from selective deafness when running free.

HOW easy to train?

Individuals vary considerably in trainability: some learn easily, while others can be very stubborn. As a breed, they were not designed for formal obedience, and the best results will be achieved with reward-based training and plenty of patience and repetition. Bullying doesn't achieve good results.

WHAT good points?

Affectionate, gentle, sweet disposition, sociable, adaptable, trustworthy with children, energetic, excellent house companion.

WHAT to be aware of?

Despite his elegant appearance, remember that this is a big, boisterous dog who can be quite clumsy around the house and tends to drool heavily. As a youngster he is very demanding and slow to mature. Without enough exercise and attention, he can be destructive and reckless.

Large dogs

WHAT medical problems?

Hip malformation (dysplasia) and lack of thyroid hormone (hypothyroidism) occur in the breed, and a small percentage of puppies are born deaf. This breed has a very sensitive skin, and skin allergies are not uncommon.

● *That beautiful plumed tail wags constantly—any ornaments placed at tail height are at risk!*

Giant Schnauzer *Other names: Riesenschnauzer*

The biggest of the three Schnauzer breeds, the Giant started out as a Bavarian farm dog, driving cattle and guarding the home, and went on to become a valuable police and army dog. He was not known outside Germany until after World War I but is now popular both as guard and companion. Like most guard breeds, this powerfully built dog is a devoted and versatile companion in the right hands but not an ideal choice for the novice. He is bold, strong willed, and dominant and needs extensive socialization and an experienced handler to ensure that his strong protective instincts do not become misdirected.

This is a high-input breed. He needs physical exercise and mental stimulation, regular grooming and, above all, plenty of interaction with his owner. If properly raised and trained, he makes an admirable family member, calm, deeply loyal, and responsive— as well as a very effective burglar deterrent.

WHAT colors?

Black, or salt and pepper (dark to light gray, the hairs being banded) with dark facial mask. White markings undesirable.

WHAT grooming does the coat need?

The harsh, wiry coat has a dense undercoat that needs weekly brushing with a stiff brush to prevent mats, and the beard, eyebrows, and leg hair need combing thoroughly. The beard usually needs cleaning after every meal! Twice a year, the coat should be hand stripped; clipping is unacceptable for show dogs as it affects coat texture, but pet owners may find it simpler.

HOW suitable are they as family dogs?

This breed can be an excellent family dog in the right hands, devoted to his owners and good with children if raised with them. However, he is not recommended for homes with toddlers, partly because of his size and partly

● *Standard Schnauzers like this are smaller than the Giants—males typically stand around 19 in (48 cm) tall.*

because a powerful and dominant guard breed is never the ideal choice for children too young to be sensible. Be careful with visiting children, as his protective instincts may lead him to misconstrue rough play.

WHAT type of home?

This is a big dog who needs space. If given enough exercise, he can be happy in city or country, but he does need a fair-sized yard that is securely fenced. Tolerant neighbors are also a necessity, as the Giant takes his guard duties seriously and believes in barking at suspicious passersby.

WHAT type of owner?

The Giant Schnauzer needs an active, strong-willed, and experienced owner with time to provide the socialization, stimulation, and company he requires. He is not a dog for novices nor for couch potatoes. He needs company and will not be happy if left alone for long periods. He also needs a job to do.

HOW compatible with other pets?

This is a dominant breed that needs extensive early socialization with other dogs as well as with people. If properly brought up, the Giant Schnauzer is usually good with other pets in the same household; care needs to be taken with strange dogs. Males often tend to be aggressive toward dogs of the same sex.

Character Trait	Poor	Average	Good	Excellent
Attitude to other dogs				
Quietness				
Not destructive				
Protective behavior				
Not likely to stray				
Good with children				
Ease of training				

Place of origin: **Bavaria**

Original purpose: Guard and general farm dog
Male height: 25.5–27.5 in. (65–70 cm)
Female height: 23.5–25.5 in. (60–65 cm)
Weight: 65–90 lb. (29.5–40.9 kg)
Life span: 10–12 years

HOW much exercise?

Energetic and athletic, the Giant Schnauzer needs plenty of exercise—at least one to two hours' brisk walk every day plus free running and active play. Puppies under 12 months should not be over-exercised to prevent damage to growing bones, but they have an inordinate amount of energy that needs to be used up in play rather than in wrecking the home.

HOW easy to train?

Training is essential for this powerful and strong-willed breed. The Giant is highly trainable but needs calm, confident leadership. He can be quite stubborn and is prone to testing his handler. Start early, and make lessons fun and interesting. This intelligent dog learns quickly and is equally quickly bored with dull repetition.

● *Bred as a working dog, the Giant doesn't take well to boring routine.*

WHAT good points?

Intelligent, bold, hardy, versatile, good-natured, reliable, deeply loyal, playful, athletic, energetic, natural guard.

WHAT to be aware of?

Can be very dominant, over-protective, and territorial; socialization essential to prevent aggression. Above-average grooming needs.

WHAT medical problems?

Generally a healthy breed; some concerns over hip malformation (dysplasia), lack of thyroid hormone (hypothyroidism), cataracts, epilepsy, skin problems, and digestive disorders.

Large dogs

Doberman Pinscher

Created in the 1880s by German magistrate Louis Dobermann as his ideal guard dog, the Dobe has become one of the most popular working breeds, serving as police and military dog and also a superb companion in the right hands.

Dobermans achieved fame as the "devil dogs" of the US Marine Corps in World War II and, like other powerful guard breeds, have often had their softer side ignored. They do need proper socialization and training. An untrained or abused Doberman is a liability and can be a genuinely dangerous dog. This is an intelligent, sensitive, and versatile breed that can be trained to a high standard but also strong-minded, dominant, and capable of walking all over an inexperienced handler—not a dog for the novice. He needs activity, both physical and mental, plenty of company and attention, and is not a dog to be left to his own devices.

WHAT colors?

Black and tan, blue and tan, brown and tan, fawn (isabella), and tan. A controversial strain of white, blue-eyed Dobermans has been in existence since the 1970s, but this color is not recognized by the KC.

WHAT grooming does the coat need?

The smooth, short coat needs minimal care; a weekly once-over with a hound glove or stiff bristle brush will keep it in perfect order.

HOW suitable are they as family dogs?

A well-trained Dobe makes a wonderful family dog, but a lot of work needs to be put into training. Affectionate and protective, he enjoys being part of family life. Adolescent Dobes are rowdy and need constant supervision to ensure that they do not play too roughly for children. The breed is not recommended for inexperienced homes with vulnerable young children.

● *Always ready for action—intense, alert, and energetic.*

WHAT type of home?

A big, active dog, the Dobe needs space and is unsuited to apartment life or a home without a secure yard. Whether he lives in the city or country, he should have access to land where he can enjoy some free galloping every day as well as walks.

WHAT type of owner?

Not a breed for novices, nor for couch potatoes, the Dobe needs an experienced, strong-willed, active and patient owner with plenty of time for him. He also needs company and should not be considered if he is to be left alone for long periods. A suitable owner will be able to provide confident leadership and plenty of affection for this strong yet sensitive dog.

HOW compatible with other pets?

Dobes are good with other pets in the same household if raised with them, but be careful about introductions. Strange cats are likely to be regarded as fair game. Socialization with other dogs is essential, and males can often be aggressive with other males.

HOW much exercise?

A great deal. These active, energetic dogs need at least two walks plus an hour's free running

Character Trait	Poor	Average	Good	Excellent
Attitude to other dogs				
Quietness				
Not destructive				
Protective behavior				
Not likely to stray				
Good with children				
Ease of training				

Original purpose: Guard
Male height: 26–28 in. (66–71 cm)
Female height: 24–26 in. (61–66 cm)
Weight: 65–90 lb. (29.5–40.9 kg)
Life span: 10–12 years

a day as well as exercise for their minds in the form of interesting, challenging training.

HOW easy to train?

Dobes are highly intelligent and highly trainable but need calm, confident leadership. They are quick to learn, full of initiative, and often one step ahead of the handler. A confrontational approach will lead to problems. Owners need to earn respect with a firm but sympathetic approach, using reward-based training to motivate the dog to want to learn.

WHAT good points?

Intelligent, loyal, bold, alert, responsive, protective, courageous, versatile, affectionate, playful.

WHAT to be aware of?

A dominant dog that needs responsible ownership. Over-popularity has produced some neurotic and aggressive strains—buy only from responsible breeders who make good temperament a priority.

WHAT medical problems?

Dobes have a regrettably high incidence of inherited disorders, including heart defects, lack of thyroid hormone (hypothyroidism), cataracts, von Willebrand's disease (a bleeding disorder), Wobbler syndrome (spinal malformation leading to swaying gait with eventual paralysis of hindquarters), and hip malformation (dysplasia)—all breeding stock should be hip scored—and a tendency to gastric torsion (bloat).

Large dogs

● An undeserved reputation for savagery owes more to unsuitable owners than to the Doberman's true nature. In the right hands, he is a loving, reliable friend.

Irish Setter *Other names: Red Setter*

His glorious color and elegant, racy lines make the Irish Setter a real eye-catcher, and his zest for life makes him a stimulating companion. Good-tempered as well as good looking, he is a fun-loving, affectionate dog who likes people, is reliable with children and gets along well with other animals—a superb family dog in the right home. He does need plenty of exercise: firm, sensitive training; and an owner with a sense of humor. A big, boisterous dog who can clear a coffee table with one sweep of his tail and bowl visitors over with his exuberant greeting, he has boundless energy that needs to be sensibly directed.

Setters developed in the age of falconry to find and mark the position of gamebirds, performing the same task later as gundogs that accompanied huntsmen. Today they are popular companions, but avoid pups from working bloodlines, which are usually too active for pet homes.

WHAT colors?

The rich red coat, ranging from chestnut to mahogany, is a hallmark of the breed. A touch of white on chest, throat, chin, or toes is acceptable.

WHAT grooming does the coat need?

Moderate. Daily brushing is required to keep the coat healthy, with meticulous combing behind the ears and through the feathering. Ears need to be kept clean, and some owners tie them back in a headband at mealtimes to save sponging dog food out of ear fringes.

HOW suitable are they as family dogs?

A well-raised, well-exercised Irish Setter makes a wonderful dog for active families with older children—small children are at risk of being knocked over by an overboisterous playmate. Families who want a well-behaved dog should probably look elsewhere, as in youth (and this is a slow-maturing breed with an extended puppyhood) Irish Setters can be quite a handful.

WHAT type of home?

Ideally this is a dog for a country home, but he will adapt to city life if enough exercise is provided—and this must include off-leash running in a secure area away from traffic. A securely fenced, fairly large yard is essential. Not suited to apartment life or to small rooms because of his size and high activity level.

WHAT type of owner?

Owners need to be firm, patient, energetic and ready to appreciate an exuberant dog who can be a real clown. Don't consider this breed unless you enjoy long walks and have plenty of time to spend with your dog. Irish Setters suffer if left alone for long periods and can become highly neurotic if denied the company they need.

HOW compatible with other pets?

His friendly nature extends to other animals as well as people, but smaller animals run the risk of being accidentally flattened.

HOW much exercise?

This is a highly energetic dog that needs plenty of daily exercise—long walks, free galloping, and active play such as retrieving games. He is not always easy to control off leash, so training a reliable recall is a high priority. If denied the exercise he needs, he may become destructive and certainly will not be happy.

HOW easy to train?

Irish Setters have a reputation for being hard to train, which is not fully deserved. The

Character Trait	Poor	Average	Good	Excellent
Attitude to other dogs				
Quietness				
Not destructive				
Protective behavior				
Not likely to stray				
Good with children				
Ease of training				

Original purpose: Locating and retrieving game
Male height: 26-28in. (66-71cm)
Female height: 24-26in. (61-66cm)
Weight: 60-70lb. (27.3-31.8kg)
Lifespan: 12-14 years

breed's original function means they are geared to range far ahead of their owners and use their own judgement, so they are not primed for rigid obedience work. However, patience, understanding, and positive reinforcement will result in a well-behaved dog who is eager to please.

● *This dog is an enthusiast— energy on four legs!*

WHAT good points?
Very affectionate, fun-loving, good-tempered, intelligent, kindly, energetic, high spirited, sociable, good with children and other animals.

WHAT to be aware of?
High commitment in terms of time and exercise. Bouncy and exuberant, especially when young. Tendency to separation anxiety. Will bring mud and water into the house. Puppies can be destructive.

Large dogs

WHAT medical problems?
Hip malformation (dysplasia), weakness of the muscle that propels food down the gullet (mega-oesophagus), degeneration of the light receptor cells in the eyes (PRA), epilepsy, skin allergies, and thyroid problems occur in this breed. Tendency to gastric torsion (bloat): safer to feed two or three small meals during the day rather than one big one.

Akita *Other names: Japanese Akita, Japanese Akita-Inu, Akita Inu, Great Japanese Dog*

The largest of Japan's native breeds, the powerful, handsome, and dignified Akita is a truly impressive dog but not one for the novice. He is a dog of strong character and a natural guard, who needs a close relationship with his owner and confident handling as well as plenty of socialization to prevent his natural dominance and aloofness from turning to aggression. In the right hands, he is a wonderful dog, intelligent, loyal, and versatile.

Originating at least 350 years ago as a hunting dog in the Akita prefecture, the Akita was introduced to the US after World War I and reached the UK in the early 1980s. Japanese and American bloodlines (both of which occur in the UK) diverged so much that they are now considered separate breeds in Europe. From 2006 the Kennel Club terms the bigger, heavier American-style dog the "Akita" and the Japanese dog the "Japanese Akita-Inu."

WHAT colors?

Any color, including white, red, black, silvery gray, pinto (any color and white) and brindle, with or without a dark mask.

WHAT grooming does the coat need?

The thick, coarse coat needs thorough grooming at least twice a week, using a firm bristle brush, with daily attention during the heavy twice-yearly molt.

HOW suitable are they as family dogs?

In experienced hands, the Akita can be a much-loved family member, but such a dominant and powerful dog is not an ideal choice around children. He can be very good with youngsters from his own family, but he has a low tolerance for mistreatment and may not care for other people's children. Many individual Akitas may be trustworthy, but it is not worth taking risks.

WHAT type of home?

The Akita is suitable for either a city or a country home. He is too big to be accommodated comfortably in an apartment, and needs a yard with a high fence, for he is a great jumper. His hunting origins mean he must be closely supervised around livestock.

WHAT type of owner?

Only owners with experience of large, dominant breeds should consider this beautiful but challenging dog. Potential owners should have plenty of time for a dog who needs sensible socialization and training, well-supervised exercise and a great deal of company—bored Akitas tend to turn to destruction to pass the time.

HOW compatible with other pets?

Be very careful. Akitas are highly dominant and can be aggressive toward other dogs. They will often live peacefully with a dog of the opposite sex, but same-sex rivalry is common. Cats and other small pets should not be considered safe in their vicinity.

HOW much exercise?

The Akita will enjoy as much exercise as you care to give—think in terms of a minimum of two half-hour walks a day, with no upper limit. His strong hunting instinct means that he should not be exercised off leash anywhere he might come across livestock, while owners should also be conscious of other dogs in the vicinity. If he is challenged by another dog he comes across, there is a strong risk that he will react aggressively.

Character Trait	Poor	Average	Good	Excellent
Attitude to other dogs				
Quietness				
Not destructive				
Protective behavior				
Not likely to stray				
Good with children				
Ease of training				

Original purpose: Hunting
Male height: 25–28 in. (63.5–71 cm)
Female height: 23–26 in. (58.5–66 cm)
Weight: 80–130 lb. (36–59 kg)
Life span: 10–14 years

HOW easy to train?

These highly dominant and strong-minded dogs are not particularly easy to train. Handlers need to be just as strong minded and very patient. The Akita will not be bullied and needs to be motivated to cooperate by a firm but kind reward-based approach with plenty of variety to keep his interest going. Training should start early while he is still a puppy and open to new ideas. Early socialization in puppy classes is strongly recommended. An unsocialized Akita is a liability!

WHAT good points?

Dignified, courageous, loyal, calm, intelligent, protective, adaptable, people oriented, loving companion.

WHAT to be aware of?

Large dogs

A challenging breed: socialization, training, and discipline essential. Can be very destructive if bored.

WHAT medical problems?

Inherited disorders include eye problems (progressive retinal atrophy), inward-turning eyelids (entropion), hip malformation (dysplasia), kneecap dislocation (patellar luxation), autoimmune disease, and skin disorders. All breeding stock should be hip scored and have current eye certificates.

● This majestic dog is revered as a national monument in Japan, where he is described as "tender in heart and mighty in strength."

Neapolitan Mastiff *Other names: Mastino Napolitano*

Magnificent or grotesque, depending upon the eye of the beholder, this Italian giant certainly makes an impact. This is a truly massive dog, with a forbidding appearance augmented by his heavy jowls and loose-fitting skin. He was bred as a guard and has a strong protective drive—a formidable burglar deterrent. Devoted to his owners, calm, responsive, and not normally aggressive unless provoked, the Neapolitan is nonetheless a breed for only confident, experienced owners. He needs extensive socialization, training and firm leadership, otherwise he can be overprotective to the point of danger.

Said to descend from Roman fighting dogs, the Neapolitan Mastiff was almost extinct by the 1940s and owes its modern survival to the painter Piero Scanziani, who sought out surviving specimens to preserve the breed. Initially known only in Italy, it reached the UK and US in the 1970s and has become increasingly popular over the last decade.

WHAT colors?
Most commonly blue (gray) or black, but also brown (fawn to mahogany; may be brindled). Small white star on chest and white toes permissible.

WHAT grooming does the coat need?
Minimal. The short coat needs only an occasional grooming with a hound glove to remove dead hair, with extra attention during the twice-yearly molt.

• *A massive dog, bred to defend his owners and their property.*

HOW suitable are they as family dogs?
Although he may fit into the lifestyle of some families, the Neapolitan is not recommended as a family dog. He is devoted to his household and generally good with children but too powerful to be left unsupervised with them. His sheer size makes it easy for him to hurt a child by accident or in play, he is not a dog whom children can walk. He can be very possessive of toys or food bowls, and in most homes he will have to be largely an outdoor dog.

WHAT type of home?
Big dogs need space, and the Neapolitan is best housed outside in a reasonably sized yard with a large, dry, comfortable kennel, and access to shade to prevent overheating. As an indoor dog his size creates problems, as does his copious drooling. Although adults spend a lot of time lying around, puppies are active, curious, and clumsy—not to be allowed near breakables.

WHAT type of owner?
This breed is for only highly committed and experienced owners who can manage a dominant dog that requires considerable socialization and training, needs his devotion to be fully reciprocated, and must have his protective drive properly channeled. Not for the fastidious: be prepared to put up with messy eating, slobbering, snoring, and flatulence.

HOW compatible with other pets?
Be careful. As adults, Neapolitans are often aggressive with dogs of the same sex, and early socialization with strange dogs is essential. They are generally good and tolerant with noncanine pets

Character Trait	Poor	Average	Good	Excellent
Attitude to other dogs	■			
Quietness		■		
Not destructive			■	
Protective behavior				■
Not likely to stray			■	
Good with children			■	
Ease of training		■		

Original purpose: Guard and fighting dog
Male height: 26–31 in. (66–79 cm)
Female height: 24–29 in. (61–73.5 cm)
Weight: 110–154 lb. (50–70 kg)
Life span: 8–10 years

in the same household if raised with them but will usually chase trespassers on their territory.

HOW much exercise?

Moderate. These heavy dogs have limited stamina and overheat easily but will benefit from regular walks (say half an hour twice a day)—lying around all day may suit their tastes but will not do them any good. Swimming is a great form of exercise that does not strain the joints. Puppies under a year old must have limited exercise to avoid damage to growing bones.

HOW easy to train?

Difficult. These strong-willed, stubborn dogs need firm leadership from puppyhood. They are intelligent but not programmed for instant obedience. Training takes patience, determination, and understanding. However, such a powerful animal must be under control at all times, and steady, consistent training will produce a well-mannered dog.

WHAT good points?

Devoted, loyal, protective, vigilant, intelligent, steady, peaceful.

WHAT to be aware of?

Tendency to be aggressive with other dogs. Messy and a champion drooler. Highly developed guard instincts mean this dog is a heavy responsibility and needs supervision.

Large dogs

WHAT medical problems?

Neapolitans are prone to hip malformation (dysplasia), gastric torsion (bloat), panosteitis ("growing pains" between four and 18 months of age), lack of thyroid hormone, eyelid disorders, and "cherry eye" (prolapsed gland in the third eyelid, requiring surgery).

Afghan Hound *Other names: Tazi, Baluchi Hound*

One of the most glamorous breeds, the Afghan Hound looks like a fashion accessory but is a demanding pet with all the needs of a big hairy hound. He needs a lot of exercise and time-consuming grooming as well as sensible discipline to control his chasing instincts. Independent, aloof, and difficult to train, the Afghan is not a dog for everyone. In the right home, however, he is a sensitive, playful companion, devoted to family and friends but regarding himself as an equal, not a subordinate. He has a great sense of fun and can be a real clown—not a dog for obedience enthusiasts!

This elegant sight-hound developed in Afghanistan to hunt large game such as antelope and leopard. In the West, where he arrived in the late 19th century, breeding for the show ring has developed a much heavier coat, but the Afghan remains a tough, powerful hunting dog.

WHAT colors?
All colors, including black, red, gold, blue, brindle, cream, and black and tan, with or without a black mask or "domino" lighter mask. White markings are frowned upon in the show ring.

WHAT grooming does the coat need?
The Afghan hound is noted for its thick coat of long silky hair, but that coat requires hours of grooming each week to maintain its beautiful appearance. A daily thorough brushing should be backed up by a thorough weekly grooming.

HOW suitable are they as family dogs?
For the suitable family, the Afghan can be a valued family member, but this is not a breed to take on lightly. Afghans are good with considerate children, though care will have to be taken with toddlers, who can easily be bowled over by a big, boisterous hound. Adolescent Afghans can be a very demanding handful and may be a problem in a busy family without the time and patience.

WHAT type of home?
Although the Afghan needs access to space for exercise, he can adapt to apartment life provided he has daily long walks. He will, however, appreciate a reasonably sized yard, which must be securely fenced. In some ways he may be more safely kept as a city dog. Country dwellers will need to be very careful to prevent livestock chasing, as the Afghan's chase instinct is very strong and it takes a great deal of patience to condition him to obey a recall.

WHAT type of owner?
Afghan owners need to appreciate a dog of independent character and must be prepared to devote considerable time and attention to the dog every day, including walks in all weather. Plenty of patience is needed to instill the basic training that will make this dog a treasured member of the family. An untrained, underexercised Afghan is a nightmare to live with.

HOW compatible with other pets?
Normally the Afghan gets along well with other dogs, and if brought up with other household pets, the Afghan will consider them part of the family. However, his high prey drive means that he should never be trusted not to chase other people's pets or livestock.

HOW much exercise?
Afghans need a great deal of exercise—at least two long walks a day plus the opportunity for off-lead galloping. However, it is essential that free exercise takes

Character Trait	Poor	Average	Good	Excellent
Attitude to other dogs		●		
Quietness	●			
Not destructive			●	
Protective behavior			●	
Not likely to stray	●			
Good with children			●	
Ease of training	●			

Original purpose: Coursing hare and gazelle
Male height: 27–29 in. (68.5–73.5 cm)
Female height: 25–27 in. (63.5–68.5 cm)
Weight: 50–60 lb. (23-27 kg)
Life span: 12–14 years, often more

place only in safe areas, as most Afghans tend to keep running and do not respond to a recall.

HOW easy to train?

Afghans score very low on trainability, which means that training is difficult but not impossible. Firm but kindly and consistent training will achieve a degree of cooperation. Harshness and lack of patience will produce a resolute stubborn lack of response.

WHAT good points?

Proud, brave, affectionate, faithful and protective toward owner, gentle and sensitive, playful, easygoing.

WHAT to be aware of?

A very demanding breed. Puppies can be slow to housebreak, adolescents may be obtrusive and very hard to control, and a bored Afghan can be quite destructive. Early socialization is essential, as youngsters left to their own devices can become quite wild.

Large dogs

WHAT medical problems?

Afghans are generally a healthy breed, although hip deformity (dysplasia), juvenile cataracts, lack of thyroid hormone (hypothyroidism), and enzyme deficiencies have been reported. The breed is sometimes prone to tail injuries and is sensitive to anesthesia.

Newfoundland

Majestic in appearance, sweet-tempered and with an admirable record of saving human lives, the Newfoundland has a well-deserved reputation as a loyal companion. The breed originated in Newfoundland as draft animals and water dogs who carried fishing nets and ships' lines ashore and rescued men and equipment which fell overboard. Modern Newfies also adore water and still serve as water rescue dogs. This is a kindly dog: intelligent, reliable and trustworthy with children; and also very adaptable to various lifestyles.

However, he is not a dog to take on lightly. He takes up a lot of space and is expensive to feed. Like any big, active dog, he needs training or he can become a liability. He is not one for the houseproud, as he is a champion drooler and sheds hair everywhere. His love of water extends to carrying a great deal indoors on his coat and feet.

WHAT colors?

Black or brown (chocolate or bronze), with or without a splash of white on chest, toes, and tail-tip. Landseer dogs (regarded as a separate breed in Europe) are white with black markings, ideally comprising a black head with narrow white blaze, saddle, rump, and upper tail.

WHAT grooming does the coat need?

The dense coat needs regular brushing and combing, at least twice weekly, with extra attention when molting. It is important to groom right down to the skin. Combing the topcoat only will look good on the surface but will leave dead hair clogging the undercoat and eventually forming mats.

HOW suitable are they as family dogs?

This is a wonderful family dog for families who have the space and

● *The gentle giant of the canine world, the Newfoundland is happiest in the heart of his family.*

time. The Newfoundland is gentle, loving, and exceptionally good with children if raised with them. Supervision is important to ensure that children do not take advantage of his good nature. Never allow youngsters to attempt to ride their giant friend, as this may injure his back.

WHAT type of home?

This giant breed is not suited for apartment living, as he needs lots of room and a large, fenced yard. Newfoundland owners need a big house to accommodate this giant breed. His heavy coat makes the Newfoundland susceptible to overheating, so he will not be comfortable in a home where the heat is always turned up high.

WHAT type of owner?

This is a breed for people who expect to treat their dog as part of the family and can give him the time and attention he needs. He loves to be part of family activities and is ideal for people with young children who want a trustworthy family dog and have the space for a giant breed. Owners do need to be capable of handling and training a physically powerful dog.

HOW compatible with other pets?

Most Newfoundlands get along well with other animals if raised with them and sensibly socialized. They are big dogs, however, so

Character Trait	Poor	Average	Good	Excellent
Attitude to other dogs				
Quietness				
Not destructive				
Protective behavior				
Not likely to stray				
Good with children				
Ease of training				

Original purpose: Draft dog, water dog
Male height: 27–29 in. (68.5–73.5 cm)
Female height: 25–27 in. (63.5–68.5 cm)
Weight: 110–150 lb. (50–68 kg)
Life span: 8–10 years

care needs to be taken to protect small pets from being trodden on.

HOW much exercise?

Moderate. Newfoundlands are not hyperactive, but they do need regular exercise to keep fit—at least half an hour a day. Puppies under 12 months should not be over-exercised as this can cause joint problems in later life. Adults will enjoy activities such as swimming and carting as well as being happy to play with children and other dogs.

HOW easy to train?

The Newfoundland is willing to please and responds well to training. This needs to start early so that by the time he achieves his full size, he is fully under control. Despite his size, he is a sensitive dog who responds better to encouragement than to heavy-handed tactics.

WHAT good points?

Gentle, docile, sweet natured, reliable, intelligent, responsive, adaptable, devoted to his family, companionable.

WHAT to be aware of?

Demanding in terms of upkeep; does not take well to being left alone; not for the house proud; susceptible to overheating.

WHAT medical problems?

Hip and elbow malformation (dysplasia) and other joint problems, heart disease, infections of the lip fold, eyelid disorders.

Large dogs

 The Landseer takes its name from animal painter Sir Edwin Landseer, who portrayed this color.

Mastiff *Other names: English Mastiff*

Descended from ferocious guard and fighting dogs, the modern Mastiff is a gentle giant. Not many homes have room for a Mastiff: this powerfully built dog is among the heaviest of all dog breeds. Calm, dignified, and loyal, he is gentle with his own family but retains all the protective instincts of his ancestors. He is a sensitive dog who just loves to please and wants to be with his owner all the time, so he is not suited for the role of outside guard dog—in fact, within his own family he is a big softy. However, because of his size, careful socialization and training are essential to ensure that he is not aggressive toward people or other dogs.

Breed historians trace the Mastiff back to ancient times, but the word "mastiff" in old texts referred to any large dog. The modern breed probably descends from medieval heavy hounds.

WHAT colors?
Apricot-fawn, silver-fawn, fawn, or dark fawn-brindle. Muzzle, ears, and nose black with black around orbits and extending upward between them

WHAT grooming does the coat need?
The short, close coat is low maintenance, needing only a weekly brushing to remove dead hairs.

HOW suitable are they as family dogs?
The Mastiff's calm, loving nature makes him a suitable companion for families who can accommodate a giant breed. He is patient and long-suffering with children, but his size should always be borne in mind. He should not be left unsupervised with youngsters, as he can easily knock over toddlers. A blow from his tail is painful even to an adult.

WHAT type of home?
Mastiffs need space—a large house with a fenced yard, preferably in the country. This is not an ideal urban dog and totally unsuitable for apartments or small houses.

WHAT type of owner?
Owners of this breed should be experienced, physically strong, and with both space and time enough to keep a Mastiff happy. Mastiffs are not for busy people, for the house proud (Mastiffs unequivocally mean mess), or for those who specifically want a guard dog, an unsuitable role for an animal who needs to be a family dog.

HOW compatible with other pets?
Mastiffs are naturally good-natured and will get along well with other pets if raised with them. Because of their size and strong protective instincts, early socialization with strange dogs is essential. Males especially can tend to be aggressive with other males if not properly trained.

HOW much exercise?
Mastiffs are often quite happy to lead a sedentary life, but they do need moderate exercise—at least half an hour's walk daily.

A fit adult will enjoy walking for miles, but avoid exercise in the heat. This breed overheats easily. Puppies under two years must not be overexercised, which is likely to cause damage to growing bones.

HOW easy to train?
Sensitive but stubborn, the Mastiff is not the easiest breed to train. With a dog this size, training is essential.

Character Trait	Poor	Average	Good	Excellent
Attitude to other dogs				
Quietness				
Not destructive				
Protective behavior				
Not likely to stray				
Good with children				
Ease of training				

Original purpose: Guarding, hunting
Male height: 27.5–30 in. (70–76 cm)
Female height: 27.5–30 in. (70–76 cm)
Weight: 175–190 lb. (79–86 kg)
Life span: 8–10 years

Keep training sessions short, frequent, and above all fun. Pile on the praise when he does right, and keep any possible disappointment low key when he doesn't to avoid negative associations.

WHAT good points?

Affectionate, loyal, protective, dignified, quiet, clean, undemanding, good-natured, intelligent, not excitable.

WHAT to be aware of?

High running costs (food, veterinary bills, and so on). Puppies need special diet designed for giant breeds to ensure growth at the correct rate without stress to bones and joints. Adults need soft bedding to prevent callused elbows. Not a dog for the fastidious: his snoring, drooling, and tendency to break wind are also on

a giant scale. Socialization essential to prevent aggression.

WHAT medical problems?

Hip malformation (dysplasia) and joint problems, tendency to gastric torsion (bloat), some eye defects, heart problems, lack of thyroid hormone (hypothyroidism), arthritis. Like other giant breeds, short life expectancy.

Large dogs

● *Mastiffs should be fit and athletic like this, not slow, lumbering fatties.*

Greyhound

The ultimate canine athlete, the Greyhound is the fastest of all dogs, with a top speed of 45 mph 72 km/h). He is famous worldwide as a racer and still used in some countries for coursing game. However, his gentle, affectionate, and surprisingly adaptable nature also makes him a wonderful companion and family dog. Much as he loves to run, he actually needs less exercise than many sporting breeds and is content to spend much of the day curled on the sofa. Ex-racing greyhounds, usually retired at three to five years old and always available for rehoming, make excellent house pets who appreciate the comforts of home life.

Long-legged hounds of Greyhound type have been valued since Old Testament times. In medieval and Renaissance Europe they were the favorites of the aristocracy, in the 20th century the heroes of popular sport on the racetrack, and throughout the ages, loving companions.

WHAT colors?

Black, white, red, blue, fawn, fallow (pale reddish yellow), brindle, or any of these shades broken by white.

WHAT grooming does the coat need?

Greyhounds are naturally clean dogs, and the fine, close coat requires minimal grooming. A daily rubdown with a hound glove to remove dead hairs will be appreciated and keep the coat in perfect condition.

HOW suitable are they as family dogs?

The average Greyhound's ideal lifestyle is to be a member of a loving family with a spare sofa and a good heating system. These gentle, sensitive dogs want to please, will adapt to family routine, and are generally very good with children. As puppies they can be boisterous and mischievous. Families with young children may prefer to avoid this stage and adopt a retired racer.

WHAT type of home?

This is an ideal country dog, but he will live happily in a city, even in an apartment, as long as he has adequate exercise and adequate company. He does need access to a park or similar secure area where he can safely enjoy an off-leash gallop.

WHAT type of owner?

A gentle, sensitive owner who will appreciate the Greyhound's undemanding companionship and who is happy with a routine of short twice-daily walks. Greyhounds like company, so owners who are regularly out for more than a couple of hours might do well to consider having two dogs—little more trouble than one.

HOW compatible with other pets?

Greyhounds are generally friendly with other dogs. However, they are bred to chase, so care needs to be taken with cats and other small pets (including small dogs). Organizations that rehome ex-racers will advise whether individual dogs are suitable to house with other pets.

HOW much exercise?

Moderate. Given two 20-minute walks a day and the opportunity to run free, most Greyhounds are

Character Trait	Poor	Average	Good	Excellent
Attitude to other dogs			●	
Quietness				●
Not destructive			●	
Protective behavior	●			
Not likely to stray		●		
Good with children			●	
Ease of training		●		

Original purpose: Hunting, racing
Male height: 27–29 in. (68.5–73.5 cm)
Female height: 26–28 in. (66–71 cm)
Weight: 60–70 lb. (27–32 kg)
Life span: 10–13 years

● In the Middle Ages Greyhound ownership was reserved for the nobility. We are more fortunate today!

happy to spend the rest of the day relaxing—although they will enjoy longer outings if these are offered. Owners need to be aware of the Greyhound's chase instinct and never trust them off leash in the vicinity of livestock—they can reach top speed in two strides, faster than owners' reaction time.

HOW easy to train?

Moderate again. Greyhounds have a reputation for low intelligence, which is undeserved. Few members of this breed are offered the opportunity to use their brains. They are not naturals for obedience work but are willing to please and ready to learn. Teaching a reliable recall is essential with a dog with such a

strong chase instinct, although it is not necessarily easy.

WHAT good points?

Easygoing, gentle, affectionate, loving, mild mannered, calm, quiet, dignified, polite with people and other dogs.

WHAT to be aware of?

With his thin coat and low body fat, the Greyhound really feels the cold, and needs a coat in cold weather. His desire to chase may be a problem, and most Greyhounds will kill small animals if they catch them.

Large dogs

WHAT medical problems?

Greyhounds are generally a healthy breed, although eye problems (progressive retinal atrophy and lens dislocation) have been reported. They are sensitive to anesthetics and may be vulnerable to gastric torsion (bloat). Racers are prone to fractures of the leg and foot bones.

Great Pyrenees *Other names: Pyrenean Mountain Dog*

For centuries this magnificent white giant guarded flocks against wolves and other predators in the Pyrenees of France. In the 17th century his imposing appearance attracted the attention of French nobility, and he became known as "the Royal Dog of France." In modern times he became mainly a companion breed, but he retains his working instincts and today is employed as a livestock protector by ranchers and farmers all around the world.

As a companion, the Great Pyrenees is built on too large a scale for the average home. His dominant nature and strong guarding instinct make him unsuitable for any but experienced owners. He needs space and a job to do, as well as ongoing socialization, to manage his protective drive. In responsible hands, he is a calm, confident, sensible presence, devoted to his family, affectionate and gentle with children, and a superb home guard.

WHAT colors?
White, or mainly white with wolf gray, badger, or pale yellow markings on head, ears, or base of tail; a few markings permissible on body.

WHAT grooming does the coat need?
The dense, weatherproof coat needs brushing down to the skin at least twice a week, taking care not to strip out too much undercoat. Daily grooming is essential during the twice-yearly heavy molt. If neglected, the coat mats—and smells quite strongly. Clipping the fur short is not advisable as the coat serves as insulation against both heat and cold.

HOW suitable are they as family dogs?
Great Pyrenees are good family dogs as long as their needs for space, employment, and confident leadership are met. They have a natural affinity with children, although they are simply too big for the comfort and safety of the

very young. Supervision is needed to ensure that they are not over-protective, putting family friends and visitors at risk.

WHAT type of home?
The ideal home for a Great Pyrenees is a farm where he can guard livestock. He is better housed in the country. In the city, he needs a large, secure yard, and is certainly not suitable for an apartment. He is essentially an outdoor dog who is happy with a kennel by the house, if he has plenty of company. He enjoys indoor visits but is too big to be comfortable in the average home and may overheat if kept permanently in the house.

WHAT type of owner?
The Great Pyrenees needs an experienced owner who is both physically strong and able to take on the role of leader. Owners must have the space to accommodate a giant breed and plenty of time for socialization, training, exercise, and grooming. The ideal owner will also have to be able to provide employment for a working dog—a flock of sheep is recommended!

HOW compatible with other pets?
Other pets in the household will be regarded as part of the Great Pyrenees's family, and his protective instincts will come to the fore. He is strongly territorial and will chase off strange dogs and cats on his property. Early socialization is essential to prevent aggression toward other dogs.

HOW much exercise?
Laid-back to the point of lethargy, adult Great Pyrenees don't demand a great deal of exercise, but they

Character Trait	Poor	Average	Good	Excellent
Attitude to other dogs				
Quietness				
Not destructive				
Protective behavior				
Not likely to stray				
Good with children				
Ease of training				

Original purpose: Livestock protection
Male height: 27–32 in. (68.5–81 cm)
Female height: 25–29 in. (63.5–73.5 cm)
Weight: minimum 85–119 lb. (38.6–54.1 kg)
Life span: 10–12 years

certainly should be exercised daily. Long walks will do them good, and they can take as much exercise at their ambling pace as their owner wishes—indeed many enjoy backpacking and hiking. Puppies under 12 months need restricted exercise to prevent damage to growing bones.

● Loyal but demanding, the Great Pyrenees deserves respect.

HOW easy to train?

Dominant, independent and stubborn, the Great Pyrenees is not the easiest breed to train. His size and strength make it essential that he is under his owner's control. Start early and establish firm but kindly leadership to win his respect—harsh or heavy-handed handling will lead to recalcitrance. This breed requires a patient, consistent approach.

Large dogs

WHAT good points?

Dignified, loyal, affectionate, protective, confident, intelligent.

WHAT to be aware of?

Barking and territorial aggression if bored. Guard instincts need careful handling. Intermale aggression likely.

WHAT medical problems?

May suffer from hip and elbow malformation (dysplasia), kneecap dislocation (patellar luxation), spinal problems, cataracts, inward-turning eyelids (entropion), and bleeding disorders.

Saint Bernard *Other names: Saint Bernhardshund, Alpine Mastiff*

Saint Bernards take their name from Saint Bernard's Hospice in the Swiss Alps, where these powerful dogs have been kept since the 17th century and became famous for rescuing lost travelers and avalanche victims. Today the Saint is a devoted companion, good-natured, child-loving, and highly protective. However, his sheer size can be a problem. This massive dog simply will not fit into many homes and lifestyles.

He is costly to feed, very messy (a heavy molter and champion drooler), and like any giant breed, needs plenty of socialization and training. The 1992 hit film *Beethoven*, starring a cute St Bernard, tempted many people to buy a Saint without considering the commitment needed. The breed deserves better.

Saints come in two coat varieties, rough and smooth. The original dogs were all smooth coats; rough coats were developed in the 19th century, when a Newfoundland outcross was introduced to combat inbreeding.

WHAT colors?
Basically a red and white dog. The red ranges through orange, mahogany-brindle and red-brindle; white patches include muzzle, facial blaze, collar, chest, forelegs, feet, and tail tip; black shadings on face and ears.

WHAT grooming does the coat need?
Smooths need only a weekly brushing, but roughs need grooming daily, combing right down to the skin. Combing only the topcoat may look good on the surface, but leaves dead hair clogging the undercoat and forming mats. This breed sheds heavily, and extra work will be required during the molt.

HOW suitable are they as family dogs?
For those who have the space and time, this gentle dog makes an excellent family dog. The Saint is gentle, loving, and famously good with children. For his size, he is amazingly careful with the little ones. He loves to be part of family activities (or inactivity–he is quite happy to doze at his owner's feet), and can become distressed and destructive if left to his own devices.

WHAT type of home?
This giant breed is happiest provided with plenty of room and a large fenced yard. They can be kenneled out-doors, but are much happier living as one of the family. Relatively inactive indoors, they can adapt to apartment life if enough exercise is provided. They are susceptible to overheating so will not be comfortable in a home where the heating is always turned up high.

WHAT type of owner?
This is a breed for people who expect to treat their dog as part of the family and can give him the time and attention he needs. He loves to be part of family activities and is ideal for people with young children who want a trustworthy family dog and have the space for a giant breed. Owners do need to be capable of handling and training a physically powerful dog.

HOW compatible with other pets?
In general, Saint Bernards are good with other dogs if sensibly socialized in puppyhood and also with cats if raised with them. They are big dogs, however, so care needs to be taken to protect small pets (including smaller dogs) from being trodden on.

Character Trait	Poor	Average	Good	Excellent
Attitude to other dogs			■	
Quietness		■		
Not destructive		■		
Protective behavior				■
Not likely to stray			■	
Good with children				■
Ease of training		■		

*Place of origin: **Switzerland***

Original purpose: Guard and mountain rescue
Male height: 28–36 in. (71–91 cm)
Female height: 26–36 in. (66–91 cm)
Weight: 110–200 lb. (50–91 kg)
Life span: c. 9 years

HOW much exercise?

The Saint's exercise needs are moderate for his size: an adult should walk a couple of miles a day. However, he can enjoy longer walks and off-leash exercise. This breed overheats easily and should not be exercised in hot or humid weather. Puppies under two years should be limited to short walks and play sessions to prevent joint problems in later life.

HOW easy to train?

Moderate. The Saint is willing to please but can be slow to respond—not a dog for obedience enthusiasts. With a dog of this size, training needs to start early and to be patient and consistent so that by the time he achieves his full growth, he is fully under control.

WHAT good points?

Large dogs

Steady, kindly, intelligent, courageous, trust-worthy, protective, notably good with children, affectionate, loyal.

WHAT to be aware of?

Expensive upkeep; does not take well to being left alone; not for the house proud; susceptible to overheating.

WHAT medical problems?

This breed has some major health concerns, including joint problems (hip and elbow dysplasia), inturned eyelids (entropion), and heart defects. Buy only from reputable breeders who screen all breeding stock.

● *The quintessential "gentle giant."*

213

Scottish Deerhound *Other names: Deerhound*

This big, rough-coated grayhound was bred to hunt red deer, a large species well able to defend itself, so he developed great power as well as speed and stamina. Today he is valued instead as a gentle and elegant companion. He is a calm, dignified dog, naturally well mannered—once past the puppy stage—and devoted to his owners. At free gallop he is poetry in motion, and the opportunity to run is essential for his well-being. Between walks he is a restful, even lazy, creature. Reserved but friendly, he makes a hopeless guard dog, though his size may deter intruders who don't know the breed!

Deerhounds were treasured by medieval Scottish chieftains and may even date back to the great Celtic hounds of pre-Roman times. They almost died out in the 18th century with the breakdown of the Scottish clans. Just in time, the Victorian love of romantic history came to their rescue.

WHAT colors?
Dark blue-gray, darker or lighter gray, brindle, yellow, sandy red, red fawn with black points. White chest, toes, and tail tip permissible.

WHAT grooming does the coat need?
This is a moderately easy-care coat, requiring only regular brushing with slicker brush and metal comb to prevent tangles and strip out dead hair. Comb facial hair and underparts, where a slicker brush may be too rough.

HOW suitable are they as family dogs?
This is a sweet-natured dog who is good with children but generally too large and too boisterous in puppyhood to be recommended to families with toddlers. Parents of young children should also consider whether they can commit themselves to the exercise needs of a powerful dog with strong chasing instincts.

WHAT type of home?
Deerhounds need space and are simply too big for apartment living. They need a house with a reasonably large yard and a high fence—this breed can easily jump a 6-foot (2-m) fence. They will also need access to areas where they can run free without the risk of chasing livestock or running into traffic.

WHAT type of owner?
Gentle dogs need gentle owners. This is not a breed that can cope with harsh handling. Deerhound owners should be patient, easygoing, and geared to a sighthound's need to run and urge to chase. They should enjoy long walks and be prepared to sacrifice the sofa to their pet's comfort.

HOW compatible with other pets?
The nonaggressive Scottish Deerhound is friendly toward other dogs, particularly other sighthounds. He will generally get along well with cats within his own household. His strong chase instinct is likely to come into play with strange cats and other small animals, including small dogs, so be careful to keep a watchful eye on him.

HOW much exercise?
Daily long walks and free galloping are essential, but it is vital to put in work on training before trusting any sighthound off leash. Many owners find that lure coursing, organized by regional clubs, is a great way of satisfying the Scottish Deerhound's need to run. Puppies under a year old should have restricted exercise to prevent damage to growing bones.

Character Trait	Poor	Average	Good	Excellent
Attitude to other dogs			■	
Quietness			■	
Not destructive		■		
Protective behavior	■			
Not likely to stray	■			
Good with children			■	
Ease of training		■		

Original purpose: Coursing deer
Male height: 30–32 in. (76–81 cm)
Female height: 28–30 in. (71–76 cm)
Weight: 75–100 lb. (34.1–45.5 kg)
Life span: 7–9 years

HOW easy to train?

The Scottish Deerhound is considered the most trainable of the sighthound breeds, which is not to say that he would be a suitable choice for competitive obedience. He is eager to please and quick to learn but easily distracted. Early socialization is important to bring out the best in him, and training needs to be gentle, calm, and consistent.

WHAT good points?

Gentle, friendly, docile, sweet tempered, affectionate, dignified, sensitive, tractable, keen, alert, nonaggressive.

WHAT to be aware of?

Can be timid if not properly socialized. Strong chase instinct: needs considerable training to be trustworthy off leash and should never be allowed to run near livestock.

WHAT medical problems?

Deerhounds are generally healthy, with bloat (gastric torsion) being one of the main causes of death. All breeding stock should be tested for liver shunt (an inherited defect whereby the liver does not get a proper blood supply). Hip dysplasia, eye problems, bone cancer, and heart disease also occur in this breed.

Large dogs

● *The novelist Sir Walter Scott, who owned famous deerhound Maida, described the breed as "the most perfect creature of Heaven"—a view with which many modern owners heartily concur.*

Great Dane *Other names: Deutsche Dogge, German Mastiff*

A giant breed of great nobility and elegance, the Dane is nicknamed "the Apollo of dogs." His ancestors were fierce boarhounds. For generations now he has been bred for the role of companion with a gentle, kindly temperament. This is a dog who conjures up images of baronial halls. Prospective owners need space on a fairly baronial scale to accommodate a dog who, when full grown, may weigh as much as a man.

Owners also need considerable commitment to socialization, training and companionship—such huge dogs need teaching and supervision to fit in with modern life. They are sociable creatures who will not thrive without company.

Despite the name, the Great Dane is a German, not a Danish, breed. It was in 18th- and 19th-century Germany that giant hunting mastiffs were polished into the breed we know today. Indeed, since 1876 he has been Germany's national dog.

WHAT colors?

Fawn, brindle, black, blue, or harlequin (white, irregularly patched with black or blue). Some countries also accept mantled, or Boston, Danes (black or blue with white shirt front and socks). Merle Danes (typically gray or fawn with dark marbling) occur but are not recognized by any Kennel Club.

WHAT grooming does the coat need?

The smooth, short-haired coat is easy care, needing only regular brushing with a firm bristle brush or hound glove to remove any accumulation of dead hairs.

HOW suitable are they as family dogs?

Danes are happy with family life if treated with consideration, but not all families will be happy with a Dane. They are good with children if raised with them, but small children are easily knocked over or trodden on. Youngsters (up to about three years old) are likely to be a hazard in households with young children or frail elderly people as they are boisterous and clumsy.

WHAT type of home?

This giant breed needs plenty of space and a large, fenced yard. Danes don't belong in small apartments or in houses with small, cluttered rooms.

WHAT type of owner?

Dane owners should be experienced and physically strong to cope with a powerful, strong-willed, and sometimes stubborn dog. They must have time to spend with him. Danes are surprisingly sensitive and need kind, stable, confident handling. They are not ideal for the house proud, as they molt and slobber—and accidental breakages tend to follow in their wake.

HOW compatible with other pets?

With proper socialization, Danes are generally good with other animals. However, because they are so big they can accidentally injure smaller animals simply by stepping on them. Although adults are generally gentle, young Danes don't know their own strength and may damage smaller dogs in play.

HOW much exercise?

Danes need a moderate amount of exercise, at least one long walk a day and the opportunity for free running—although if you have large grounds, they will largely exercise themselves. They will enjoy longer walks if that fits in with your lifestyle and can enjoy athletic activities such as agility and flyball. However, puppies under a year old must have their exercise limited to prevent damage to growing bones.

Character Trait	Poor	Average	Good	Excellent
Attitude to other dogs				
Quietness				
Not destructive				
Protective behavior				
Not likely to stray				
Good with children				
Ease of training				

Original purpose: Boar hunting
Male height: 30–34 in. (76–86 cm)
Female height: 28-32 in. (71–81 cm)
Weight: 100–180 lb. (45.5–81.8 kg)
Life span: 7–10 years

HOW easy to train?

Danes are highly trainable but can be stubborn. Training needs to start early—never allow a cute puppy to get away with behavior such as jumping up at visitors which will be unacceptable when he weighs as much as you do. This is a sensitive breed. Training needs to be based on encouragement and praise. Harsh methods are counterproductive.

WHAT good points?

Friendly, gentle, intelligent, dignified, affectionate, easy-going, noble, imposing appearance.

WHAT to be aware of?

Early socialization essential to prevent shyness or aggression. Some individuals are very territorial and dominant. Despite the elegant appearance, Danes are prone to slobbering and flatulence.

WHAT medical problems?

Danes, like other giant breeds, are prone to health problems and often short-lived. Medical problems include joint disorders (hip and elbow dysplasia), heart defects, gastric torsion (bloat), tumors, lack of thyroid hormone (hypothyroidism), von Willebrand's disease (a hereditary bleeding disorder), eye problems and tail injuries. Breeding stock should be hip tested. Buyers are advised to seek pups from long-living breeding lines.

Large dogs

● *Usually thought of as dignified, Danes can also be clowns at home—inspiring the creation of two cartoon favorites, comic strip character Marmaduke and Hanna-Barbera's renowned Scooby-Doo.*

Borzoi *Other names: Russian Wolfhound*

This powerful Russian sighthound was bred to course wolves, but today is a gentle companion and glamorous show dog. As a house pet, once past the puppy stage he is calm, dignified, and well mannered. He is deeply attached to his family and very sensitive to their moods. However, he retains his chasing instincts and loves to run, which can be a problem for homes not geared to a sighthound's needs. Although happy to lounge around restfully between walks, he needs regular exercise and free galloping. Early socialization is vital to prevent his natural suspicion of strangers escalating into shyness. With all his virtues, this is not really a dog for the novice.

As a breed, the Borzoi dates back to at least the 16th century, with the first written standard appearing in 1650. It was introduced to the UK in the 1860s and to the US in the 1890s, with instant impact.

WHAT colors?

Any color acceptable, including red, white, brindle, and tricolor. White with colored markings is most common.

WHAT grooming does the coat need?

The silky coat will mat and tangle if neglected but requires less maintenance than many long-haired breeds to keep it in good condition. A brush and comb through every few days will suffice, except during the molt, when extra work will be required.

HOW suitable are they as family dogs?

The Borzoi is not the ideal pet for the average family because of his high exercise needs, strong chasing drive, and highly strung, sensitive nature. He is better suited to the role of companion to adults. He is good with sensible children if raised with them, but he dislikes rough handling. He is very touch sensitive, tending to snap if startled.

● *In Czarist Russia, Borzois were favorites of the nobility.*

WHAT type of home?

A Borzoi needs space, so a home with a large, secure yard is best. He can cope with city life provided enough exercise is provided, although he is unsuited to apartment living. He does need access to areas where he can run free without danger to himself (i.e., no dashes across busy roads) or to local livestock. Farmers will not welcome unleashed Borzois near their animals.

WHAT type of owner?

This is a breed for an active person with access to land where a Borzoi can run free, who will appreciate the needs of this sensitive dog, and has the time and patience for socialization and training. Not a good choice for anyone who favors strict obedience.

HOW compatible with other pets?

Borzois are generally good with other dogs, especially other sighthounds. They can be good with cats within their own household if raised with them. However, their natural instinct is to chase and kill anything that looks like prey, so they should not be trusted with small pets or livestock.

HOW much exercise?

A great deal. Borzois need at least an hour's walk every day, plus free running. However, their strong hunting drive and deafness to the recall mean that areas where they can be trusted off leash are hard to find. Many owners find that the answer is to join a lure coursing club, where hounds pursue an artificial hare.

Character Trait	Poor	Average	Good	Excellent
Attitude to other dogs		●		
Quietness				●
Not destructive			●	
Protective behavior	●			
Not likely to stray		●		
Good with children			●	
Ease of training	●			

Original purpose: Hunting
Male height: 29 in. (74 cm) minimum
Female height: 27 in. (68.5 cm) minimum
Weight: 75–105 lb. (34–48 kg)
Life span: 11–13 years

HOW easy to train?

Difficult. The Borzoi is independent, stubborn, and not naturally docile—not the breed for obedience enthusiasts. Nonetheless, careful socialization and training are essential to make him a pleasant companion. Training must be gentle, patient, and consistent. Borzois are very sensitive to stress and respond badly to harsh treatment.

WHAT good points?

Dignified, gentle, quiet, loving, independent, calm, faithful, alert, sensitive, graceful.

WHAT to be aware of?

Strong hunting drive; hard to recall when off leash. Highly strung and does not react well to stress. Early socialization vital to prevent shyness.

WHAT medical problems?

Borzois are generally a healthy breed, although like other deep-chested breeds they may be prone to bloat. Hip malformation (dysplasia) and progressive retinal atrophy (degeneration of the light receptors in the eyes) have been reported. Sensitive to anesthesia.

Large dogs

Irish Wolfhound

This impressive giant is the tallest breed of dog and not one to take on lightly, representing a major commitment in terms of time, space, exercise, and food costs. Given a home that meets his large-scale needs, he is a loving companion. Despite his huge size, he is gentle and friendly, good-natured with children, and very affectionate toward his owners. With a dog this size, who may weigh as much as his owner and is extremely powerful, good socialization and training are essential. Although adult Wolfhounds are generally mannerly, pups (up to two or three years old) are boisterous and mischievous and can be hard work before they mature.

The Wolfhound harks back to the great Celtic hounds of pre-Roman times, which served as war dogs as well as hunters. However, the breed was almost extinct by the 17th century. The modern Wolfhound is largely an effort of 19th-century reconstruction.

WHAT colors?

Gray, brindle, red, fawn, wheat, and steel gray. Solid black and pure white are also recognized colors but rarely seen today. Puppies may change color as they grow their adult coats.

WHAT grooming does the coat need?

The harsh, shaggy coat is fairly low maintenance but needs grooming at least weekly with a pin wire brush and wide-toothed comb in order to remove dead hairs and to keep it healthy.

HOW suitable are they as family dogs?

In the right home, where sufficient priority can be given to his needs, the Wolfhound is an excellent family dog. However, a dog this size is not recommended for households with small children as he can easily knock them over. Even a blow from his tail may cause bruising. Young Wolfhounds can often be too rough for children's comfort and safety.

WHAT type of home?

Ideally the Wolfhound is a country dog, but he can adapt to city living if given sufficient exercise. He is unlikely to be comfortable in an apartment. Big dogs need space. This breed will cause problems in a home with small rooms where he has to maneuver around furniture and needs to be stepped over all the time. He also needs a reasonably sized and securely fenced yard, as well as access to areas where he can run off leash in safety.

WHAT type of owner?

This is not a dog for owners who have to leave him while they go to work. He needs company and can develop bad habits if bored and lonely. Wolfhound owners need to have time, space, and money to maintain this breed. They need to enjoy daily walks in all weather, and in order to train and control a young Wolfhound, they need to be fit and strong.

● *A gentle giant, but he may not always realize his own strength.*

HOW compatible with other pets?

Wolfhounds are good with other dogs, although they may accidentally injure small or fragile breeds simply by treading on them. They will generally get along well with cats

Character Trait	Poor	Average	Good	Excellent
Attitude to other dogs			▓	
Quietness	▓			
Not destructive			▓	
Protective behavior	▓			
Not likely to stray			▓	
Good with children				▓
Ease of training	▓			

Original purpose: Hunting and guarding
Male height: 31–35 in. (79–89 cm)
Female height: 28–33 in. (71–84 cm)
Weight: 90–120 lb. (41–54 kg)
Life span: 5–7 years

and other pets within their own household, but they have a strong hunting instinct and may not resist the temptation to chase a moving target.

● *Giant dogs need space— not the right choice for a small home.*

HOW much exercise?

Daily long walks and free galloping are essential for an adult Wolfhound, say an hour's walk a day plus the same amount of off-leash running. Like all sighthounds, this breed needs a lot of work on the recall, as he develops selective deafness once he has built up speed. Puppies under a year old should have restricted exercise to prevent damage to growing bones.

HOW easy to train?

Difficult. Training is essential, as a dog this size must be under control, so start early and stick

to it. Wolfhounds are stubborn, and owners need both patience and persistence. Lessons should be reward based, with lots of praise. Physical punishment will simply make the Wolfhound distrust you.

WHAT good points?

Gentle, kind, friendly, powerful, brave, affectionate, dignified, sensitive, not aggressive.

Large dogs

WHAT to be aware of?

Not a breed for everyone. Be sure you can cope before taking on a Wolfhound. Rapid growth rate means puppies need specialized diet. Long tail easily damaged in confines of home, and once injured can be slow to heal. Needs supervision!

WHAT medical problems?

The breed is vulnerable to bloat (gastric torsion), liver and heart problems, and bone cancer (osteosarcoma).

Index

Note: Page numbers set in *italic type* refer to pictures and/or captions; page numbers set in **bold type** indicate the main entry for the breed.

Picture Credits

The publisher wishes to thank the individual photographers and picture libraries who have contributed photographs for this book. Their pictures are credited here by their page number. Any pictures that are not listed below come from Interpet Publishing's own photographic archive. Note: t = top, c = center, b = bottom.

Jane Burton, Warren Photographic: 1, 3, 5 all, 6 all, 9, 10-11, 11, 12t right, 15b, 17, 19b, 25b, 27b, 35b, 39b, 47b, 50c, 51b, 53b, 55b, 56t, 57t and b, 59b, 61b, 65t, 66c, 72b, 76c, 79b, 81b, 83b, 93b left and right, 97, 98c, 99b, 100t and c, 101b, 105b, 114t and c, 115b, 117t and b, 119b, 120c, 121b, 122c, 123t and b, 131b, 132c, 133b, 135, 140b, 141b, 143b, 152b, 153b, 162b, 163b, 165b, 166c, 171b, 176c, 178c, 179b, 183b, 186c, 187b, 194c, 196t, 197b, 201b, 206c, 207b, 216c, 218t, 219t.

David Dalton: 30t, 33b, 36t, 37b, 43t, 62b, 71b, 89t, 108t and c, 109b, 110b, 111t, 144c, 145t and b, 155b, 164c, 173b, 214c.

John Daniels: 21b, 29b, 32t, 33t, 43b, 48b, 49b, 52t, 53t, 56c, 62t, 63b, 67b, 68t and c, 69t and c, 75b, 86b, 87b, 88t, 89b, 94t, 95b, 102t and b, 103b, 106t and c, 107t and b, 110t, 111b, 112c, 113b, 124t and c, 125b, 130b, 131t, 148t and c, 149t and b, 154c, 155t, 156c, 157b, 158c, 159t and b, 161b, 166t, 167t and b, 168c, 169t and b, 174t, 175b, 180c, 181t and b, 184t and c, 185t and b, 187t, 188c, 189t and b, 190c, 191t and b, 192t and c, 195b, 199t and b, 202t, 203b, 204c, 205b, 210c, 211b, 212b, 213b, 214t, 215t, 217b, 218c, 219b, 220c, 221b.

Frank Lane Picture Agency: 28c (Mitsuaki Iwago, Minden Pictures), 45t (Mitsuaki Iwago), 63t (David Hosking), 70c (Gerard Lacz), 94c (Mitsuaki Iwago, Minden Pictures), 95t (Gerard Lacz), 109t (Foto Natura Stock), 125t (David Dalton), 128c (Bruce Coleman Inc.), 165t (Foto Natura, Alice van Kempen).

The Kennel Club Picture Library: 30c (CA Johnson), 31t (David Dalton), 31b (CA Johnson), 32c (Marc Henrie), 37t (John Hartley), 42b (David Dalton), 44t (Colin Seddon), 44c (Marc Henrie), 45b, 48t, 49t (David Dalton), 52c (David Dalton), 64t (David Dalton), 64c, 65b, 70t, 86t, 87t, 88b, 90b, 91b (CA Johnson), 103t (Marc Henrie), 144t (Colin Seddon), 164t (Colin Seddon), 174c (David Dalton), 193t and b, 215b, 221t.